LABELING PEOPLE

McGILL-QUEEN'S STUDIES IN THE HISTORY OF IDEAS
SERIES EDITOR: PHILIP J. CERCONE

LABELING PEOPLE

French Scholars on Society, Race, and Empire, 1815–1848

Martin S. Staum

McGill-Queen's University Press
Montreal & Kingston · London · Ithaca

© McGill-Queen's University Press 2003
ISBN 0-7735-2580-7

Legal deposit third quarter 2003
Bibliothèque nationale du Québec

Printed in Canada on acid-free paper.

This book has been published with the help of a grant from the Humanities
and Social Sciences Federation of Canada, using funds provided by the
Social Sciences and Humanities Research Council of Canada. Funding has also
been received from the Faculty of Social Sciences, University of Calgary.

McGill-Queen's University Press acknowledges the support of the Canada Council
for the Arts for our publishing program. We also acknowledge the financial support
of the Government of Canada through the Book Publishing Industry
Development Program (BPIDP) for our publishing activities.

National Library of Canada Cataloguing in Publication

Staum, Martin S., 1943-
Labeling people: French scholars on society, race and empire, 1815–1848/Martin S.
Staum.

(McGill-Queen's studies in the history of ideas; 36)
Includes bibliographical references and index.
ISBN 0-7735-2580-7

1. Racism – France – History – 19th century. 2. Learned institutions and societies –
France – Paris – History – 19th century. 3. Social sciences – France – History – 19th
century. 4. Société phrénologique de Paris – History. 5. Société de géographie de Paris
– History. 6. Société ethnologique de Paris – History. 7. France – Colonies – History –
19th century. 8. Imperialism – History – 19th century. I. Title. II. Series.

GN345.3S73 2003   305.8'00944'09034   C2003-901465-7

This book was typeset by Dynagram Inc. in 10/12 Baskerville.

To Sarah and Nina

Contents

Illustrations

Preface and Acknowledgments

When the first echoes of the *Bell Curve* controversy arrived in 1994 I was working on a study of French phrenology. A paper by the historian of French psychiatry and psychology Jan Goldstein had inspired me to investigate phrenology more closely. I could not believe that, at the end of the twentieth century, there were still efforts to make ethnicity a significant variable for intellectual aptitudes. The continual recurrence of these same controversies makes the nineteenth-century disputes presented here timely. Classifying people, contrary to the philosopher Michel Foucault, may be necessary for any knowledge at all, but how often does it result in tendentious hierarchies? This study shows that the builders of early French social sciences constructed questionable images of "other" people within French society as well as those in the wider world.

After my first publication on phrenology, I had the good fortune to meet Marc Renneville, a historian formerly at Université de Paris – 8, whose expertise in the cultural history of French phrenology is unparalleled. His good colleagueship and generosity have benefited my own research, whatever our differences in interpretation. My forays into the history of geography have profited immeasurably from the research of Anne Godlewska of Queen's University, author of a massive work on French geographers. She kindly introduced me to the Association of American Geographers. A very special note of gratitude goes to Claude Blanckaert, whose knowledge of the history of French anthropology and of French social sciences made this study possible. I have very much appreciated his hospitality in Paris.

A word of thanks must go to the staff of the Département des Cartes et Plans of the Bibliothèque nationale de France (Richelieu), who made research there pleasant and productive. Similarly, I am grateful to the librarians at the Bibliothèque de l'Arsénal and the Bibliothèque centrale du Muséum d'histoire naturelle, who were most helpful. I am very much indebted to the research assistance of Jillian Maciak Walshaw, an Honours graduate of the University of Calgary, who will soon receive her doctorate from the University of York (UK). The Faculty of Social Sciences of the University of Calgary provided a much-needed term of teaching release. Finally, without the research funding of the Social Sciences and Humanities Research Council of Canada, this project would not have been feasible.

Throughout the stages of producing this book, I have been grateful to the staff of McGill-Queen's University Press. I would like to thank the executive director, Philip J. Cercone, for his encouragement, co-ordinating editor Joan McGilvray for her eminently useful instructions, and copy editor Lesley Barry for her diligent efforts to improve style and consistency.

I acknowledge The Johns Hopkins University Press, which has permitted use of some materials from my article "Physiognomy and Phrenology at the Paris Athénée," *Journal of the History of Ideas* 56 (1995): 443–62. Similarly, I would like to acknowledge Elsevier Science, publishers of the *Journal of Historical Geography*, for use of an earlier version of chapter 4 – "The Paris Geographical Society Constructs the 'Other,' 1821–1850," *Journal of Historical Geography* 26, no. 2 (2000): 222–38 – and the *Canadian Journal of History* for an earlier version of chapter 5 – "Paris Ethnologists and the Perfectibility of 'Races,'" *Canadian Journal of History* 35, no. 3 (2000): 453–72. I extend special thanks to Ross Woodrow and the University of Newcastle, Australia for permission to reprint a plate from the "Digital Lavater."

Abbreviations

AEE	Archives, Ministère des Affaires Étrangères
AN	Archives nationales
ASG	Bibliothèque nationale, Cartes et Plans, Archives de la Société de géographie
BA	Bibliothèque de l'Arsénal
BSAP	*Bulletin de la Société d'anthropologie de Paris*
BSEP	*Bulletin de la Société ethnologique de Paris*
BSG	*Bulletin de la Société de Géographie de Paris*
Dumoutier, Journal	Bibliothèque du Musée de l'Homme, MS 72, Dumoutier, Journal de son voyage à bord de l'Astrolabe [1837–40]
JSSP	*Journal de la Société phrénologique de Paris*
MSAP	*Mémoires de la Société d'anthropologie de Paris*
MSEP	*Mémoires de la Société ethnologique de Paris*
NAV	*Nouvelles annales des voyages*
OSSE	*Oeuvres de Saint Simon et d'Enfantin*

LABELING PEOPLE

1

The Bell Curve *and the*
Nineteenth-Century Organic Society

THE BELL CURVE

The impulse of humans to relate the physical appearance of their fellow beings to categories of intelligence and personality seems to flourish more than ever in times of social insecurity. So it was in nineteenth-century post-revolutionary France and so it has been more recently in the United States during the 1990s. The resurgence of interest in IQ test results as guides to social policy is symptomatic of concern in the United States over inter-ethnic tensions, immigration, and high divorce and illegitimacy rates. Richard Herrnstein and Charles Murray in *The Bell Curve* asserted the relative immobility of the IQ during an individual lifespan.[1] They rested their assumptions on arguments dating to the early twentieth century about the existence of a significantly heritable (40 to 80 per cent) single generic intelligence variable underlying IQ tests.[2] This cognitive ability, they tried to show, is the single most important predictor not only of educational potential but also of job performance. They argued that this ability correlates more reliably than socioeconomic status with the so-called culture of poverty, including the likelihood of incarceration, long-term stagnation on the welfare rolls, likelihood of bearing an illegitimate child, and heading a home as a single parent.

These arguments were sufficient to provoke a national furor, but the authors even more sensationally claimed that the well-known differences in average IQ scores of American "whites" and "blacks" are not the

---

1 Herrnstein and Murray, *The Bell Curve*; for the controversy, see the reviews and commentary in Jacoby and Glauberman, eds. *The Bell Curve Debate.*
2 Herrnstein and Murray, *The Bell Curve*, 18–23, 105.

product of deprived or enriched social environments but of inherent and largely unchangeable cognitive ability.[3] The apparatus of notes even endorsed the racial intelligence rankings of Ontario psychologist J. Philippe Rushton, who correlated brain size with intelligence in a rank-ordered series – with Asians at the top, followed by whites and blacks. Rushton ordered the sex drives of these groups inversely, so that the incidence of AIDS or illegitimacy could be explained by higher or lower sex drive, and correspondingly lower or higher intelligence.[4] These contentions look strikingly similar to those of nineteenth-century European (and American) racial theorists and craniologists.

The critique of *The Bell Curve* arose partly because of challenges to the idea of a single measurable variable for general intelligence that counted for so much.[5] But understandably, most angry responses came from the assumption – similar to many nineteenth-century authors' estimates of inherent intelligence – that the differences in average group IQ scores are not likely to change appreciably over time. Other critics also contended that policy recommendations did not logically follow from the allegedly value-free scientific arguments. The authors suggested ending welfare support for otherwise incorrigible single mothers and ending affirmative action programs in education and at work. But the same premises could lead to wholesale efforts to remedy whatever IQ deficiencies were correctible by educational, medical, and social support.[6]

The importance of *The Bell Curve* for this study is that it renewed and displayed the surprising vitality of nineteenth-century debates about whether a single variable or set of variables could be used to order the intelligence and character of individuals and peoples. In the late eighteenth century, the estimate of character by facial profile – physiognomy – was a popular fad and often a literary exercise. In a variant accepted by many artists and naturalists, the so-called "facial angle" – made by drawing a line from ear to upper lip or jaw and another line from the latter point to the foremost projection of the forehead – could diagnose cranial capacity and therefore intelligence. Early in the nineteenth century, the examination of head shapes and of the prominence of multiple cerebral organs – phrenology – allegedly revealed information about character, intelli-

3 Ibid., 269–315, 387.

4 Ibid., 666–7; see Rushton, *Race, Evolution, and Behavior.*

5 For questioning of *g* see Stephen Jay Gould in Jacoby and Glauberman, eds. *The Bell Curve Debate,* 7–11; for information about theory of multiple intelligences, see Gardner, ibid., 64–6.

6 Ibid., 325–92 for conservative commentary and critical press editorials.

gence, and almost all aspects of personality. All of these intellectual efforts continued the perennial nature versus nurture controversy. They attempted to rank peoples as well as individuals, with often unfortunate consequences for those assessed as "retarded" or primitive.

These early efforts at formulating the social sciences of psychology, human geography, and anthropology formed a fascinating counterpoint to a Romantic subculture of buoyant, even utopian hopes for social reform. While phrenologists in particular sought to enable individuals to realize their own potential, many of them stressed the obvious corollary – that some individuals should be content with their lot. In contrast to the excellent recent study by Marc Renneville, *Le langage des crânes, Une histoire de la phrénologie*, which examines the progressive implications of French phrenology, this discussion illustrates the tendency of phrenologists to summarily denigrate the capacities of non-European peoples. Building on Anne Godlewska's work on the discursive formation of the French geographic community but contrary to the recent French study of Dominique Lejeune, *Les sociétés de géographie en France et l'expansion coloniale au XIXᵉ siècle*, I point out an impulse even in the early Paris Geographical Society toward the practical pursuit of commercial interest and imperial adventurism. At the same time, the geographers employed the models of racial theorists to rank the peoples they encountered. Some ethnologists went to the extreme of considering non-European "races" as separate species that depended on Europeans to achieve whatever limited civilization they could attain. Supplementing the pioneering studies of French anthropology by Claude Blanckaert, we shall go beyond previous estimates of the continuity of discourse of the Paris Ethnological Society with Paul Broca's Anthropology Society.

While historians have sometimes associated forebodings of national decline, fears of degeneration, and medicalized social pessimism with the Third Republic era after the defeat in the Franco-Prussian War, here we shall find elements of social pessimism inherent in the early social sciences even before 1848. There were deep divisions among the "progressive," utopian, republican, or reformist thinkers associated with the political and anti-clerical left. Some thought an egalitarian society feasible. Others wished to preserve the hierarchy at least of meritocracy or to limit opportunity for social mobility. In addition, the encounters of the French with other peoples had already induced a sense of the civilizing mission that would form the cultural cornerstone of the Third Republic era of imperial expansion. While these conservative and adventurous impulses might seem contradictory, they were really just two facets of

constructing the "Other" – the feared "dangerous classes" at home and
the unassimilable "savage" or organically deficient peoples abroad.[7]

This chapter touches upon the nature of nineteenth-century classification, the conjectural history model of social development, and the
background of the Saint-Simonian vision of an organic society. The second chapter introduces the most influential advocates of physiognomy,
the facial angle, and a multiplicity of human species. The third chapter
examines how the French phrenological society aspired to social reform, but how some members promoted a society controlled by experts
and minimized the abilities of non-European peoples. The fourth and
fifth chapters illustrate how scholarly societies of geography and ethnology constructed their visions of any people deviating from the European
norm. The concluding chapter relates ideas expressed before 1848 to
the scholarly literature on psychological, geographical, and anthropological ideas of the late nineteenth century.

WHY CLASSIFY?

There were both intellectual and socioeconomic contexts for the nineteenth-century impulse to classify. From ancient times, philosophers
had developed the idea of a "Great Chain of Being," or ladder of nature, based often in the Christian context of a benevolent Creator filling
the world with all possible creatures. At the top were the Deity and spiritual angelic beings, while partly material and partly spiritual humans
occupied an intermediate rank. Animals, vegetables, and mineral sub-
stances completed the structure.[8] Philosopher Michel Foucault argued
in *The Order of Things* that the entire "classical" mode of knowledge in
the seventeenth and eighteenth centuries was classification of species,
especially in natural history, according to static, external criteria. The
new systems of naming species, as exemplified by the Swedish naturalist
Carl von Linné (Linnaeus), represented this impulse, and extending it
to humans seemed a logical corollary.[9] Yet naming has never been inno-

---

7 Renneville, *Le Langage des crânes*, 2000; Godlewska, *Geography Unbound*; Blanckaert, "On
the Origins" and many other articles cited below on the history of anthropology; on medicalized social pessimism, Nye, *Crime, Madness, and Politics*; on the civilizing mission, Conklin, *A
Mission to Civilize*; for the subtleties of the Republican left, Pilbeam, *Republicanism*.

8 Lovejoy, *The Great Chain of Being*; Stepan, *The Idea of Race*, 1–19; Renneville, *La Médecine du crime*, 2:805 cites a passage from the essay of Emile Durkheim and Marcel Mauss
(1903) on primitive classification about how this impulse is not self-evidently natural.

9 Foucault, *Les mots et les choses*, 57–9, 66–7, 230, 276, 284; Kristner, "Georges Cuvier,"
175–90.

cent. As Londa Schiebinger has argued, the naming of parts of plants as well as animals could be fraught with gendered assumptions.[10] Nor were naturalists such as Buffon predestined to classify, when classification seemed to them artificial. Classification was not an inherent impulse of the mind, but often directed toward a specific purpose.

In a remarkable survey of the historical concepts of "race," a team of historians in 1997 set out to explore race "not as biogenetic category" but as "socially constructed, an ideology embedded in and expressed through, specific social relations of power." For David Brion Davis, races are "fortuitous and arbitrary inventions ... by-products, primarily, of Europe's religious, economic, and imperial expansion across the seas of the earth."[11] Throughout history, some groups in dominant power positions have chosen deliberately to focus on external physical features of others and to classify them accordingly. The norm became the attributes of the dominant group, in this case Europeans. James Sweet has argued that, even before exploration of the Americas, Muslim slave traders, Iberians in feudal Andalusia, and Portuguese traders considered as inferior beings not just the culturally "backward" but those with black skin colour. Without having a fully developed ideology of race, they practised racism in the sense that "biological assumptions that were familiar to a nineteenth-century Cuban slaveowner would have been recognizable to his fifteenth-century Spanish counterpart."[12]

There has been much disagreement about whether such racial assumptions preceded the existence of plantation slavery in the Americas. Winthrop Jordan developed the thesis of continuity of negative images of blacks, including the Biblical curse of Ham and Canaan, Noah's son and grandson, which legitimized enslavement in a religious framework at least by the late sixteenth century. That is, Europeans could enslave the reputedly African descendants of Canaan because God had cursed them.[13] Other historians have stressed the contingency of the rise of slavery according to new economic demands, with the curse invoked only when slavery had to be justified. The only emerging consensus is agreement on a mutual reinforcement of attitudes toward "race" and the denigration of enslaved groups.[14] Some specialists in the history of

---

10 Schiebinger, *Nature's Body*, 11–75.

11 McGiffert, "Editor's Preface," 3; Davis, "Constructing Race," 7.

12 Sweet, "The Iberian Roots,"143–66, esp. 165.

13 Jordan, *White Over Black*, stresses the pre-existing negative images of "blackness" helping to justify slavery rather than the emergence of slavery from capitalist development.

14 Davis, "Looking at Slavery"; Davis, *The Problem of Slavery*.

North American natives contrast positive portrayals of their dignity and worthiness with the extreme denigration of Africans.[15]

The commercial and imperial impulse that promoted slavery also led to an enforcement of European dominion over peoples considered less advanced.[16] The advance of Europeans into the Pacific or into the African interior, even if for trading posts rather than colonization, created new contacts and new subjects to classify. This study shows that there was temporarily a tendency to consider these new subjects in terms of biological determinism rather than to classify them according to their degree of cultural "retardation," or savagery. Between 1800 and 1850, the more strictly physical criteria triumphed. And with the newly indelible nature of "race," there was no way out of the labeling. Later in the nineteenth century, as these physical criteria persisted, evolutionary theory both in biology and sociology provoked a resurgence of the retardation model. By that time, however, the difficulties of "catching up" placed a grave handicap on any benevolent image of non-Europeans.

Fully developed classification of humans by skin colour emerged only among the naturalists of the late eighteenth century. Ordering "races" by superiority could serve to assuage guilt about slavery, although even anti-slavery authors generally believed in racial hierarchy and African inferiority.[17] However, such classifications did not necessarily mean fixed capacities in each people. By the late eighteenth century, many European philosophers, such as Adam Smith and Anne-Robert-Jacques Turgot, were no longer enamoured of the "noble savage" myth, used as a foil for European imperfections. They assumed that all peoples followed the same life cycle toward greater development – hence "savages" were "primitives" with a simple mode of subsistence as they clambered along the stages toward civilization.[18]

The classification of individuals in a non-hierarchical manner had been the staple of the medical profession since ancient times. In the

15 See Liebersohn, *Aristocratic Encounters,* 9; cited there are Stephen Greenblatt, *Marvelous Possessions: The Wonder of the New World* (Chicago: University of Chicago Press, 1991); Stuart B. Schwartz, ed. *Implicit Understandings* (Cambridge: Cambridge University Press, 1994); Karen O. Kupperman, ed. *American in European Consciousness 1493–1750* (Chapel Hill: University of North Carolina Press, 1995); Robert Berkhofer, *The White Man's Indian: The History of an Idea from Columbus to the Present* (New York: Knopf, 1978).

16 Pagden, *European Encounters.*

17 Banton, *Racial Theories*; Hannaford, *Race;* Malik, *The Meaning of Race*; Stepan, *The Idea of Race,* 1–19.

18 Meek, *Social Science.*

corpus of Hippocrates and the works of Galen a certain physical temperament or reaction of the body with illness correlated with character
(irascibility, melancholia, or a phlegmatic nature), though not necessarily with intelligence. Inborn temperaments were indelible, though external variables such as climate, diet, and lifestyle could modify them.
Moreover, there was no reason why each individual could not strive to
counteract the nature of an endowed temperament.

But there were also specific reasons from the social context for a renewed interest in classifying people by external appearances in the eighteenth century. Ladies and gentlemen of the Court and of high society
were easily distinguished from artisans and servants by the fabric, cut,
and colour of clothing. But in this era in most European countries,
sumptuary laws were lapsing and consumer tastes were changing. Sumptuary laws had limited the luxury of rich silk fabrics and gilt ornamenta-
tion to the rich and prohibited non-nobles from dressing as nobles.[19] In
France intermediate social groups such as the wealthy bourgeoisie increasingly imitated aristocratic fashion, and even urban artisans just
above impoverished status increased spending on articles of clothing. In
Paris a veritable industry with partly illegal methods of production and
marketing grew to supply "cheap copies of aristocratic luxury items."
The Revolution merely accentuated existing trends that made distinguishing social status by clothing more difficult.[20] The wider distribution of luxury silk fabrics and brighter colours made the theatrical
comedy confusion of valets and masters more plausible in real life.[21]

In this situation, reading people's faces and head shapes was all the
more crucial for assessing future employees or even marriage partners.
The French Revolution definitively removed all prohibitions on orna-
mentation and dress for those who could afford them. Phrenology flourished in the era of industrialization in Britain and France, when new
fears of the "dangerous classes" in overcrowded cities haunted well-
heeled members of society.[22] At the same time, artisans with aspirations

19 On the consumer revolution, see Maza, "Luxury, Morality," esp. 214; Fairchilds,
"The Production and Marketing," 228–48; Pardailhé-Galabrun, *La naissance*; Roche, *The
Culture of Clothing*, 26–7, 49 on sumptuary laws.

20 Roche, *The Culture of Clothing*, 33, 39, 58, 92–3; Fairchilds, "The Production and
Marketing," 228.

21 Roche, *The Culture of Clothing*, 108, 111, 399 on Louis-Sébastien Mercier's fears
about "popular" tastes for luxury.

22 Pinkney, *Decisive Years*; Chevalier, *Laboring Classes* and re-assessment by Ratcliffe,
"Classes laborieuses."

for self-improvement could seek to realize their own potential by knowledge of their own capacities. Both the desire for stabilization and the desire for self-improvement could reinforce the impulse to classify individuals.

In an era of social turmoil and commercial rivalry on a global scale, the temptation to label people heightened interest in the emerging human sciences. The Revolutionary and Napoleonic eras had brought sustained efforts in the French National Institute and in contemporary learned societies to understand regularities in human behaviour as a part of the natural world. In fact, the relation of physical temperament or bodily characteristics with moral and mental phenomena was one of the chief goals of the Idéologues, a circle of physicians and philosophers especially active from 1795 to 1803.[23] Hostile spiritualist philosophers attacked the materialist implications of Destutt de Tracy's Rational Ideology while perpetuating an introspective mode of psychology. Victor Cousin, the most famous lion of the lecture platform at the Sorbonne in the 1820s and early 1830s, wished to save a special place for the mind and self while reasoning about mental faculties. He and his disciples were able to insinuate psychology into the University curriculum by making it a branch of philosophy.[24]

It would be several more generations before the new social science disciplines were officially institutionalized in the French university system. Previous studies of the social sciences in this era have focused on the re-establishment of the Academy of Moral and Political Sciences, with its debates among economists and philosophers and the diatribes of materialist physicians such as François-Joseph-Victor Broussais against Eclectic spiritualist philosophers.[25] While other institutions, such as the lecture forum of the Collège de France, were sometimes more innovative, it was in the small learned societies and public lecture forums such as the Athénée de Paris that tentative steps toward forming new disciplines occurred.[26] These furnished a means for generating new cognitive authority and legitimizing new "knowledge." They also actively communicated such knowledge, to educate the public and exchange

23 On the Idéologues, see Staum, *Minerva's Message*; on the more general enterprise of a science of man, Williams, *The Physical and the Moral.*

24 Goldstein, " 'Official Philosophies' "; Goldstein, "The Uses of Cousinian Pedagogy."

25 Leterrier, *L'institution des sciences morales*, 185–93.

26 On the different dynamic of provincial learned societies, see Fox and Weisz, eds. *The Organization of Science*; Fox, "Learning, Politics, and Polite Culture"; Chaline, *Sociabilité et érudition.*

knowledge with similar societies. A study of the British Royal Geographical Society refers to Bruno Latour's concept of "centers of calculation" in arguing that these societies "function as pivots in flows of information, co-ordinating ever larger networks of communication, diffusing standard techniques of observation and centralizing the results of data collection."[27] The Paris Geographical Society (Société de Géographie de Paris), the group founded first, in 1821, brought together an assortment of active explorers, armchair geographers, and linguists to continue the study of describing both the physical and human world and representing its surface.[28] In their enthusiasm to describe the peoples of the world, they also articulated the objective of subjecting the rest of the world to French commercial intervention. They helped develop theories that ranked peoples and made French dominion over them thinkable.

After 1830, a second and much narrower group, predominantly of physicians, established the Paris Phrenological Society (Société phrénologique de Paris), which aspired to diagnose intelligence and character from head shapes – a new means of studying physical-mental relations.[29] While the introspective, academic philosophy of mind remained in the respectable mainstream, this group won only limited recognition from the scientific, medical, and intellectual luminaries of the day. Its activities of assessing personalities were more like some branches of modern psychology than the lectures of Victor Cousin at the Sorbonne.[30] They believed that the shape of the cranium disclosed the prominence or deficiency of multiple cerebral organs and therefore inherent dispositions of individuals. A trained observer could diagnose the capabilities for self-improvement and unavoidable limitations of each person or group.

In 1839 another physician, William Frédéric Edwards, gathered a group of geographers and linguists to establish the Paris Ethnological Society (Société ethnologique de Paris) with the explicit motive of studying human variety and assessing the perfectibility of different races.[31] Often paralleling the conclusions of explorers in the

27 Driver, *Geography Militant*, 29.
28 On the Society see Fierro, *La Société de Géographie*; Lejeune, *Les sociétés de géographie*; on French geographers of this era, see Godlewska, *Geography Unbound*.
29 Renneville, *Le Langage des crânes*.
30 See Richards, *Mental Machinery*, 270: "In its disciplinary and its cultural aspects, phrenology anticipated Psychology in remarkable detail."
31 Blanckaert, "On the Origins"; Williams, "The Science of Man," 55–67.

Geographical Society, the ethnologists branded some groups as uncivilizable, while others could benefit from European contact. In the process, they set the stage for the discourse of anthropologists later in the
century. They also helped eventually to undermine the traditional
French theory of empire, which considered all subject peoples as educable as French citizens at home.

As exercises in discipline-building, the efforts of these societies laid
foundations without completing enduring structures. The eventual expansion of the geographical societies and the strategic rivalries for empire would produce public pressure to include geography in French
university education. Phrenology could never easily transform itself into
experimental psychology because the majority of the scientific and medical communities did not rally to its support. However, it set the precedent for later efforts in psychopathology and criminology to search for
indicators of individual capacity. All such attempts weighted innate dispositions as well as sociocultural influences on individuals. Phrenologists also created a body of literature that made invidious distinctions
among peoples and "races." The art of reading crania, even without the
principles of phrenology, then became one of the principal pursuits of
anthropologists, whether they were dealing with exotic people or socially undesirable citizens. The shock and apparent discontinuities of
the 1848 revolution disrupted both the Phrenological Society and the
Ethnological Society, but the discourse of the ethnologists provided a
blueprint for the approach to physical anthropology championed by
Paul Broca in the Paris Society of Anthropology after 1859.

The common theme among these three societies was the very problem raised by *The Bell Curve* – the perfectibility of individuals and races.
None of the three societies was monolithic on this issue. Some of the
phrenologists were inclined to stress educability and humanitarian goals
of social reform, while others were more disposed to slot people into a
society controlled by the experts. As with *The Bell Curve*, policy conclusions were not implicit in "scientific" investigations. Nor did the conventional "party of order" versus "party of movement" division determine
the conclusions. Even "progressives" sometimes accepted that those
with limited capacities should be content with their role, though others
stressed the importance of educability, which might even influence the
state of the brain itself.

Some geographers and ethnologists used the facial angle as an indelible marker of fixed limited capacities; some stressed the benefits of European tutelage. Political progressives often were likely to circumscribe

the abilities of non-Europeans, while Christian conservatives could ally with anti-slavery radicals to hold forth the prospect of universal perfectibility. In all three societies, however, could be seen the temptations of a physical or biological determinism that could enshrine European superiority, and which would ultimately make the "civilizing mission" painful for "inferior" peoples.

THE CONJECTURAL HISTORY OF PEOPLES

Eighteenth-century conjectural history is an essential background for understanding the mid-nineteenth-century changes toward physical indicators of intelligence and character. Baron Charles-Athanase Walckenaer, a founding member and future president of the Paris Geographical Society, compiled a typical essay of conjectural history in 1798, when he was only a young Polytechnique graduate. A royalist and Catholic who was imprisoned during the Revolution, he was an often painstakingly erudite historical geographer.[32] He divided peoples by stages of development from savagery to civilization. There was no overtly racial criterion. As with other naturalists, there were "degrees of civilization" according to the "more or less progress societies have made in the arts, industry, and knowledge necessary for subsistence."

The most primitive societies, illustrated by those on what is now the Philippines and Marianas Island, were gathering societies, with little effort necessary for subsistence. The more advanced North American or New Zealand natives were hunters. As with Adam Smith, the more advanced the mode of subsistence, the more stratified the society. The division of labour was also an important mechanism for change. In India and Africa, the more complex relationships of a pastoral society prevailed. There was no simple gradation of peoples by continent or skin colour. Some African peoples, such as the Mandingo, were already in the fourth (agricultural) stage. The most advanced European and American peoples had attained the fifth stage of the commercial and manufacturing economy, but all peoples were vulnerable to a sixth stage of decline brought on by excessive luxury and corruption. By implication, all peoples would attain the division of labour, more complex government, and increased moral sympathy already evident in the fifth stage.

32 Godlewska, *Geography Unbound*, 273–5.

This conjectural account restated the naturalist Georges-Louis Leclerc, comte de Buffon's environmental differentiation of the races. Climate, diet, and lifestyle altered skin colour over the long term, so that darker-skinned peoples generally lived closer to the equator. Occupations and lifestyles could modify body proportions and even skull shapes. The degree of civilization was neither racially determined nor fixed. For example, as Walckenaer maintained, it is not the "destiny of Tartars always to be a pastoral people; if their soil is fertile, they will become cultivators."[33] Walckenaer was thus open-minded toward others, if certainly no advocate of political democracy or of the "revolt of the classe immonde" that occurred during the Revolution.[34]

Conjectural history could serve the important function of rationalizing the need for European guidance to other less advanced peoples, since it ranked peoples by the development of the arts, sciences, and industry peculiar to Europe. But at least it did not condemn them to indelible stagnation based on limited intelligence.

TEMPERAMENT AND ORGANIC DISPOSITIONS

Fear of instability and post-revolutionary disillusionment with egalitarianism and aristocratic idleness soon fostered in the early nineteenth century the new ideal of an organic society. In this model, each individual would play an assigned functional role, much as each organ does in the body. The model also strongly criticized Buffon's conviction that altered climate and lifestyle could change human varieties. The result was a theory of fixed races or even perhaps several differing fixed human species. This section considers the interplay between an alteration in traditional temperament theory and the model of the organic society.

Hippocratic-Galenic temperament theory had included the possibility of opposing harmful excesses and deficiencies among four fundamental human temperaments. The sanguine temperament displayed excellent circulatory strength in the body and fostered an open, optimistic, and courageous character. As such, it was clearly the most healthful and desirable. The bilious temperament made for angry and impetuous dispositions. Phlegmatic or lymphatic temperaments led to lassitude characteristic of the elderly or of typical women. Melancholic people

33 Walckenaer, *Essai sur l'histoire*, 7–8, 22–4, 67, 88, 183, 254, 357, 360, 365. The citation is from 367–8.
34 Ibid., 312.

suffered obstacles to the flow of their humours, so that they were sombre and fearful but capable of profound meditation. To some extent, a skilled physician could read external signs of temperament, such as the large chests of the sanguine. Hippocratic climate theories allowed for alterations in temperament because of air temperature, winds, soil, and even habits: certain climates made people docile, and the nomadic lifestyle affected the fertility of Scythian women. There could conceivably be a tendentious classification of national characters by climate, if not temperament proper.[35]

Eighteenth-century physicians, such as Louis de Lacaze and Théophile de Bordeu of Montpellier, added the concepts of nervous or muscular temperaments. Nervous temperaments were more characteristic of all women and contemplative men, and were more likely to promote moral sensitivity and sociability. Muscular temperaments of athletic types might characterize savage peoples who acted without reflectiveness. Advanced social organization was supposed to develop the more sensitive temperament.[36] The temperament theory was conspicuously discriminatory against women and cast aspersions on "savage" peoples, although it did not differentiate by race.

Hygienists in the late eighteenth century based their advice on making the best of one's innate temperament. Moving, exercising more, and eating heartier foods would stimulate sensitive temperaments, while sleeping more or dieting more would calm muscular temperaments. Another famous Montpellier physician, Paul-Joseph Barthez, displayed the germ of a new organic philosophy. He asserted that the radical forces of a so-called vital principle could be concentrated in some organs and deficient in others. Individual variability could then assume a more pronounced importance and be less correctable, though Barthez never correlated the vital principle with race.[37]

The Idéologue physician Pierre-Jean-Georges Cabanis was among the first to use in French the word "anthropology," defined by him as an amalgam of physiology, analysis of ideas, and ethics. He based his idea of temperament and underlying physical sensitivity, like the Montpellier physicians, on so-called "dispositions of the organs," including states of excitation or illness. In this way, the state of a subcentre of sensitivity

35 Hippocrates, "Airs, Waters, Places" in *The Works of Hippocrates*, 1:109–11, 121–37; Temkin, *Galenism*, 175–82.

36 Lacaze, *Idée de l'homme*, 225–6, 394–8, 420.

37 Barthez, *Nouveaux élémens*, i–xviii, 285–6, 289–92.

such as the uterus could be responsible for "hysteria," while the state of other internal organs could produce other passions, and pathological states of the brain itself could provoke hallucinations.[38] Though temperaments were not completely alterable, Cabanis strongly believed that they could be modified through hygiene. Medical intervention, changes in diet, climate, and lifestyle could affect organic dispositions, and, by sympathy, the brain and cerebral nervous system. Therapeutic efforts and changes in regimen could in this way make most men, in any case, potentially capable citizens.

The temperament theory produced its own invidious distinctions. The disastrous medical reading of women's temperaments made them supposedly unfit for philosophical meditation and public life.[39] Physicians also issued warnings about unsociable occupations that would foster ardent, implacable temperaments, such as butchers or slaughterers. There was the conventional bias against the pre-agricultural lifestyle of pastoral and hunting peoples for their lack of appreciation of property. Cabanis exhibited little openness to "primitive" peoples, but had no concept of indelible, racially determined qualities. Rather, he agreed with Buffon that climate influenced skin colour and therefore "race," as supposedly evidenced by darker-skinned descendants of the Portuguese in the Cape Verde Islands.[40]

Not all Idéologue physicians were immune to the newer forms of racial theory. Cabanis's pupil Balthasar-Anthelme Richerand and his sometime disciple Jacques-Louis Moreau de la Sarthe became enthusiasts for using the facial angle to classify peoples and, in Moreau's case, of physiognomy to make judgments about individuals.[41]

How, then, did the inflection of traditional temperament theory help introduce the concept of an organic society? Michel Foucault has designated the more famous contemporary of Cabanis (though not an Idéologue) Xavier Bichat as one of the critical representatives of the Paris Clinical School. Bichat probed the nature of the living by dissecting cadavers and practising pathological anatomy, and he is also important for developing the organic philosophy that influenced phrenologists, the

---

38 Cabanis, *Oeuvres philosophiques*, 1:189, 196–7, 205–8, 562, 578–80, 593–5 and 2:77.

39 On women, Cabanis, *Oeuvres philosophiques*, 1:291.

40 For Cabanis on climate, ibid., 1:452–6, 474–8, 482, 489, 502–4; on race and Portuguese, 475–6. For the theory of climate as moralizing, Livingstone, "The moral discourse of climate."

41 For Moreau on perfectibility see "Mémoire sur plusieurs maladies"; for Moreau on anthropology, see "Extrait du Traité"; on Lavater in the Moreau edition, see Lavater, *L'Art de connaître*, 1:192, 208; 4:64.

Saint-Simonian movement, and many ethnologists. Less optimistic than Cabanis, he did not see that intelligence could be changed by medical and environmental stimuli to the internal organs. He separated "animal life," the realm of intelligence, from the "organic life" of the internal organs. Therefore, there could be no acquired temperaments, only the power of habit on animal life.[42]

The most important general principle that Bichat contributed to the model of the organic society derived from the work of Lacaze and Barthez in the Montpellier tradition: "the perfection of one part of the body is acquired only at expense of that of all the others." In some people the passions dominated; in others, the sensations and perceptions, or intelligence, or the will. Only a limited amount of energy would be available for the functions of the senses, activity, and reason. The sensitive are gifted for poetry, the fine arts, and botany. The rational have a talent for geography, history, the analytic sciences, and refined judgments. The muscular temperaments display skill in dancing, riding, and the mechanical arts. Rarely can one develop muscular capacities and the brain at the same time. Bichat also accepted the possibility that the facial angle measured by of the Dutch anatomist Petrus Camper seemed to indicate the stage of development of the higher "animal" functions in human beings.[43]

SAINT-SIMONIANS: CLASSIFICATION OF INDIVIDUALS AND PEOPLES

The consequences of Bichat's tripartite divisions surfaced in the energetic speculations of the comte Henri de Saint-Simon (1760–1825), who ceaselessly solicited interest from political and scientific figures for a new scientific social order. For him Bichat was the "immortal physiologist who established as a law of human organization that the different capacities of the human mind are mutually exclusive." As different tissues played different roles in the body, so did different groups perform different social functions.[44] At stake in this observation was the

42 Haigh, *Xavier Bichat*; Dobo et Rôle, *Bichat*; see Bichat, *Recherches physiologiques*, 38–43 on separation of animal and organic functions; 29, 59 on perfection in part at expense of others; 94–5 on sensitive, active, and rational equilibrium.

43 Bichat, *Recherches physiologiques*, on Camper, 49, 58, agreed the angle was a measure of perfection of animal life.

44 Saint-Simon, "Du système industriel" (1821) in *OSSE* 22:56–7; interpretation of the key significance of Bichat appeared in the work of Manuel, "From Equality to Organicism," esp. 61–2, 65; see also Haines, "The Inter-Relation," 27–8 on Bichat and 30–1 on functionalism.

difference between a liberal, individualist society with equality of opportunity and in which all could be fit for citizenship and an organic society
in which the relatively fixed abilities of each individual set limits to a
functional role.[45] In his last work, the *New Christianity* (1825), Saint-
Simon designated the forces of development in the new social organization as the sciences, the fine arts, and the great industrial combinations.
This organic society could not establish an "equality which is absolutely
impracticable" and had to be directed by "the most capable men in the
sciences of observation, in the fine arts, and in industrial calculations
for the general interest."

   In the new industrial age that was replacing the feudal era, active
"*industriels,*" workers and especially entrepreneurs, representing the "lo-
comotive function," ("motor," or active men) would become the administrators and directors of practical projects, as well as heads of "temporal
power." Men of theory, the scientists and scholars (savants), would rep-
resent the rational activity (cerebral men) that planned the new society
and assured the progress of philosophy. Theologians, poets, and artists
(sensory men) would stimulate the emotive function needed to accept
the new doctrines and to arouse patriotism. Together they would form a
"spiritual power" coordinated with the temporal government. Only such
a natural aristocracy would successfully substitute talents for the obsolete aristocracy of birth. Others would find happiness in fulfilling duties
to assist those more talented. Saint-Simon's proclaimed purpose was the
"improvement of the physical and moral existence of the most numerous class," which was also the "poorest class."[46] Supporters of this
organic society could claim to be responding to the most grievous
exploitation by the privileged or the wealthy.

   The physician and phrenologist Etienne-Marin Bailly de Blois became
an enthusiast for Saint-Simon. He explained how society is "a veritable
organized machine all of whose parts contribute differently to the oper-
ation of the whole."[47] Modern politics could then be equated with a
"general physiology," with hygienic precepts to assure the unity and harmony of all organs for the general interest. In the past, peoples and
monarchs struggled ceaselessly against each other. Now, with the abolition of slavery and equality of rights, administrators needed to consult

45 Manuel, *The Prophets of Paris,* 124–9; Manuel, *The New World,* 304, 415n21.

46 Saint-Simon, "Nouveau christianisme" in *OSSE* 23:170, 173, 182, 302; see also
"Mémoires sur les sciences de l'homme," 40:305.

47 Bailly de Blois, "De la physiologie," esp. 177; Carlisle, *The Proffered Crown,* 27–8.

those they administered. Saint-Simon's notes on Bailly indicate the desire to purge the nobility and clergy from leadership. To "stimulate as much as possible all classes to perform the work most useful to society," the Saint-Simonians needed peace-loving men "most capable of directing national interests," the "artists, scholars, and *industriels.*"[48] There was a natural fit between Saint-Simonian believers in an organic society and tendencies in phrenology. The flirtation of the young physician and future Christian socialist Philippe Buchez with both Saint-Simonianism and phrenology confirms this view.[49]

After Saint-Simon died in 1825, his immediate disciples were mostly an array of young bankers, engineers (often Polytechnique graduates), and frustrated revolutionaries who found no effective way of shaking the regime of Charles X. Among them was a future member of the Ethnological Society, the banker Olinde Rodrigues. He had been closely involved with the writing of the *New Christianity*. A mathematician and tutor at the Polytechnique, he could not advance in an academic career because of his Sephardic Jewish origins. He had helped introduce the future secretary and guiding spirit of the Ethnological Society and another scion of a banking family, Gustave d'Eichthal, to Saint-Simon and to the count's brilliant former secretary, Auguste Comte. Rodrigues became an enthusiastic partisan of easier credit for workers and, before his break with one of the Saint-Simonian leaders – the priesthood of Barthélemy Prosper Enfantin – a prophet of the new Saint-Simonian religion established in 1828. Some scholars still attribute to Rodrigues a conversation among an artist, scholar, and industrialist published the same year as the *New Christianity*. In this work, the author stresses that the Saint-Simonians seek a moral revolution, not a social revolution. They would never promote disobedience to the "natural leaders" of society. Everyone would value work and be attached to industrial entrepreneurs.[50] Eventually, however, Rodrigues represented the most egalitarian tendencies present among the Saint-Simonian cohort.

The equivalent of the organic view of society in any one nation was an organic view of the peoples of the world. In his first major publication, *Letters of an Inhabitant of Geneva* (1802), Saint-Simon already called Europeans the "children of Abel, while the children of Cain inherit Asia and

48 Saint-Simon, *OSSE* 39:193–4.

49 On Buchez, see Isambert, *De la charbonnerie*; Buchez et Trélat, *Précis*.

50 Rodrigues, "L'Artiste, Le Savant, et l'Industriel" in *OSSE* 39:210–58, esp. 232; for the argument that Léon Halévy was the author of this pamphlet, see McWilliam, *Dreams of Happiness*, 45n38.

Africa." The Africans are bloodthirsty, and the Asians indolent.[51] In 1808 Saint-Simon lamented the "great errors" by the "heads of government during the Revolution" who "failed to appreciate facts which physiologists observed. They established in principle that Negroes were equal to Europeans, and this necessarily fallacious principle is based on a fact which observations falsify."[52] Saint-Simon treated Africans as if their physiology made them inherently incapable of rising to the European level. He did concede that the Saracens made important contributions to the sciences, but the peoples of China and India "stayed in childhood, and are not needed for the history of the human mind."[53]

In a somewhat later work, Saint-Simon accepted the traditional eighteenth-century picture of the ladder of being, with surviving peoples representing stages in the march of time as if they were parts of one great being of humanity. The voyage of Captain Cook was thus like a lesson in the development of human intelligence, from its lowest form along the straits of Magellan, to the northwest American coastal Indians, to the Friendly, Society, and Sandwich Pacific islanders, and on to the previously known Peruvian and Mexican civilizations and the sophisticated monuments of ancient Egypt.[54]

His disciples certainly accepted as a European task the imposition of civilization on the Orient. Michel Chevalier, the loyal friend of the charismatic Enfantin, developed a complex scheme by which Europeans would achieve these objectives peacefully by railway and port construction rather than by military force.[55] Saint-Simonian ethnologists could easily turn into enthusiasts for French expansion. However, the case of Rodrigues shows that sympathy for the deprived and exploited could sometimes take precedence over the imperatives of an organically constituted society, and even over the development of racism.[56]

Although the small group of Saint-Simonians was by no means a mass phenomenon, they attracted thousands to their lectures, meetings, and spectacles in Paris from 1828 to 1832. Bailly de Blois among the phre-

---

51 Saint-Simon, "Lettres d'un habitant de Genève" in *Oeuvres choisies,* 1:38.

52 Saint-Simon, "Introduction aux travaux scientifiques" (1808) in *Oeuvres choisies,* 1:173; Manuel, *The New World,* 162, 408 calls attention to a similar passage in the first edition of *Lettres d'un habitant de Genève.*

53 Saint-Simon, *Oeuvres choisies,* 1:178, 188.

54 Ibid., 2:97–9, 115–16, 127.

55 Carlisle, *The Proffered Crown,* 77, 198–204.

56 Ibid., 22, 42, 89, 120, 170, 176 on Rodrigues.

nologists, d'Eichthal and Rodrigues among the ethnologists, and the young naval officer Théophile Lefebvre among the geographers and ethnologists represented important examples of Saint-Simonian influence in the learned societies. Saint-Simonianism became a viable outlook because, after the upheavals of revolution, many young people, including some women, were looking for a new, emotionally stirring quasi-religion to fill the void of egoistic individualism that seemed the lot of post-Revolutionary society.

In this context, they welcomed a new means to classify people by organic dispositions. As W.R. Albury has argued, one of the distinctive features of the Paris clinical school was the belief that individual variations became pathological. He sees this conviction particularly in the works of Napoleon's distinguished physician Jean-Nicolas Corvisart, clinical medicine professor at the Paris Ecole de Santé, and in the works of the *enfant terrible* of Establishment medicine, François-Joseph-Victor Broussais. No natural healing force of nature or compensating variable could adjust for the idiosyncrasies of temperament: experts would have to intervene to correct the situation.[57] Physicians had increasing pretensions to diffuse their insights into the general philosophical realm.

With Bichat, variability in organic dispositions became a signal that no one person could excel in all capacities. The only answer for a productive society, therefore, was specialization in which the naturally talented would rise to the top. On a world scale, Europeans would be the global brains, at the head of economic development, while other peoples might attain guidance to climb the ladder of being or advance through the several stages of development. In a harsher view, however, some would always remain uncivilizable. The medically based phrenology of Franz-Joseph Gall amplified this organicist conception of society. The medical profession, as L.S. Jacyna has argued, would be qualified to make wide-ranging pronouncements about education and penal codes.[58]

---

57 Albury, "Corvisart and Broussais."

58 Jacyna, "Medical Science and Moral Science," esp. 115, 119; for a provocative attempt to classify physiologists along axes of centralized versus devolved models and of functional differentiation, and to correlate these theories with political positions, see Pickstone, "How Might We Map"; the problem with Pickstone's schemas is that major political divergences occur even among people endorsing the same general physiological models, as among phrenologists or among theorists of the unity of the human species.

The development of new measures to assess and classify peoples by profiles and facial angles accentuated more rigid attitudes toward non-Europeans. A more aggressive racial theory also elaborated the rudimentary classification of peoples by continents by suggesting that there was more than one human species. The result was convenient justification for either dominating other peoples in good conscience or arguing that they needed the guardianship of colonization and the projected benefits of commercial relationships.

2

The Facial Angle, Physiognomy, and Racial Theory

NATURAL HISTORY

Classification in natural history preoccupied several notable eighteenth-century efforts to investigate the living world, and Michel Foucault has argued convincingly that the typical eighteenth-century discourse of representation relied on readable external signs and interrelations. Early nineteenth-century discourse shifted to internal significance, functional capacity, and historical development.[1] In the earlier period, external signifiers took precedence over internal function of organs. The arrangement of life forms, either by structural morphology or capacity to interbreed, was a static hierarchy of fixed species, rather than species open to transformation. Foucault's model leads to oversimplification, particularly in considering human physiology, where notions of internal functioning already were important in the eighteenth century. But he placed in a valuable context of discourse the hierarchical schema of a Great Chain of creatures arrayed from the simplest to the most complex.

The work of Swedish naturalist Carl von Linné (Linnaeus; 1707–78) certainly exemplified that quasi-hierarchical division among human varieties that would later be defined by the geometry of the facial angle and the art of profile physiognomy. In the first edition of *Systema naturae* (1735), Linnaeus had classed man and ape in proximity in an order of "anthropomorpha." The pious Linnaeus had no irreligious intention, though he opened the way for many future classifiers of human varieties to denigrate certain human varieties as intermediate to the apes.

1 Foucault, *Les mots et les choses*, 57–9, 66–7, 230, 276, 284.

Linnaeus's own fascination with apes, chimpanzees, and orangutans led him to study that sensitive boundary between the merely animal and the admittedly superior human being. Critics found unacceptable not only this alleged insult to human dignity but the collection of other species in company of homo sapiens. Besides the orangutan (man of the woods), Linnaeus added pathological specimens such as the albino (feral man of the night) and "monstrous" tailed humans.

Whatever the opinions on coexisting species, Linnaeus met a more agreeable response in subdividing homo sapiens into varieties. The most convenient indicators were skin colour and geographic location, with matching temperaments. Europeans were white and sanguine, "gentle, acute, inventive"; Asians, "sallow," greedy, and melancholic; Americans, copper-coloured and choleric; and Africans, black and phlegmatic, but also "crafty, indolent, and negligent." Characteristically, Linnaeus as a classifier could not apply neutral and innocuous labels. Only Europeans had the favoured position of being "governed by laws," while implicitly less sophisticated Asians were "governed by opinion," Americans by "custom," and Africans by "caprice."[2]

However, as Claude Blanckaert and other scholars have argued, not all naturalists of the eighteenth century welcomed excessive classificatory activity. Georges-Louis Leclerc de Buffon (1707–88) found any tendency to set arbitrary boundaries misguided, and in particular questioned Linnaeus's efforts. This criticism failed to prevent Buffon himself from identifying human varieties, each subject to modification. For Buffon, there was "degeneration" among humans from the ideal and temporally prior figure of the white European, and he labeled savages "ugly." But he did not typify a view that "races," based on geography or skin colour, were the desired units of classification within the human species. Nor were there predetermined logical categories for "races."[3] Observers had to construct characters of races if they did not reveal themselves spontaneously. This construction occurred as classifiers postulated hereditary morphological differences.

Buffon, for his part, used the terms "race" and "species" almost interchangeably when discussing human beings in his early work, but eventually race came to designate subgroups within the species. Both race and species were lineages, with species expressing more notable similarities

2 Linné, *A General System of Nature*, 1: 9; see Broberg, "Homo sapiens."
3 Buffon, "Premier discours," *Histoire naturelle* in *Oeuvres de Buffon*, 1:12–13; see also Blanckaert, "Contre la méthode," esp. 111–13, 118.

and being capable of producing fertile offspring, while races were more changeable. Skin colour alone was never sufficient for Buffon to designate a variety, as there had to be a global judgment on physiognomy, hair, or stature – that Lapps were small, for example. So great was Buffon's contempt for this northern race that in 1749 that he labeled them a degenerate "particular species whose individuals are only incompletely developed." While accepting the unity of the entire human species, Buffon attributed changes in skin colour to climate in the most general sense, nutrition, and particular customs. Without creating rigid divisions, he discussed varying groups of humans, including the Northern peoples, Tartars, Chinese, Malaysians, Mogols (of India), Blacks (Negroes, Caffirs [southeast Africans], and Hottentots [south African Khoi]), whites (Europeans, Arabs, north Africans and north Asians, etc.), and Americans. William Frédéric Edwards, the founder of the Ethnological Society, shared these complex criteria for distinctions but articulated the polar opposite view in believing in the permanence of racial types despite climatic differences.[4]

CAMPER'S FACIAL ANGLE

The French naturalist Louis-Jean Daubenton (1716–1800) in 1764 also explained the superiority of humans to animal species. He measured the inclination of the occipital cavity or foramen magnum in the brain with a line drawn from the back of the cavity to the lower edge of the orbit of the eyes. This procedure evaluated the orientation of the head.[5] Several years later, Daubenton's effort may have inspired the Dutch anatomist, artist, and physician-surgeon Petrus Camper (1722–89) (though Camper magnified his own originality). Camper wished by a similar geometric exercise to differentiate humans from animals and varieties of humans from each other. His lectures at the Amsterdam Drawing Academy in 1770 (repeated at the Paris Academy of Sciences in 1777) had the practical objective of enabling artists accurately to depict the distinctive traits of non-Europeans.

4 On the Lapps and Eskimos, see Buffon, *Histoire naturelle* (1750–89) 3:372–3, 379; on climate and skin colour, 446–8, 528; on the unity of the species, 529–30; on early theories of race and nationality, see Hudson, "From 'Nation' to 'Race,'" esp. 252–3; on degeneracy in Buffon, see also Sloan, "The Idea of Racial Degeneracy."

5 Blanckaert, "'Vicissitudes,'" esp. 417–19; for general interpretation of Camper, Virey, and facial angles in the context of "scientific racism," see Cohen, *The French Encounter with Africans*, 226.

The great German art historian and archaeologist Johann Joachim Winckelmann had very much affected Camper's cultural environment. To Winckelmann, the ancient Greek sculptures revealed the most harmonious geometric proportions for the human face and the standard for all conceptions of beauty. On the surface, Camper rejected this view when he admitted that beauty was culturally relative to the beholder.[6] Moreover, in a Groningen lecture of 1764 that announced discovery of the facial angle, Camper defended the unity of the human species. He refused to tolerate the idea that Africans had more in common with the Asian orangutan than with the European.[7] Like Buffon, he assumed that climate, particularly temperature, could account for variations in skin colour. He speculated that after a thousand years, whites in the tropics might turn black. In addition, he thought differences in skin colour and facial angle superficial, natural variations not necessarily denoting differences in intrinsic worth.[8] Camper hardly seems a candidate for the accusation of being midwife to racism.

Despite his own apparent egalitarianism, Camper's dissertation on human varieties (revised definitively in 1786 and posthumously published in French in 1791) became the touchstone for many subsequent theories of hierarchical racial classification. To his art students he pointed out that the most notable difference among human faces, particularly those of central Asian Kalmuks and Africans, was the placement and projection of the upper and lower jaws. Camper himself arranged skulls on his shelf in an order from African to Greek, with the African close to the orangutan.[9] However, the Camper scholar Miriam Meijer contends that he accepted natural variety as a providential blessing without designating an "abnormal" race and without creating a hierarchical Chain of Being. Still, Camper could not help underscoring his perception of the "greater conformity of the Negro head with that of the ape than that of the European or antique." For Camper himself apes were

6 On Winckelmann, see Baridon and Guédron, *Corps et arts*, 74; on relativity of beauty, see Camper, *Dissertation*, 84.

7 Meijer, "Petrus Camper," 3–9 and *Race and Aesthetics*, 1, 3; Camper also published a dissertation, *De l'orang-outang*, in 1782, which affirmed its separation from any variety of the human species.

8 Camper, *Dissertation*, 18, 29; Meijer, "Petrus Camper," 6–7 and *Race and Aesthetics*, 159–60.

9 Schiebinger, *Nature's Body*, 149–52; she also comments on Camper's belief in a wider pelvic angle for Africans, Asians, and American natives (156).

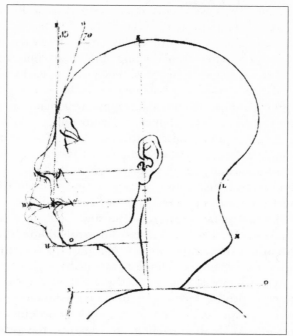

Facial angles of Europeans and Africans. P. Camper,
*Dissertation sur les variétés naturelles qui caractérisent
la physionomie des hommes dans des climats et des différents âges.*

always distinct from humans, and he disdained any fable of African origins from crossing apes and whites.

To clarify the comparison, he drew two lines in a two-dimensional profile of the heads, comparing birds and other vertebrates, the single-tailed ape, the orangutan, and African, Kalmuk, and European heads, including Roman and Greek statues. The "facial line" extended from the most prominent point of the forehead to the front of the upper incisor teeth. Outside the face, it met a "horizontal line" from the opening of the ear to a point under the root of the nose. The image of ideal beauty appeared with an obtuse facial angle of 100° in the Greek sculptures, never observed in nature. The typical observed angles were 80° for Europeans (though 85° appears in some plates), 75° for Asians such as the Chinese, and a minimum for humanity of 70° for Africans and Kalmuks, 58° for a young orangutan, and 42° for the African single-tailed monkey. Less advanced species such as a dog and a bird (woodcock) had even more acute facial angles.[10]

According to Camper, the prominence of the lower jaw in the "Negro" and Kalmuk required the flattening of the nose. Since the occipital part of the head is larger in Africans, they must tilt backward to maintain their balance. A paradox never confronted by later Pacific travelers was that Camper's single sample of a Tahitian head had a facial angle of 90°, a value he attributed to "chance."[11] Camper also expressed interest in making the art of physiognomy into an empirical science even before the influential publication of the Swiss pastor Lavater.[12]

The scientific blessing for the facial angle and a more insidious interpretation of racial hierarchy came out of the anatomical researches of Georges Cuvier and Etienne Geoffroy Saint-Hilaire on the natural history of the orangutan (1795). Cuvier and Geoffroy first used the angle to classify apes. They intersected a horizontal line from one earhole to the other through the incisor teeth, with a second line from the most prominent forehead bone between the eyebrows or root of the nose to the incisors. For them, the angle was not a geometric construction in profile but a part of a three-dimensional triangle constructed on paper with a compass and with a definite vertex at the front teeth. With these new measurements, the primates now registered an angle from 56° to 63°, closer to the 70° of Africans. Cuvier now asserted that the prominence of the jaw could only occur with a smaller cavity available for the frontal lobes of the brain. A larger jaw was therefore a sign of a brute nature with less brain mass and intelligence.[13]

While Cuvier stressed internal function rather than external signs, he seemed to be replicating in another realm Bichat's principle of finite distribution of functions in the formation of the organism. By 1800, in Cuvier's *Leçons d'anatomie comparée*, the facial angle of the young orangutan measured 70°, identical to the "Negro," the adult orangutan 67°, and the adult European 80°. A lower facial angle indicated domination by the sensory apparatus, while higher angles showed the liberation of intellect from the senses. In 1817, when Cuvier definitively established his three great "races" (Caucasic, Mongol, and Ethiopian), he thought

10 Camper, *Dissertation*, 8, 12, 40 and plates; Meijer, *Race and Aesthetics*, 48–9, 55; on the influence of Dürer's similar graphic profiles, which did not stress the jaw, see Meijer, 103–4; on apes 124; on relative beauty, 163–4.
11 Camper, *Dissertation*, 44, 47–8, 56.
12 Meijer, *Race and Aesthetics*, 117–18.
13 Blanckaert, "'Vicissitudes,'" 432–5.

Portrait of Georges Cuvier (1769–1832),
naturalist and advocate of facial angle

the "salient muzzle and large lips of the Negro race manifestly relate to
the apes, and the peoples who compose it have always remained barbarous."[14] Despite the sceptics, the facial angle would become a cornerstone of racial theory, a choice tool for geographers and explorers
interested in reporting the advanced or retarded nature of peoples of
Africa and the Pacific.

14 Cuvier, *Le Règne animal*, 95; for his earlier view, *Leçons d'anatomie comparée*, 2:1–8.

THE ART OF PHYSIOGNOMY

The revival of interest in the ancient art of physiognomy would intensify the focus on variants of the facial angle. Of Aristotelian vintage, physiognomy in the medieval and Renaissance eras compared animal and human profiles, and sometimes dabbled in astrology. In seventeenth-century France the court physician Marin Cureau de la Chambre and the painter Charles Le Brun also sought to classify and depict the expression of the passions on the human face.[15] Perhaps not coincidentally, the eighteenth-century intellectual fashion for physiognomy occurred at the same time as popular fascination for facial portraiture by projecting the darkened shadow of a profile on white paper. In the 1750s, the interest of French finance minister Etienne Silhouette encouraged this popular pastime and gave it a name.[16]

The Zurich pastor, theologian, and mystic Johann Caspar Lavater (1741–1801) revived physiognomy ostensibly for an elite, not for the masses, but his self-promotion skills made it a phenomenon of popular culture. The court physician of Hanover, Johann Georg Zimmermann, encouraged Lavater to develop his interest in skulls and crania. Very much aware of the Swiss naturalist Charles Bonnet's notion of a Great Chain of Being, Lavater subscribed to the notion of a graded series of creatures from animals to humans, culminating in ideal beauty. After collecting hundreds of portraits and profiles, he published a sketch of his theories in 1772 and a costly four-volume German edition in 1775–78.[17]

The book caused much excitement in the German-speaking world in the 1770s, and Lavater's work went through fifteen French editions by 1810. Among the renowned authors who commented on it were Louis-Sébastien Mercier, Madame Roland, Madame de Genlis, Madame de Staël, the novelists George Sand and Honoré de Balzac (in *Eugénie Grandet* and *La peau de chagrin*) Stendhal (in *Le Rouge et le noir*), Chateaubriand, and the artist Anne Girodet.[18] Physiognomy was politically acceptable to conservatives such as Balzac because, unlike phrenology, it did not challenge belief in the human soul. Balzac sometimes reflected on physiognomy and phrenology at the same time. He owned

15 Delaunay, "De la Physiognomonie" Baridon and Guédron, *Corps et arts*, 15–59.

16 Renneville, *La Médecine du crime*, 1:65.

17 Blanckaert, " 'Vicissitudes,' " 429.

18 Tytler, *Faces and Fortunes*, 6, 99–100; Baridon and Guédron, *Corps et arts*, 90, 102; for Balzac, see Rivers, " 'L'homme hiéroglyphié': Balzac, Physiognomy, and the Legible Body" in Shookman, ed. *The Faces of Physiognomy*, 144–60.

the Moreau edition of Lavater, and attempted to chart the physiognomy of each profession.[19]

Physiognomy intended to see through the trappings of dress and status to assure wise choices of friends, spouses, or business associates. In an urban environment threatened by social turmoil, where clothes were less and less distinctive across status or class boundaries, physiognomy could rely on facial features to provide unalterable testimony. As Balzac put it in *Une fille d'Eve*, "the caste system gave each person a physiognomy which was more important than the individual; today the individual gets his physiognomy from himself."[20]

For Lavater, nature revealed the Divine in the human soul, and the human face was a mirror to the soul. Physiognomy was a semiotic art, reading the invisible intellectual and moral attributes of any person by observing the external signs of facial profile.[21] While Lavater shared the artists' concern to portray passions (the art of pathognomy), he preferred the more reliable interpretation of static physiognomy. The silhouette, true to nature rather than the vagaries of artistic representation, would be its ideal tool, and the bone structure of the cranium, shaped by the brain, would be its irrefutable solid foundation. However, the silhouette could only reveal the natural dispositions, not the actual state, of a person's character.[22]

Lavater hoped to make physiognomy a "true science, founded on nature," a "science with fixed rules ... characters in a language" revealing intellect.[23] Among these general principles were that the shape of the forehead was the key to intellectual capacity, the region of the nose denoted taste, feeling, and moral sensitivity, while the mouth, lips, and chin were symbols of the instincts and sensuality. It was important to see if foreheads were retreating, straight, or prominent. Proportions were also critical: "a horizontal line from the point of the nose to the extremity of the head held straight should not exceed in length the

19 Wechsler, *A Human Comedy*, 25, 183; Tytler, *Faces and Fortunes*, 66; for Moreau's supplement to Lavater on professions, see Lavater, *L'Art de connaître*, 6:224–55, 8:12.

20 Peter Brooks, "The Text and the City," *Oppositions* 8 (1988): 7–11, cited in Wechsler, *A Human Comedy*, 29.

21 Baridon and Guédron, *Corps et arts*, 16. See also Siegrist, "'Letters of the Divine Alphabet,'" esp. 30–1 and Ellis Shookman, "Pseudo-Science, Social Fad, Literary Wonder: Johann Caspar Lavater, and the Art of Physiognomy," both in Shookman, ed. *The Faces of Physiognomy*.

22 Lavater, *L'Art de connaître*, 2:26 on the cranium; see also 7:1–12 and 8:13; Hart, "Physiognomy and the Art of Caricature" in Shookman, ed. *The Faces of Physiognomy*, 129; McKechnie, *British Silhouette Artists*.

23 Lavater, *Essays on Physiognomy* 1:7, 59 and 2:168–9.

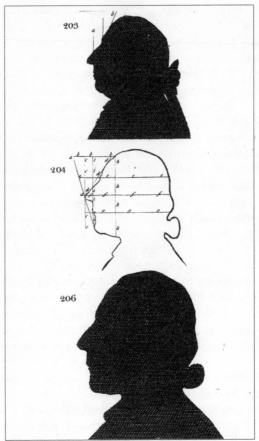

Profile of a Man of Truth and Expression, from
Johann Caspar Lavater, *Essays on Physiognomy*

perpendicular extending from the summit to the place where the chin
and neck join." Already the "finesse or roughness of the upper jaw" was
critical, as was as the occipital bone. Even before Camper, Lavater
claimed to have measured the angle of a line from the tip of the nose to
the first molar of the mouth and a second line with a perpendicular to
the eyes, an angle that related more to the nose than the jaw shape.
Camper had corresponded with Lavater in 1776, though his confidence
in Lavater's physiognomy is somewhat doubtful.[24]

24 Lavater, *L'Art de connaître*, 2:42–3; 8: 30; Meijer, *Race and Aesthetics*, 120–1.

The overriding assumption was that physical beauty connoted moral worth, or, as Lavater himself put it, "the morally better constitution is most beautiful, the morally worse, uglier."[25] The individual could not expect, as Helvétius did, that education was capable of complete transformation of a person. For Lavater, freedom was no more than "the liberty of a bird in a cage." Despite the potential for Christian repentance that illuminated the visage as much as dissipation degraded it, certain faces could never be capable of great achievements.[26]

Such a concept had remarkable consequences for the limitations of certain human groups. Lavater reasoned extensively about the finer points of "national physiognomies." In addition he quoted extracts from Buffon's natural history about climate as the key to racial differentiation, and in revised editions he adopted from Johann Friedrich Blumenbach the idea of five principal races and a variety of ideal beauty.[27] Each group could be "ennobled according to its primitive nature."[28] Any deviation from the Greek ideal, representing the most beautiful incarnation of humanity, was degeneration, as Buffon himself had implied. After hearing from Camper, Lavater could promote the use of the facial line.[29] For Lavater, the ancient Greeks really had been superior beings, and all modern humans were degenerate.

With knowledge of Camper and Blumenbach, Lavater expressed his belief in a serial hierarchy of the "immense ladder" of the Chain of Being. Image by image, Lavater metamorphosed a frog in twenty-four steps through the first glimmer of human reason to the Apollo Belvedere. Halfway through the gallery, the first rung of humanity had a facial angle of 60°. The more the angle was acute, the more the image was like an animal. There was a characteristic minimum and maximum in each human race. As the low angle of 70° in Camper's Kalmuks and Angolan Negroes decreases, the images "insensibly lose all trace of human analogy." The twenty-first image was eminently reasonable, and the twenty-second most beautiful. The last three figures represented

25 Lavater, *L'Art de connaître*, 3:239, 249–50; on the ideals of Winckelmann, 7:131–2; see also Baridon and Guédron, *Corps et arts*, 72.

26 Lavater, *Essays on Physiognomy*, 2:23; *L'Art de connaître*, 1:113; *cf* Baridon and Guédron, *Corps et arts*, 10; Tytler, *Faces and Fortunes*, 70.

27 Lavater, *L'Art de connaître*, 4:34–40, 45–53; 160–4.

28 Lavater, *Physiognomische Fragmente*, 4:325, cited in Flavell, "Mapping Faces," esp. 17.

29 Lavater, *Essays on Physiognomy*, 2:148–9; and Lavater, *L'Art de connaître*, 4:35, 72, 281–2.

PLATES LXXVIII. LXXIX.

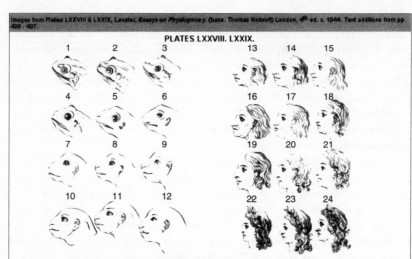

To render these ideas more intelligible and evident, the reader needs only cast a glance on the annexed plates of profiles, which will explain and elucidate my theory. The gradual transition from the head of a frog to the Apollo-. which, when we compare the 1st and 24th figures alone, must appear almost impossible without a *salto mortale*, an extravagant leap and unwarrantable violence-exhibits itself, as I may say, in them, in such a manner that we are more surprised it should be so natural than that it is abrupt and forced, and we immediately find the commentary on what we see in our own feelings, without a single word of explanation. Fig. 1, is entirely the frog, the swollen representative of disgusting bestiality; 2, is likewise a complete frog, but a frog of an improved kind; 3, may be considered as a more intelligent frog; 4, has still somewhat of the nature and appearance of the frog; 5, is no longer a frog; 6, is still less so; the round eye has lengthened. In 7, there is a sensible advance towards a nose and chin. In 8, the progress is small, but the angle between the mouth and eye is impossible in any animal of very low degree. The progress is much more conspicuous in 9. The lips of 10, are much more defined. Here commences the first degree of the cessation of brutality. In 11, a greater progress is made towards a forehead and a mouth. In 12, begins the lowest degree of humanity; the angle of the countenance is indeed not much larger than sixty degrees, very little raised above brutality, yet nearer to the negro than the orang-outang; and the projecting nose and defined lips decisively indicate commencing humanity. 13, expresses weak limited humanity; the eye and forehead are not yet sufficiently human. 14, has the expression of benevolent weakness. 15, has all the attributes of humanity, and the angle of the countenance contains seventy degrees. 16, gradually advances towards reason. 17, is still more rational; but the eye, forehead, and chin are feeble. The signs of intelligence are manifest in 18; but still more conspicuous in 19. In 20, the progress is not discernible nor expressed as it ought to be: it is in fact an unmeaning supplementary countenance. Much more intelligent is 21. The three last heads are on the whole elegant, but ill-delineated: so dull a forehead, so vacant an eye, as in 24, is not suitable to the far-striking, the penetrating divinity.

From the Frog to Apollo, from Johann Caspar Lavater, *Essays on Physiognomy*

Greek ideals with obtuse facial angles, high foreheads, and non-projecting jaws, better than the average living European.[30]

On a more practical level, Lavater's belief in the ideal Greek norm meant denigrating those who deviated from it. Citing Leibniz and Newton in his early sketch *Von der Physiognomik*, Lavater found it inconceivable "that the one could have conceived his theodicy in the skull of a Lapp, and the other pondered the planets and split a beam of light in the head of a Moor (Negro) whose nose is squashed, whose eyes protrude from his head, whose lips, as much as they pout, barely cover his teeth, and who is fleshy and round all over." In the subsequent *Fragmente* Lavater removed the offensive reference to the "Negro" and replaced with it a "Lapp who can't count to six and calls everything beyond it innumerable."[31]

PHYSIOGNOMY IN FRANCE

The facile acceptance of Lavater's views in France is evident in the work of Jean-Joseph Sue fils (1760–1828), anatomy lecturer at the École des Beaux-Arts and, from 1784 to 1807, at the public forum of the Lycée and Athénée. A student of pathognomy, Sue also taught anatomy to painters. In 1797 he produced an *Essai sur la physiognomonie des corps vivants considérés depuis l'homme jusqu'à la plante*. For him Lavater was "very philosophical," but not theoretical enough. Sue accepted the cardinal principle that the form of the face, such as a beautiful nose, was a sign of excellent character or intelligence.[32] Clearly he also identified with Winckelmann's aesthetic values, since ancient Greek statues manifested superior form. Sue was not well disposed toward non-Europeans: "bizarre customs only add to the natural ugliness of these different peoples, which in the moral as well as the physical seem to have no affinity with perfection." He asserted that a low facial angle by Camper's standard was the badge of inferiority. He also accepted the commonplace that Asian peoples such as the Chinese needed to kidnap more beautiful "Caucasians" from Georgia to

---

30 Lavater, *L'Art de connaître*, 9: 10–13; see also Blanckaert, " 'Vicissitudes,' " 430; Baridon and Guédron, *Corps et arts*, 75–6; Judith Wechsler, "Lavater, Stereotype, and Prejudice" in Shookman, ed. *The Faces of Physiognomy*, 106–7.

31 Lavater, in *Von der Physiognomik* (Leipzig: Weidman and Reich, 1772), 14 and *Physiognomische Fragmente*, 1:46, cited in Carsten Zelle, "Soul-Semiology: On Lavater's Physiognomic Principles" in Shookman, ed. *The Faces of Physiognomy*, esp. 58; Lavater, *L'Art de connaître*, 2:188.

32 Sue fils, *Essai sur la physiognomonie*, v, 172–3, 183.

enhance the beauty of their own race.[33] Like Lavater, he thought that the greatest knowledge of passions could be obtained from inmates of prisons or asylums. Lavater's status as prison chaplain and early visits to prisons by the inventor of phrenology, Franz Joseph Gall, would make such institutions the ideal arena with a captive audience par excellence for physiognomic and phrenological studies.[34]

Idéologue physician and hygiene lecturer at the Athénée in 1799–1801, and eventually biographer of Cabanis, Louis-Jacques Moreau de la Sarthe (1771–1826) launched one of the most widely distributed scholarly editions of Lavater in France from 1806 to 1809.[35] An ex-surgeon in a military hospital, due to an injury Moreau became more renowned as a medical journalist and author. He contributed to the Idéologue periodical *La Décade philosophique* and also occupied the positions of assistant librarian and librarian at the Paris Faculté de Médecine.

Strongly committed to continuing Cabanis's exploration of physical-moral relations, Moreau had even been among the first writers of French to use "anthropologie," in a review of Philippe Pinel's treatise on "insanity." He divided anthropology into physical and moral. The physical branch included the natural history of human beings, anatomy, physiology, the applied physiology of hygiene, and medicine. The "moral" branch was partly "experimental" – biography, history, and travelers' reports, but also included analysis of the intellectual faculties (ideology) and sentiments (ethics), applied ethics, public economy, and legislation – a net wide enough to encompass a good part of the emerging social sciences.[36] Moreau's lifelong enterprise was the use of the passions, feelings, and sentiments to influence the physical (the reverse of Cabanis) in the hopes of therapies both psychological and physiological. While Moreau was extremely conservative in his assessment of gender roles, otherwise he thought a "physiological theory of ethics" could bring "improvement in morals and happiness," in short the "limitless perfectibility of the human species."[37]

---

33 Ibid., 20, 26, 59.

34 Ibid., 185.

35 For the most recent work on Moreau, see Signoret, "Moreau de la Sarthe," where she cites "Remarques philosophiques et médicales sur la nature de l'homme (rubrique Physiologie), remarques formant l'un des principaux supplémens ajoutés dans la nouvelle édition de Lavater," *La Décade philosophique* no. 26 (11 sept 1807): 449–57, no. 27, (21 sept 1807): 513–28.

36 Moreau, review of "Pinel, Traité médico-philosophique."

37 Moreau, "Esquisse d'un cours d'hygiène," *Recueil périodique* 8 (1800): 75; "Mémoire sur plusieurs maladies," *Recueil périodique* 6 (1799): 389–90, 392, 396.

Moreau turned with great alacrity to Lavater to help formulate a true "science of observation." Such a subdivision would be part of Cabanis's more extended "science of man" (physiology, analysis of ideas, and ethics), which in turn occupied the interval between physical and moral sciences.[38] However, Moreau converted Lavater's physiognomy into a more secular or even anti-clerical pursuit with more striking physiological consequences. Moreau also added an interest in pathognomy to investigation of profiles. Both Moreau and Lavater thought one could see the effects of remorse, melancholy, and sadness imprinted on facial expressions. Hospitals and prisons provided excellent fields of observation for seeing the "uneducated man strongly occupied with their interests and passions." The habits of frequently renewed expressions marked characteristics on the face – the acquired ugliness of the hateful, the agitation of the financial speculator, the alterations of drunkenness and debauchery.[39]

Moreau believed some causes of inequality to be inherent, while others were the products of milieu, education, or social organization. Referring specifically to Bichat, he noted that to "educate particularly and to improve, by apprenticeship and exercise of any profession, a type of organ and faculty is to weaken the others, in hoarding by a kind of usurpation the powers of life in certain privileged regions of the organization." Human castrati or alterations of plants for double flowers furnished examples. Professions exercising the intellect obtained the first rank, while those allowing "animal life" all its activity attained only the least advantaged places in society.

While open to Bichat's anticipation of the organic society model, Moreau was not committed to purely physical determinism. He still gave modes of life overriding importance. So, on the one hand, traditional temperament theory gave grounds for "natural and organic causes of inequality among men"; on the other hand, living conditions, habits, and occupations could determine "acquired temperaments or even constitutional degeneracy."[40]

In interpreting the weakness of "savages" found by the naturalist François Péron on Nicolas Baudin's voyage to Australia from 1800 to 1804, Moreau thought that "crafts and professions" were responsible for modifying and possibly strengthening the muscles. The progress of civilization also affected feminine nature. In the "early epochs of civilization,"

38 Lavater, *L'Art de connaître*, 1:64–5.
39 Ibid., 1:110, 112; see also Moreau, "Encore des réflexions," esp. 71.
40 Lavater, *L'Art de connaître*, 8:148.

women appeared less feminine because of "violent exercise, exposure to the weather, slavery, and persecution."[41] In fact, to appreciate properly the nature of beauty itself, one would need a "properly disposed brain, a peaceful soul, and a very much advanced civilization."[42]

To the degree he accepted inescapable organic inequality, Moreau justified Lavater's belief in the difficulty of modifying temperaments, especially of non-Europeans.[43] In his edition of Lavater, he augmented considerably the sections concerning Camper's facial line. He also added Georges Cuvier's contention that the shape of the forehead was an index of intelligence and a sign of the predominance of brain or senses. The degraded man was correspondingly closer to the animals. Africans had receding foreheads, protruding jaws, and less room for frontal lobes, with smaller facial angles. The "Ethiopian" (African) physiognomy was "contrary to well-developed human nature" and the Kalmuk Tartars "far from the perfection of the human species."[44] Moreau's endorsement of Camper's facial angle was far from idiosyncratic in France. The facial angle would be used by both English and French physicians who wrote on anthropology from 1813 through the 1830s, including the physician Pierre-Nicolas Gerdy in a physiology text of 1832. Gerdy was the teacher of the renowned anthropologist Paul Broca.[45]

BLUMENBACH AND CRANIA

Aside from Buffon and Cuvier, the most influential early racial theorist for the French was Johann Friedrich Blumenbach (1752–1840), the physician of Göttingen commonly designated the father of physical anthropology. He repeated the four geographic divisions of Linnaeus in the first edition (1775) of his *De generis humani varietate nativa*, but by his third edition of 1795 had added a fifth (Malay) variety.[46] Blumenbach separated humans from apes, excluded the wild and monstrous species of Linnaeus, and avoided purely geographic categories. Like Buffon, he

41 Ibid., 6:230–1, 240–1; 7:18.

42 Ibid., 7:86–7.

43 Ibid., 1:11, 63.

44 Ibid., 1:192, 206–8, 243, 287; 4:160–4; see also Moreau, *Histoire naturelle*, 1:40n, 110, 241–2.

45 Blanckaert, " 'Vicissitudes,' " 438.

46 Blumenbach, *De generis humani varietate nativa* (Göttingen: Vandenhoek and Ruprecht, 1795) translated in Blumenbach, *The Anthropological Treatises; De generis*, 114–22, cited in Bertoletti, "The Anthropological Theory," esp. 116.

demanded complex criteria for varieties, including not only skin colour but also hair type and eye colour, stature and proportions, physiognomy, and facial structure relating to cranial form. Rather than observe the face in profile like Camper, he insisted on comparing crania from behind and above. Blumenbach could thus measure the width of the cranium and face, as well as take other measures of the forehead, jawbone, eye sockets, nasal bones, and teeth. For him, Camper's angle was too limited and unreliable, since individuals of the same race varied too greatly and those of different races could have the same angle. Even by Blumenbach's own measures, there was much diversity within each race, so a "type" was difficult to formulate.[47]

Blumenbach found the skull of Georgians from the Caucasus most harmonious, so he created the term "Caucasian" for the white variety of humans found in north Africa and west Asia as well as Europe. He based his judgment of "the most beautiful stock" with the whitest skin on a Georgian woman.[48] He assumed this form was the norm and the most primitive, while the four other varieties deviated from it because it would be easier to transform a white person into a coloured person than the reverse. At two extremes were the "Ethiopian" and the "Mongolian" (including Finns, Lapps, and "Eskimos"). Intermediate between the Caucasian and Mongolian were the "Americans" and intermediate between Caucasian and Ethiopian were the "Malay" of the Pacific islands, Indonesia, and the Malay peninsula. The Malays shaded off into Ethiopian in the south and west Pacific, where Papuans and New Hollanders could as easily be classified as Ethiopian.

While Blumenbach was among the most non-hierarchical of racial theorists, he attributed to the influence of climate a kind of "degeneration" of the primitive Caucasian type as it adjusted to new environments. Climate, nutrition, and lifestyle affected the formative force (*nisus formativus*) in all beings. Like Buffon, Blumenbach thought colour changes reversible, until he adopted from Kant the idea that varieties became hereditary. At that point he called varieties "races" (*gens* in his Latin usage), which he thought from time immemorial were virtually interchangeable with "species."[49] However, Blumenbach always insisted on the morphological unity of the species, with insensible gradations of types. In his

47 See also Schiebinger, *Nature's Body*, 119.

48 Ibid., 129.

49 Blumenbach, *The Anthropological Treatises*, 211 on air exposure and colour; Blanckaert, "Monogénisme et polygénisme," esp. 3024–5.

dissertation on "Negroes," he particularly insisted that Negroes were capable of education and culture and could associate with the most educated peoples on earth.[50] In that sense, Blumenbach was a moderating influence compared to the rigidly hierarchical views characterizing two French racial theorists, Virey and Bory.

VIREY, BORY, AND MULTIPLE HUMAN SPECIES

A completely different sensitivity informed the conclusions of the indefatigable popularizer Julien-Joseph Virey (1775–1846). Virey was a pharmacist who taught natural history at the Val-de-Grâce military hospital and at the public forum of the Athénée. In 1814 he also received a medical degree from the Paris Faculty. Although very much fascinated by physical-mental relations, Virey, unlike the Idéologue Cabanis, was a vitalist and Providentialist. His political tendencies at least in the 1830s identified him with the centre-left in the Orléanist Chamber of Deputies, where he served from 1831 to 1837.[51] Claude Blanckaert's previous study of Virey demonstrates the difficulty of firmly classifying him either as a polygenist or as a monogenist climate theorist.[52] There is no doubt of Virey's importance for polygenist writers such as Bory de Saint-Vincent and Honoré Jacquinot. He was also a prime target of critical monogenists such as Armand de Quatrefages and egalitarians like the abolitionist Victor Schoelcher. Virey's peculiar diatribes against blacks may be partly explained by the atmosphere after the ferocious massacres by both sides in the Haitian revolts and Bonaparte's re-establishment of slavery in 1802. But Virey's immediate motivations in 1800 seem to be an endorsement of selected eighteenth-century polygenist racial theorists and a critique of theories of racial differentiation by climate.[53]

As early as 1800, in the first edition of *Histoire naturelle du genre humain*, Virey argued that skin colour persists no matter what the change in climate is for a given group. Nor was colour apparently correlated to climate, since Siberians in a cold climate were as brown as Malays in the

50 Blumenbach, *Beiträge zur Naturgeschichte* (1806), 97, cited in Bertoletti, "The Anthropological Theory," 98.

51 Jacques Léonard, "Pour situer Virey" in Bénichou and Blanckaert, eds. *Julien-Joseph Virey*, 17–22.

52 Blanckaert, "J.-J. Virey," in ibid., 97–182.

53 Sources cited in Virey, *Histoire naturelle* (1800), 1:86n include, besides Charles White, Linnaeus, Buffon, Blumenbach, J.R. Forster, Zimmermann, Kames, de Pauw, Daubenton, Camper, Kant, Smith, and John Hunter.

Portrait of Julien-Joseph Virey (1775–1846),
pharmacist, physician, and advocate of two distinct
human species

tropics.[54] Blanckaert established that at the same time, Virey accepted
some role for climate in limiting development, establishing varieties,
and affecting temperament. Virey also seemed to endorse the conjectural history model used by Walckenaer of the development of savage
peoples toward civilization.[55]

Despite these contradictions, the dominant model even in the first
edition of the book was the distinctiveness of each race. While no
human was equivalent to an ape, "some races were closer to the apes."
Virey was aware of Charles White's gradation of races in 1799 by

54 Virey, *Histoire naturelle* (1800), 1:23, 126.
55 Ibid., 1:125–6, 128, 132–7.

Camper's facial angle.[56] Virey accepted Cuvier's interpretation that "a more acute facial angle" of certain races resulted in reduced brain mass. Using a slightly different measure, from the base of the forehead to the upper jaw and from the occipital cavity to the alveoli of the upper incisors, Virey assessed the facial angle at 85° for Europeans, 75° for Negroes, and 65° for the orangutan of Borneo. A tendentious illustration taken from Anne-Claude de Tubières, comte de Caylus's antiquities (1752), and reprinted by other authors, also exaggerated the resemblance between the orangutan and the "Negro."[57]

Virey was already considering the idea of separate species. He cited Lord Kames's designation of the "Negro" as a distinct species, with "muzzle of apes and a flattened nose" and added an indicator of "larger sexual organs," like some tropical peoples and "northern Scots." Therefore, "some of the five or six [Blumenbach's five plus a Northern race] primordial races could be considered distinct species, since they are constant in their sequence of reproduction, independently of any cause of variation," including climate, nutrition, and custom. Indeed, fertile hybrids proved nothing about the unity of the species. Negroes were closer to "animality" with their posterior occipital cavity and larger nerves draining the brain of energy. Perhaps most striking in view of the future enterprises of geographers, he thought the "world would be a vile rabble of barbarians without Europeans, hence world empire is European destiny."[58] In his ladder of humanity, polar peoples, the Hottentots, and the savage tribes of South America and the South Seas ranked even below African Negroes, and might never be civilized. Clearly, the moral perfectibility of peoples was related to their physiological and physical make-up. He conceded, however, that some climates induced weakness and irritability, and therefore kept the "Negro and Lapp in barbarity."[59]

In his article "Negro" in 1803 in Deterville's *Nouveau dictionnaire d'histoire naturelle,* Virey even proclaimed the eternal destiny of the Negro to be enslaved.[60] By 1817, in his article "Homme" in the Deterville *Dictionnaire des sciences médicales,* Virey was more overtly polygenist. The full implications would be spelled out in the second, enlarged edition (1824) of his

56 Ibid., 1:86–91 on apes and humans, including use of Charles White, *An account of the regular gradation in Man* (London: C. Dilly, 1799); see also Claude Blanckaert, "J.-J. Virey" in Bénichou and Blanckaert, eds. *Julien-Joseph Virey,* 109–11.

57 Virey, *Histoire naturelle* (1800), 1:121, 157–8, 182, 297; 2:42, 184.

58 Ibid., 1:23, 126, 138, 143, 146.

59 Ibid., 2:121; 167; 266–7.

60 Blanckaert, "1800–Le moment 'naturaliste,'" esp. 120.

natural history. There were now definitely two human species, not degeneration from a primitive type, and the facial angle was the distinctive dividing line. The races of Europeans, with an angle of 85–90°, and Asians, Malays, and Caribs (Americans), with angles of 80–85°, qualified for the first species. The "Ethiopians" (including east African Galla and Caffirs), Papuans, and Hottentots were a second species, with "two black and blackish races" deficient in brain size and intellect (a facial angle of 75–80°), as well as courage, industry, and skill. The second race of the second species (Hottentots, Bushmen, Papuans, Australians, and New Caledonians) comprised the "last of men, closest to the orangutan."[61] Now the universal development of savages toward civilization had disappeared. In an assertion to be repeated in discussions of the Paris Ethnological Society, for Virey, "Negroes do not civilize themselves." They lived as "big children," without laws or constitutions.[62]

By 1824, the curious inverse relationship of the brain and sexual organs would explain how sexual passions accounted for the "natural inferiority of the Negro race with regard to whites in respect to all talents and industry, and which, though equal in the eyes of humanity and nature, degrades the black man toward animality."[63] As with Moreau, Bichat was also a source for this equilibrium of functions: Bichat's "determinate sum of faculties and powers" assured that "man loses in one sense what he gains with another." Condorcet's dream of human perfectibility was therefore misguided.[64]

Still, like so many nineteenth-century racists, by the 1820s Virey would give aid and comfort to pro-slavery theorists without himself advocating slavery. He devoted thirty pages of the edition of 1824 to outlining the abuses of the slave trade and to assertions such as "no one is born a slave." Indeed, Europeans should "extend a protecting hand [to the emancipated slaves] to elevate them to an honourable rank in the ladder of perfection ... they could then enjoy a social life with the degree of enlightenment and happiness to which they can aspire."[65] Virey in this manner endorsed a position that would echo through anthropologists' manifestoes of the late nineteenth century. Inequality was assumed, but Europeans could assist inferior races to reach their full, if limited, potential.

61 Virey, *Histoire naturelle* (1824), 1:408–9, 438; 2:2n, 5, 22, 46, 52–3.
62 Ibid., 2:56, 60, 173, 193.
63 Ibid., 1:136–7, 142, 249.
64 Ibid., 3:232.
65 Ibid., 2:72, 83–107, and esp. 106–7.

Virey became a sourcebook for every cliché of hatred for non-Europeans. His personality was reserved, however, compared to the carousing cavalry officer and cartographer in the military headquarters of the Dépôt de la Guerre, Jean-Baptiste-Geneviève-Marcellin Bory de Saint-Vincent (1780–1846). A boastful Gascon field-mapper and statistical expert, Bory regretted not inflicting more mayhem on the enemy after the battle of Austerlitz. He lived with mistresses apart from his wife, and was bailed out of debtors' prison by a son-in-law.[66] A self-proclaimed deist, he was possibly an atheist, and had a reputation as a materialist after writing a book on the nature of matter. An enthusiastic Bonapartist and possibly a republican during the Restoration, Bory gained fame through cartographic expeditions to the Canaries and other islands off the African coast. His membership in the House of Representatives during the Hundred Days cost him a four-year exile from 1816 to 1820 in Prussia and the Low Countries. In addition to editing a multi-volume dictionary of natural history, Bory capped his career with major work on two French scientific expeditions. As head of the physical sciences section of the scientific commission, his botanical work in the Morea in Greece in 1829–31 secured him election to the Academy of Sciences in 1832. He also engaged in botanical and anthropological study in Algeria from 1839 to 1842, stormily supervising civilian subordinates such as the former Saint-Simonian leader Prosper Enfantin. There Bory prepared unpublished anthropological documents that have not been found.[67]

While Virey may have trumpeted European destiny, Bory was a practicing imperialist who often seemed to adjust his racial theory to suit French interests.[68] In 1825 he published a classic article on "man," cataloguing separate human species in the *Dictionnaire classique d'histoire naturelle.* Two years later this article became a separate work, *L'homme* (homo), *Essai zoologique sur le genre humain.*

Basing his findings on travel reports and his own experience, Bory advocated the existence of fifteen distinct human species, each divided into races and varieties. Using the old Aristotelian standard of straight versus woolly hair, he saw a fundamental division between the eight straight-haired and seven woolly-haired species. Otherwise, skin colour

66 Rôle, *Un destin hors série,* 29, 113, 116; Godlewska, *Geography Unbound,* 176–86; Thomson, "Bory de Saint-Vincent."

67 See Bory de Saint-Vincent, *Relation du voyage de la Commission scientifique de Morée dans le Péloponnèse, les Cyclades et l'Attique,* 2 vols (Paris: F.-G. Levrault, 1836–38) cited in Broc, "Les grandes missions."

68 Thomson, "Bory de Saint-Vincent," 286.

Portrait of J.-B.-G.-M. Bory de Saint-Vincent

and continent were insufficient markers, although facial angle would play a critical role.[69] Against the standard view of Blumenbach or of the English physician and anthropologist James Cowles Prichard, Bory believed each species to have an independent origin.

The first human species was the "Japetic" (after Japheth, third son of Noah), representing the Europeans with four races (Caucasic in the east, Pelagian Greeks and Romans in the south, Celtic in the west, and Germanic in the north, both Teutonic and Slavonic). There also was an "Arabic" species with two races – western ("Atlantic" – Barbary coast) and eastern ("Adamic" – Jews and mideastern Arabs).[70]

Bory changed his mind on north African racial classification after his visit to Algeria. In 1827, he placed Moroccans, Algerians, and Libyans in the Atlantic race,[71] but by 1845, he had discerned three distinct species in Algeria: (1) native Atlantic, whom he called "Kabyles" or "Berbers,"

---

69 Bory de Saint-Vincent, L'Homme.

70 See also Thomson, "Bory de Saint-Vincent," 274, 277.

71 Bory de Saint-Vincent, L'Homme, 1:174–8, cited in Thomson, "Bory de Saint-Vincent," 283.

settled mountain dwellers in contrast to the "Moors," shepherds or peasants in valleys or city dwellers; (2) the Adamic, conquering Arab or wan-
dering Bedouin; and (3) the Ethiopic blacks.[72] The Atlantic species,
with great skill in the arts and sciences and a "nearly straight facial angle," now included Moors, Berbers, ancient Iberians, and even Celts
(therefore the French). The "more acute facial angle" of the Adamic
made common classification with the Atlantic impossible. The Ethiopians, on the other hand, still demonstrated "signs of animality" with their
"kind of muzzle."[73] The renewed classification of the Kabyle, close to a
kindred French people, was consonant with French designs: the French
now envisaged unconquered Kabyle outposts as eager to accept French
civilization. Indeed, thought Bory, if the French regime cannot produce
a European civilization in Algeria, it "will at least produce a civilization
suitable for the climate."[74] This conclusion matched the viewpoint of
Virey on Africans.

In addition to the Europeans, Arabs, and Berbers, Bory postulated
the Hindu, Scythic (Turkish and Tartar peoples), Sinic (Chinese and
east Asian), Hyperborean (northern), and Neptunian (Malaysian, Oceanic or Polynesian, Papou, and Australasian) species. Completing the
straight-haired species were those of the New World (Colombic or eastern North American, American, or north and coastal South American,
and Patagonian, or eastern coastal South American). The curly-haired
species included the Ethiopian, Caffir (southeast African), Melanian
(dark-skinned Pacific peoples with a facial angle less acute than the
Papous), and Hottentot.

Like Virey, Bory made use of Cuvier's observation that the facial angle
of 65° of the orangutan was only a bit less than the 70° of the Ethiopian
species, while the "Japetic" were closest to a right angle. Ethiopian brain
mass was consequently at least 11 per cent less than the Japetic species.
Ethiopians were "quite inferior to the Japetic, Arabic, Hindu, and Sinic
species in relation to intellect and sociability." Either Ethiopians had
poor organic conformation or had no suitable basis of civilization to develop moral faculties.[75]

72 Bory de Saint-Vincent, "Sur l'anthropologie de l'Afrique française," *Comptes rendus
des séances de l'Académie des sciences* 20, no. 26 (1845): 1812–24, reprinted in *NAV*, 5ᵉ sér., 6
(1846): 108–24; see also his agreement with General Guyon on the existence of white, fair-
haired descendants of Vandals and Goths in Algeria in *NAV*, 5ᵉ sér., 5 (1846): 116.

73 *NAV*, 5ᵉ sér., 6 (1846): 114, 119–20.

74 Ibid., 124; on construction of the Kabyles, see Lorcin, *Imperial Identities*.

75 Bory de Saint-Vincent, *L'Homme*, 1:48–9, 102; 2:29–30, 38.

There was some disparity between the lowest facial angles and "the most brutish of men," since the Australasian species had a higher facial angle at 75° than the "Ethiopians" yet allegedly lacked all religion, law, and the arts.[76] However, Bory portrayed the Hottentots with "hideous profiles of animality," so primitive that they consumed vermin and the unwashed entrails of beasts. In all fairness, Bory was not charitable to European peasants either, who were homegrown savages. "Nine-tenths of the Japetic species are not superior to the Hottentots in the development of their reason," he warned, and some Haitians had now risen to the Anglo-American level.[77] The equation of peasants with "savages" would be a continuing theme in a discourse in which marginalization of "lower" classes proceeded apace with disdain for non-Europeans. However, there is no evidence here that the language of "class" developed from the language of race.[78]

Like Virey, Bory doubted that climates affected the skin colour of Negroes and whites, since the Portuguese had remained white in Africa for 300 years.[79] He similarly insisted that differences among human species did not authorize mistreatment or a slave trade, since Bory would "not admit mistreatment of the least of animals." The condition of blacks did not "condemn them to be beasts of burden." In fact, had they not been corrupted by the slave trade, "they might quite quickly be rendered to the state of civilization."[80] And he excused the defensiveness of the Colombic peoples, who "repulse civilization to which one tries to introduce them," perhaps because "of the harm civilization did them." But if all human beings were from the same Creator, their kinship did not mean descent from a single couple like Adam and Eve. "Younger species" like the Australasians, Hottentots, Melanians were less advanced.[81]

In this manner Bory did not despair of the civilizability of many inferior species, nor did he consciously advocate their subjection. Yet the laying out of such a finely graded hierarchy could only induce a

76 Ibid., 1:319, 323.
77 Ibid., 2:127–8.
78 For a discussion of Foucault's lectures relating class, sexuality, and race, see Stoler, "Towards a Genealogy of Racisms: The 1976 Lectures at the Collège de France" in *Race and the Education of Desire*, 55–94; see also, however, the equation of conquered and conquering "races" and classes in François Guizot and Augustin Thierry in Piguet, "Observation et histoire," esp. 96.
79 Bory de Saint-Vincent, *L'Homme*, 1:71.
80 Ibid., 1:68; 2:52.
81 Ibid., 2:150, 161, 174.

superiority complex in Europeans. As a practising imperialist in Algeria, Bory, like Virey, would convey an early version of the late nineteenth-century theorists of imperial "association." The Algerians were capable of a certain kind of civilization, but would never develop to European norms.

From Petrus Camper's innocuous intentions, there emerged an entire industry of classification of peoples in which the facial angle assumed a critical role. While few theorists completely discarded climatic influences, physical conformation in the shape of facial profile was now a great restraint on the capacity for civilization. Lavater's physiognomy would have many reincarnations in the late nineteenth century, although many later anthropologists repudiated Lavater's unscientific method. But no less a pillar of the Société d'anthropologie de Paris than Charles Letourneau would praise the work of the painter Jean-Baptiste Delestre and the anatomist Pierre-Louis Gratiolet in developing a more scientific physiognomy, which could be used to aid comparative craniology of races.[82] If the profile itself were not enough of an indicator, the features of faces that were allegedly "criminal" figured in the later debates on the criminal anthropology of Cesare Lombroso. There, too, would be parallels between the criminal as having animal-like "atavism" and the savage.[83]

Before assessing the consequences of the facial angle for geography and ethnology, we must examine a different method of external labeling. Here the practitioners combined external head shape with internal functionality of the brain. The "organology" of Franz-Joseph Gall and Johann Caspar Spurzheim arrived with great fanfare in Paris in 1807 and would stimulate the classification of both individuals and races well into the 1840s.

82 Anne-Marie Drouin-Hans, "La physiognomonie des anthropologues; art divinatoire ou discipline légitime?" in Blanckaert, *Les Politiques de l'anthropologie*, 29–53; both Gratiolet and the Italian Paolo Mantegazza studied the expression of sentiments, or mobile physiognomy.

83 Claude Blanckaert, "Des sauvages en pays civilisé, L'anthropologie des criminels (1850–1900)," in Mucchielli, ed. *Histoire de la Criminologie française*, 55–88.

3

The Ambivalence of Phrenology

Franz Joseph Gall (1758–1828), born in the German state of Baden, studied medicine in Strasbourg and Vienna. A practising physician, he began lecturing in 1796 in Vienna on what he called "organology," the cerebral localization of mental faculties. Others called his palpation of skulls to ascertain the prominence or deficiency of these organs "cranioscopy." After the Habsburg emperor banned Gall's lectures as a danger to religion in 1801, Gall in 1805 embarked on a tour of Europe and finally arrived to a sensational public, but mixed scholarly, reception in Paris in October 1807.

From 1804 to 1812, his younger colleague, Johann Gaspar Spurzheim (1776–1832), also from a German village near Trier, was his anatomist and collaborator. Spurzheim received his medical degree only in 1813, from Vienna. For reasons never fully uncovered, Gall repudiated Spurzheim around the same time, but it was Spurzheim who most notably diffused a revised version of Gall's doctrine. By 1815, the English physician Thomas M. Forster had baptised these ideas "phrenology." Most British and French "phrenologists" followed Spurzheim's augmented listing of mental faculties.[1]

THE FOUNDATION OF PHRENOLOGICAL SOCIETIES

The major effort to institutionalize phrenology as a science came from the cooperation of physicians and a group of liberal philanthropists late

---

1 On the careers of Gall and Spurzheim, see van Wyhe; Giustino; Temkin, "Gall"; and Erwin H. Ackerknecht and Henri V. Vallois, *Franz Joseph Gall, inventory of phrenology and his collection*, Madison: University of Wisconsin Medical School, 1956. On the term "phrenology," see Cooter, *The Culture of Popular Science*, 59; Renneville, *Le Langage des crânes*, 27.

in 1830 (officially in January 1831), when they founded the Société phrénologique de Paris.[2] Among the leaders were the teacher and prison reformer Benjamin Appert (1797–1873), a protocol chief in the royal household who believed phrenology could help explain crimes, and factory owners and primary education reformers baron Guillaume Ternaux (1763–1833) and comte Charles de Lasteyrie du Saillant (1759–1849).[3] Within a year there were 82 physicians in a membership of 150, with a sprinkling of six lawyers, six artists, a few pharmacists, sculptors, architects, officials, even one priest. They committed themselves to "propagate and improve the doctrine of Gall" and to "promote the progress of enlightenment."[4] By the late 1830s, Paris had at least five phrenology courses, other departments had at least three, and there were provincial societies in Lyon, Toulon, Metz, Epinal, and Saint-Brieuc.[5] While three professors of the Paris Faculty of Medicine joined the Society, the summit of success came with ministerial approval for a phrenology course under Faculty auspices by François-Joseph-Victor Broussais (1772–1839). If phrenology never gained great acclaim, it was hardly a fringe-group phenomenon.

Extensive studies of British phrenology reveal the impact of Spurzheim's converts, the lawyer George Combe of Edinburgh and his brother Andrew, a physician. Phrenological societies were founded in London in 1820 and Edinburgh in 1823, and by 1840 there were at least twenty-eight societies with a total of over 1,000 members. George Combe's *On the Constitution of Man and its Relationship to External Objects* (1828–29) was one of the most successful popular philosophy volumes of the nineteenth century, with sales over 200,000 through at least nine editions.[6]

Unlike the Paris membership, the Edinburgh society had a large grouping of middle-class lawyers, merchants, and manufacturers, while only one-sixth were physicians. The medical contingent of members consisted of younger physicians, of lower social status or with less prestigious medi-

2 On the impulse behind learned societies, see Fox, "The Savant Confronts his Peers"; for provincial societies of amateur men of letters, see Chaline, *Sociabilité et érudition*.

3 Renneville, *Le Langage des crânes*, 120–7.

4 "Liste des membres de la Société phrénologique de Paris," *JSPP* 1 (1832): 21–8, 80; the unsuccessful application for a "society of public utility" in 1833 claimed 150 out of 200 physicians (AN F173038); see Renneville, *Le Langage des crânes*, 129–37 on the composition of the Society; Williams, *The Physical and the Moral*, 182–8.

5 *La Phrénologie* 1 no. 17, (20 sept 1837), suppl. p. 3; Renneville, *La Médecine du crime* 1:389–90.

6 Cooter, *The Culture of Popular Science*, 26–9; and generally Giustino, *Conquest of Mind*.

cal degrees and professional reputations than the medical opponents of phrenology. They were more likely to be Whig or dissenters rather than Tory or Anglican.[7] In France, the paucity of information concerning large numbers of opponents of phrenology makes comparable conclusions difficult. Fragmentary evidence yields no significant age difference between vehement supporters of Gall (usually from the generation reaching maturity from 1815 to 1825) or members of the Society and the most vocal critics (see appendix 1). As in Britain, however, the most prestigious scientists were staunch opponents (permanent secretaries of the Academy of Sciences included Cuvier, who was unfriendly to Gall in 1808, and François Magendie [1783–1855] from the older generations, Marie-Jean-Pierre Flourens [1794–1867] from the younger generation; Frédéric Dubois d'Amiens [1799–1873], secretary of the Academy of Medicine, was another opponent). But aside from Broussais, stalwart advocates of phrenology in the Paris Faculty of Medicine included Jean-François Bouillaud (1796–1881) and Gabriel Andral (1797–1876), and J.-B. Mège (1787–186?) and Félix Voisin (1794–1872) in the Academy of Medicine. Some of the older-generation adherents of the Société phrénologique were deputies, journalists, or other non-medical figures. Many physicians who were early members of the Society were in their thirties, but figures for a comparable number of opponents are difficult to obtain.

The culture of phrenology in Britain allowed both attacks on aristocratic privilege and aspirations for social control. Radical, even Owenite socialist thinkers supported its naturalistic anti-clericalism and promise of self-help for workers. But Combe made thrift, temperance, discipline, and respect for property preferable to animal desires. Roger Cooter has consequently designated phrenology a vehicle to naturalize division of labour by slotting diverse personalities into their appropriate role in the modernizing industrial economy.[8] However, in Britain there was less fear of revolutionary upheaval through social mobility, especially in Combe's spiritualist version of phrenology.

The aforementioned political slant in France assured that phrenologists similarly came from the Orléanist centre-left after 1830, the liberal left, or even the ranks of Fourierist socialists. In contrast to Britain, however, there does not seem to be any evidence of widespread popular enthusiasm in France, at least after the initial fascination with Gall. Closer

---

7 Cooter, *The Culture of Popular Science*, 42–7, 114; see also Shapin, "Homo Phrenologicus," esp. 55–63; and Shapin, "Phrenological Knowledge."

8 Cooter, *The Culture of Popular Science*, 114–16; 204–8; Giustino, *Conquest of Mind*, 139–42; Cooter, "Phrenology and British Alienists."

study of opinions of Society members points to a very restrained vision of social reform and in most cases the compatibility of social hierarchy with the "progressive" politics of republicanism and anti-clericalism. While Combe may have given British workers another tool for cultivating the self, the fears of social elites in France could turn French phrenology into a denigration of the Other, whether of different social classes or different ethnic origins.

THE FOUNDERS: GALL, SPURZHEIM, AND RELATION TO PHYSIOGNOMY

A brief description of Franz Joseph Gall's "organology" will help clarify discussion of its social and cultural significance. Gall asserted that distinct, localizable organs in the brain (twenty-seven, augmented to thirty-five in Spurzheim and even forty-two in Joseph Vimont) conditioned individual intelligence and character by related dispositions of particular instincts, sentiments, and abilities. By allegedly empirical observation, Gall had correlated bulging eyes with the aptitude for visual memory, for example, or a large cerebellum (protruding neck) with sexual appetite. He ascertained the relative development of each organ by its size. Since the cranium moulded around the brain in the fetus, an observer could palpate the cranial protuberances and depressions of an individual (a procedure known later as cranioscopy).[9] For example, an overdeveloped organ for the faculty of possessiveness, legitimate in the attachment to property, could lead to a penchant for thievery. An excess of the animal-like "carnivorous instinct" could show homicidal tendencies. Some individuals would excel in specifically human religious feeling, linguistic skill, or calculation. When Gall launched his public Parisian career with lectures to 150 people at the Athénée de Paris in 1807–08, the press caught the mood of sensationalism. There was a plethora of caricatures, production of craniological snuffboxes, and student masquerades in which stock comic characters touched each others' heads.[10]

9 Gall and Spurzheim, *Anatomie et physiologie*, 1:iii, xv; see also Letter to Retzer, translated in *JSPP* 3 (1835): 116–37; on the early career of Gall and the suggestion that he sought social prestige and gentlemanly status, see van Wyhe, "The authority of human nature."

10 Renneville, *Le Langage des crânes*, 83–96 on the popular sensation of phrenology in Paris; Wegner, "Phrenologische Schnupftabakdosen," esp. 71, 78 and "Franz Joseph Gall"; for the Athénée records, see Bibliothèque historique de la Ville de Paris, MS. CP 3948; MS. 920, 13 Nov., 8 Dec. 1807, 2 and 12 Feb. 1808; and MS. 772, fol. 102; see also *Gazette de France*, 23 janvier 1808, 92.

Gall

Amativité

Phrenological assessment of Franz Joseph Gall
(1758–1828), founder of phrenology

Gall attempted to parry the charge of materialism by arguing that he never speculated on the essence of matter or the soul, and even demonstrated God's existence by postulating a brain organ for receptivity to Divine Revelation.[11] However, such a strict dependence of the soul on the body would never satisfy believers in an immortal soul. And many critics agreed with pro-Kantian author Louis-Sébastien Mercier, who feared that criminals, distorting Gall, would have a ready-made argument from their irresistible organic impulses that they could "be a thief, be a murderer, God wanted it." For analogous reasons even the Idéologue physician Louis-Jacques Moreau de la Sarthe found Gall a dangerous social menace.[12]

There were three significant aspects of the relationship between the art of physiognomy and phrenology. First many authors confused and conflated the two. Second, there was an analogy between the reading of faces and crania, even though phrenology was more "scientific." Finally, physiognomy, with its related use of the facial angle, could accentuate the tendency in phrenology to establish a rank order of races and nationalities along a scale of perfection.

Despite Gall's denunciation of Lavater's anatomical ignorance, even Spurzheim's early description of organology used terms such as "physiognomical system."[13] But while Spurzheim called physiognomy a "true science" of external signs and valued facial expressions as clues, he carefully distinguished his own measurements of the relative size of the regions of the cranium from Lavater's external profile measurement of the shape of the forehead, nose, or hands.[14] In fact, Gall and Spurzheim had no experimental techniques to locate the cerebral organs: in Foucauldian terms they executed an incomplete shift from the external surface reading that characterized Lavater's assessment of profiles.

11 Gall, *Fonctions du cerveau*, 1:9, 223, 225–8, 231, 237, 266; 5:325–6, 366, 399.

12 *Journal de Paris* 2569 (27 nov 1807); see the similar arguments in *Journal de l'Empire* (27 janvier 1808), 3; (1 février 1808), 3–4; (27 février 1808), 3–4; Moreau, "Exposition et critique"(30 nivôse an XII): 129–37; 40 (10, 20 pluviôse an XII), esp. 257–8, 260–3; see also Williams, *The Physical and the Moral*, 109–10; *cf* the spiritualist phrenologist Bailly de Blois, *L'Existence de Dieu*, 26, 54–6.

13 Tytler, *Faces and Fortunes*, 352–3, on Lavater, see Gall, *Fonctions du cerveau*, 1:1–2; 2:148, 394–8; 3:161; 5:429, 431, 434; 6:420–2.

14 Spurzheim, *Phrenology in Connexion*, 7, 12–15; Spurzheim, "Lectures on Phrenology," *The Lancet*, 7 (1825): 99–100.

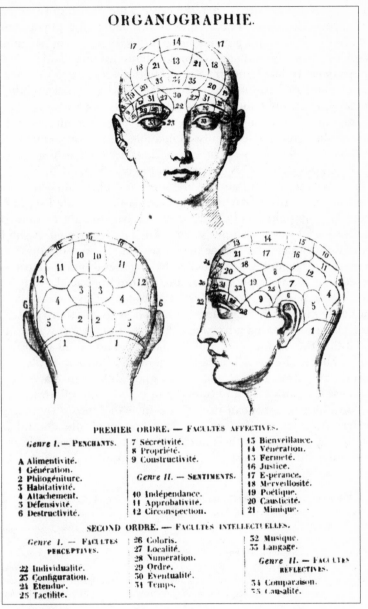

ORGANOGRAPHIE.

PREMIER ORDRE. — FACULTES AFFECTIVES.

Genre I. — PENCHANTS.

A Alimentivité.
1 Génération.
2 Philogéniture.
3 Habitativité.
4 Attachement.
5 Défensivité.
6 Destructivité.

7 Sécretivité.
8 Propriété.
9 Constructivité.

Genre II. — SENTIMENTS.

10 Indépendance.
11 Approbativité.
12 Circonspection.

13 Bienveillance.
14 Vénération.
15 Fermeté.
16 Justice.
17 E-perance.
18 Merveillosité.
19 Poétique.
20 Causticité.
21 Mimique.

SECOND ORDRE. — FACULTES INTELLECTUELLES.

Genre I. — FACULTES PERCEPTIVES.

22 Individualité.
23 Configuration.
24 Etendue.
25 Tactilite.

26 Coloris.
27 Localité.
28 Numeration.
29 Ordre.
30 Eventualité.
31 Temps.

32 Musique.
33 Langage.

Genre II. — FACULTES REFLECTIVES.

34 Comparaison.
35 Causalité.

Phrenological organs according to Johann Caspard Spurzhem, from
T. Poupin

Later popularizations, such as the essay of the physician Isidore Bourdon (1796–1861), gave equal value to phrenology and physiognomy.[15] Even Gall's close supporters tended to justify the use of physiognomy as a supplement to phrenology. When the anatomist Bouillaud reported to the Academy of Medicine in 1841 on Voisin's reading of the heads of young criminals, several sceptical academy members suggested Voisin should have covered the inmates' faces so as "not to be reading the physiognomy." Bouillaud countered that "physiognomy and cranioscopy could agree." The alienist Guillaume Ferrus (a member of the Academy) as well as the prison physician Hubert Lauvergne heartily supported physiognomy as a supplement to cranial analysis.[16]

The tendency to conflate physiognomy and phrenology despite vigorous warnings from Gall and Spurzheim assumes added significance since physiognomists habitually used the facial angle to rank races. Gall himself rejected Camper's angle since it measured only the front brain, rather than intelligence manifested in all brain organs. The existence of intelligent Africans belied hasty generalizations. He also suspected that hardly 2 per cent of any national or racial group would have the same proportion of forehead to face; Chinese would differ among themselves in facial angle as much as from other races.[17] Nor was Gall an unthinking advocate of European superiority, since he asserted that the Iroquois Six Nations had civil and political institutions comparable to the French Estates-General.[18] In principle, phrenology should have advocated racial equality, since all humans have the same faculties. But both Gall and Spurzheim could lend scientific prestige to conventional European prejudices. In Jean-Baptiste Demangeon's transcriptions of Gall's lectures, Gall spoke of the central Asian Kalmuks as disposed to theft and ruse and the West Indian Caribs as cruel, superstitious, and stupid. Spurzheim adopted the ancient Greek

15 Bourdon, *La Physiognomonie et la Phrénologie*, 23–4; Poupin, *Caractères phrénologiques et physiognomiques*, 7–8, 29–31, 33–5; Ysabeau, *Lavater et Gall*, 3, 35, 165, 177–9.

16 *Bulletin de l'Académie royale de médecine* 7 (1841–42): 163–4, 166–7; Lauvergne, *Les forçats*, 78.

17 Gall and Spurzheim, *Anatomie et physiologie* 2:230-1 (1812); on Camper, see *Fonctions du cerveau*, 2:301, 303–6; 5:418–20; see also Blanckaert, "'Vicissitudes,'" 449–50; for Spurzheim, see the *Lancet* 7 (1825): 363 on the brains of Africans; on beauty and Camper, see *Essai sur les principes*, 10, 12; *Philosophical Catechism*, 26–7, 86; *Manuel de phrénologie*, 35, 39, 56–7.

18 Gall, *Fonctions du cerveau*, 6:462.

Measurement of Regions of Head. Caspar Spurzheim,
Phrenology in Connexion with Physiognomy

ideal of beauty, like Julien-Joseph Virey and Lavater. He also disdained the "ignoble Samoyeds," and summarily judged national characters, such as the "destructiveness" of Caribs.[19]

Later phrenologists continued to differentiate between educable Europeans and unredeemable savages. In Britain, the Edinburgh *Phrenological Journal* celebrated the superiority of Teutonic to Celtic Europeans and warned that existing primitive races in the British empire posed a threat to British soldiers and officials who might be tempted to intermarry. In this view, Hindus and other Asians were "stationary" and unlikely to improve, while Africans would always be intellectually and morally inferior.[20] Although a firm believer in the power of education and even inheritance of acquired characteristics, George Combe himself suspected that the "development of the brain sets limits to the spontaneous development of civilization in different races." He qualified any hasty judgment of Africans, though, by admitting that they had never been justly treated.[21]

The popularizers who valued physiognomy were the most likely to use the facial angle to establish an intelligence hierarchy. Bourdon heralded European destiny to educate or subjugate other less intelligent races. He thought after many generations Africans might achieve similar intelligence, but "Hottentots" were hopeless, "stupid ... intermediaries between humans and apes."[22]

Spurzheim's own stepson, the painter Hippolyte Bruyères, believed in the "vicious cerebral conformation" of certain races (animal-like nature and amorality) living along the Indian Ocean, on the South American coast, and in Africa. There were "immense differences" between the "miserable and frightful savage of New Holland" and the "superb and virtuous Germanic race" favoured by a fertile soil. And in a common analogy of the marginalized, Bruyères also commented on the immense difference of more favoured Frenchmen from the "rachitic and de-

19 Demangeon, *Physiologie intellectuelle*, 288, 312, 319; Spurzheim, *Essai sur les principes*, 18; Spurzheim, *Phrenology in Connexion*, 23, 45; Spurzheim "Lectures on Phrenology," *The Lancet* 7 (1825): 171.

20 *Phrenological Journal* 2 (1824): 3, 5, cited in Giustino, *Conquest of Mind*, 69–70.

21 Combe, *The Constitution of Man*, 217, 321; for his citations of French ethnologist William-Fréderic Edwards on national character, see 471–2.

22 Bourdon, *La Physiognomonie et la Phrénologie*, 24–6, 263; on Saartje Baartman, see Sander Gilman, "Black Bodies, White Bodies" in Gates, ed. *"Race," Writing and Difference*, 223–261.

formed worker of our cities."[23] Victor-Frédéric-Alexandre Ysabeau referred directly to Lavater's comparison of crania of a "German," Hindu, African, and Kalmuk Tartar that demonstrated the "natural, regular proportions" and "intellectual superiority" of the European.[24]

PHRENOLOGY AND NON-EUROPEAN PEOPLES

Such reflections were far from exceptional among phrenologists. Broussais's phrenology course in 1836 attracted such interest (an audience of 3,000) that he had to move to a rented auditorium away from the Faculty of Medicine.[25] Unlike other disciples of Gall, he adopted as true and valuable Camper's facial line. In his lectures he proclaimed that the Caucasians were the "most beautiful," while the "New Hollander" (Australian) and Maori would "never become civilized."[26] The Maoris, like the Caribs, had no cerebral organ for producing great poets or great painters. While Africans might advance with European guidance, the "Hottentots" were under the complete domination of animal instincts. Broussais certainly advocated justice and benevolence for the entire human species, but he warned that he could not share the beliefs of a "sect" in "indefinite perfectibility."[27] His disciple, the physician Pierre-Marcel Gaubert, continued to justify the ranking of talents by racial criteria in a memoir to the Society in 1839.[28] When Broussais's son, the physician Casimir-Anne-Marie Broussais (1803–47), in 1832 measured the cranium of a Bedouin chief captured in Algeria, he found a "lack of intellectual faculties and murderous instinct."[29]

The prison physician Hubert Lauvergne, a conservative convert to Gall, believed the modern Greeks worthy successors to the ideal ancient Greek head, but claimed an unflattering "immutability of the Jewish type." The people called "Makoeas" [Makua] of southeast Africa were

23 Bruyères, *La Phrénologie*, 398, 470.

24 Ysabeau, *Lavater et Gall*, 66–7.

25 Renneville, *Le Langage des crânes*, 113–14; for 1,200 attending in 1838, see Charles Place, "Éloge de Broussais,"*La Phrénologie* 3 (août-sept 1839): 65–70.

26 Broussais, "Lectures on Phrenology," *The Lancet* issue 2 (1835–36): 930–2; Broussais, *Cours de phrénologie*, 516.

27 Broussais, *Cours de phrénologie*, 753–4, 789–96, 835 (see "Lectures on Phrenology," *The Lancet* issue 2 (1835–36): 917, 929–32, 986, 941); on intelligent Africans, *La Phrénologie* 2, no. 12 (30 juillet 1838).

28 Belhomme, "Compte-rendu des travaux," 78–9 summarizes Gaubert.

29 *JSPP* 1 (1832): 160.

Broussais

Estime de soi

Phrenological portrait of F.-J.-V. Broussais, notorious
physician and partisan of phrenology

"at the bottom of the human chain ... hardly superior to animal instincts." For Lauvergne, there was "more resemblance between the heads of certain Negroes and of great apes than between Negroes and Europeans." Unlike most observers of Algeria, who attempted to construct the Kabyles as closer to whites, Lauvergne found the Arabs in the Toulon *bagne* "noble and beautiful," while the Kabyles were "more instinctive than intellectual" and "very inferior to the European race."[30]

Some of the most potentially tolerant attitudes emerged in the journals and publications of the anatomist and medical assistant Pierre-Alexandre-Marie Dumoutier (1797–1871). His private phrenological museum, "open to workers" on the rue de Seine, in 1836 had a collection of 600 wax heads and 300 crania. He captivated both scientists and the public with his clever technique at moulding the heads of indigenous peoples as a naturalist accompanying Dumont d'Urville to the Pacific from 1837 to 1840.[31] When four Charrua Indians, survivors of a massacre in the Plata region of Uruguay in 1832, arrived in Paris, Virey had summarily condemned them as savages, "big children" with animal affections and inferior crania. Dumoutier's study for the Phrenological Society affirmed the humanity of the Charruas' dignity and courage. Moreover, if their crania were assessed by volume rather than circumference, they showed no significant difference from Europeans.[32]

On the Dumont expedition itself, Dumoutier refused to condemn the Patagonians for thievery or immorality, willingly spent a night ashore with them, and found them less unjust than the European "civilized beggars" who exploited the trade with them. Yet our accounts of geography and ethnology in subsequent chapters will show that Dumoutier's journals on Polynesians and Melanesians were far less complimentary to exotic peoples. Therefore, his alleged tolerance remains problematic.[33]

Joseph Vimont (1795–1857), the most distinguished comparative brain anatomist among the phrenologists, rejected Camper's angle but accepted a differential educability among peoples. He concluded, "no phrenologist could admit rapid progress of civilization, whatever the

---

30 Lauvergne, *Les forçats*, 32, 41, 52, 127, 136.

31 Renneville, *Le Langage des crânes*, 25 on the 4,000 viewers of his busts at Toulon in 1840; see Dumoutier's private lecture course program in AN F17 3038 and discourse at the opening of his museum in AN AJ15 562, reprinted in Renneville, "Un musée anthropologique oublié"; Ackerknecht, "P.M.A. Dumoutier."

32 *JSPP* 2 (1833): 74–103; Renneville, "Un Terrain phrénologique," 101–10; Renneville, *Le Langage des crânes*, 159–64 and *La Médecine du crime* 1:388n60.

33 Renneville, *Le Langage des crânes*, 216–23, 237.

institutional forms or care in education, with the cerebral apparatus illustrated in the images of the Carib or New Hollander." The naval surgeon René-Primevère Lesson of the Duperrey expedition had observed
the "excessively limited intellectual faculties" of the Australians. Only
"crossing with races better endowed" could bring improvement.[34] Given
the alleged failures of Sierra Leone and Haiti due to "deficiency in organization" of the black "race," Vimont was one of the few to argue that
emancipation of the slaves was undesirable. However, with white admix-
ture, there could be some intellectual progress. Vimont cited the intelligent creoles on Martinique in his own experience and the allegedly
more reflective and European "Cafres" (southeast Africans). Characteristically, residents of the West Indies denigrated even more the potential
of "pure" Africans. Similarly, naval surgeons Jean-René Quoy and J. Paul
Gaimard of the Freycinet expedition had found more educable brain
organization in the "Papous," black-Malay hybrids, rather than in other
dark-skinned islanders.

Other Society members recorded equivalent assessments. An editor of
the phrenologists' journal, the physician Adhémar Bérigny, in 1838 reviewed favourably the work of the amateur ethnologist Victor Courtet
de l'Isle, who highlighted race as a key factor in civilization. Bérigny
agreed that each of the races "may be called to fulfill a mission marked
by Providence in unequal conditions." For him, too, only fusion of races
would efface inequality. Courtet also recommended the persistence of a
mitigated slavery with avenues to emancipation. Bérigny approvingly
noted, "nothing better favours the division of labour than inequality of
faculties." Each may be placed in the proper sphere, within society or
among peoples of the world. He reiterated Broussais's display of differences in the cerebral conformation of the races.[35] The Fourierist Adrien
Berbrugger (1801–69) ranked various peoples for their faculty of poetic
"ideality," and, unsurprisingly, found Europeans the most gifted, with
the "Negro" and "New Hollander" the least endowed. The native American, however, was more "destructive" than the "Negro."[36] The alienist
and phrenologist Voisin, even as late as 1858, stressed the hierarchy
from primitive to civilized humanity. The "mutilated heads" of "barbarous nations" that were brought to France illustrated the lowest rungs

34 Vimont, *Traité de phrénologie*, 2:471, 509, 514, 516–21.

35 Adhémar Bérigny, "Compte rendu du livre *La Science politique*, par Victor Courtet de
l'Isle" *La Phrénologie* 1, no. 35 (20 mars 1838): 3–5.

36 Adrien Berbrugger, *JSPP* 2 (1833): 312–14.

of the ladder, since they showed only an obtuse intelligence and brutish penchants that considered theft as natural.[37]

Inevitable organic deficiency could close off avenues of improvement from savagery to civilization. Even those who subscribed to the older cultural retardation model, like the Fourierist journalist Julien Le Rousseau (1812-?), agreed with the commonplace that some races are more "beautiful and intelligent than others," an explanation for the enslavement of inferiors. The only distinctive feature of Le Rousseau is that he welcomed, rather than merely speculated about, a colonization that would lead in the distant future to racial fusion, thus eliminating both the differences and the prejudices.[38] A similar utopianism appeared in the lectures in Metz of the physician Henri Scoutetten (1799–1871). Scoutetten thought Cuvier had proven Europeans superior because of their higher ratio of the face to the cranium. He lamented the amorality of Hawaiian cannibals and thieving central Asians. He nevertheless predicted that gradual elevation from the savage state would bring the triumph of universal morality diffused to all peoples.[39]

Certainly, belief in phrenology did not inevitably bring about advocacy of racial hierarchy. But it became a likely consequence when so many phrenologists concluded that some "savages" were innately uncivilizable due to undeveloped brain organs, and that Europeans were obligated to guide others or interbreed with them to assure their progress toward civilization.[40]

For unexplained reasons, Spurzheim resigned his membership in the Phrenological Society and helped the physician and ethnologist William-Frédéric Edwards establish a short-lived Société anthropologique de Paris in 1832. The known members included Dumoutier, the deputy Emmanuel Las Cases fils (1800–54), the philanthropist de Lasteyrie, the physicians Roberton and Pierre Foissac (1801–86), the Society secretary, and the sculptor David d'Angers. We know only, from an article by Foissac forty-five years after the fact, that they discussed the effect of racial mixing on the "laws of organic heredity," already a topic of Edwards in 1829. In practice, the group seems to have combined phrenological

---

37 Voisin, *De l'homme animal*, 392–4.

38 Le Rousseau, *Notions de phrénologie*, 5–7, 272.

39 Scoutetten, *Leçons de phrénologie*, 5, 168.

40 For a philosophy of Providential racial struggle and triumph among phrenologically assessed European Gauls, Romans, and Franks correlating to popular, bourgeois, and noble ranks in society, see Alphonse Esquiros, described in Rignol, "Anthropologie et progrès."

interests with classification of races. But Foissac indicates that the Society broke up shortly after a notorious misreading of the cranium of the great anatomist Xavier Bichat as that of a common criminal.[41]

PHRENOLOGY AND GENDER STEREOTYPING

The Society's less concentrated focus on the capabilities of women did not indicate less prevalent gender stereotyping. The founders of phrenology accepted only conventional feminine roles. Gall approved the reasons of the Idéologue physician P.-J.-G. Cabanis for excluding women from the army, public speaking, or teaching at universities. Gall also thought that, since women's heads were larger in the back and their foreheads lower and smaller than those of men, they therefore sensed and judged differently, and their inferior organization made them superstitious.[42] Spurzheim similarly found women "destined by nature to certain functions," since they had larger organs for love of children, perception, friendship, benevolence, circumspection, idealism, and secretiveness. Correspondingly lower foreheads of women indicated less active faculties of reflection, needed for the arts and sciences. According to Spurzheim, even the powerful "influence of habit cannot in itself annihilate the modifications presented by the sentiments of the two sexes."[43] Talented women presented no proof of equality. Women should therefore keep to the virtues demanded by their condition in the social order.

Bruyères conveyed an equally clear message that women had less developed faculties, and should devote their time to child rearing or education of daughters.[44] Even the Fourierist Le Rousseau, whom one might expect to be a feminist, repeated the same cliché that women were dominated by affective instincts and sentiments: "Nature did not specially confide to her the mission of searching for the causes and laws of facts ... to one sex, serious, grave, strong occupations, to the other those of charm and the most exquisite delicacies of art."[45] Voisin main-

---

41 *JSPP* 3 (1835): 182; and Foissac, "La tête de Bichat," esp. 954–5; Renneville, *Le Langage des crânes,* 189–90.

42 Gall, *Fonctions du cerveau,* 2:160–1; 5:220–31, esp. 221, 225.

43 Gall, *Fonctions du cerveau,* 1:205–6; 2:160, 439; 3:271; 5:220–231; Spurzheim, *Essai sur les principes,* 98–9, 206–7, 209, 215; Spurzheim, *Phrenology in Connexion,* 17–19, 40, 43; *cf* Russett, *Sexual Science,* 19–22.

44 Bruyères, *La Phrénologie,* 414.

45 Le Rousseau, *Notions de phrénologie,* 269–72.

tained his belief in the clear evidence of male superiority in intellectual matters.[46] For the prison physician of La Roquette in Paris, Emile Debout, the female role was complementary to the male, though women did not have inferior intelligence. Their love of children, "ideality" (the source of morality and religion), and their sense of attachment designated them for special social duties. He quoted Cabanis approvingly to the effect that women could not participate in administration. As for the supposed counterexample of Catherine the Great, she had the head of a man.[47] For Scoutetten, women had the important role of educating children from the cradle onward, a recognition of their moral value: they "will become the most useful instruments for the future improvement of society, since one has to recognize that morality is the basis of civilization."[48]

Renneville has highlighted one of the most positive evaluations of women, in 1841 by the military officer Charles-Jacob Marchal de Calvi (1815–73). Marchal clearly repudiated Virey's strictures on female inferiority and recognized that women had the same organs as men. Further, favourable circumstances and cultivation of women's faculties would be crucial to their development. However, the superiority of their affective faculties neutralized their intellectual faculties and indicated no justification for citizenship or active political participation.[49] In this manner, even the most sympathetic of the male phrenologists advised women to accept their political and social status.

PHRENOLOGY – SOCIAL REFORM OR SOCIAL ORDER?

The more general social implications of phrenology rested on a balance between a pessimistic, deterministic view of innate inclinations and the optimistic conception that faculties could be cultivated or repressed by education. The founders themselves, Gall and Spurzheim, established this polarity, albeit with fewer differences between them than is sometimes alleged. Gall gloomily predicted that the powerful drives to enjoyment of the senses, conquest, and destructiveness would, for most people, "limit moral perfectibility by organization." On the other hand,

46 Voisin, *Analyse de l'entendement humain*, 237, 242, 273; see also *De l'homme animal*, 125–9, on maternal love and women's destiny.
47 Debout, *Esquisse de la phrénologie*, 78–88.
48 Scoutetten, *Leçons de phrénologie*, 28.
49 Renneville, *La Médecine du crime*, 1:490–2 and *Le Langage des crânes*, 258–60.

he would not exclude individual rehabilitation for those not congeni-
tally handicapped.[50] He identified himself as the "first proponent of
education," since an "artificial conscience" could emerge by religion,
morality, school discipline, and the laws.[51]

While Gall expected phrenologists to diagnose the mentally disturbed
or the criminal, in other respects he was far from a political or social reformer. He thought humans had unequal capacities to govern, and so
"envy, jealousy, and the passion to dominate" controlled republicans. In
addition, "wherever rules, decisions, and laws are the work of the plural-
ity of votes, mediocrity wins out over genius." Sounding like the Saint-
Simonian functionalists, Gall insisted that people "are not destined to
exercise upon each other the same reciprocal influence ... nature, in
giving each different organization, influence, and faculties, has assigned
to each of them a different position."[52] Hence, for classes unable to educate themselves, it would be enough to assure "good food, enough exercise, training in crafts, and love of work."[53] These attitudes persisted
in the functionalist outlook of French disciples of Gall.

Spurzheim, who had influenced the majority of French phrenologists,
was more openly confident that one could reinforce the faculties of benevolence and religious veneration and control the faculty of destructiveness. He also reiterated that "all faculties are good in themselves";
only their abuses were blameworthy.[54] Inherent temperament theory
still had a role in determining the degree of activity of the thirty-five faculties.[55] Followers like Broussais warned that a phlegmatic temperament
could rob the energy of a well-formed brain, but Broussais also held out
the hope that education, exercise, and strong nerves could "produce a
Talleyrand in a weak constitution."[56]

Nevertheless, one need not overestimate the contrast between the approaches of Gall and Spurzheim. While Spurzheim seemed more confident in educability, he did not foresee better moral outcomes in society

50 Gall, *Fonctions du cerveau*, 1:127, 139, 143–4, 325, 426; 2:143–8; 4:379–405,
esp. 385; 6:447–9, 463.
51 Gall, *Fonctions du cerveau*, 1:239, 253, 266, 280, 282–8; 2:106, 151; 4:280, 413; for
Spurzheim against predestined actions see *The Lancet* 8 (1825): 200–1.
52 Gall, *Fonctions du cerveau*, 4:255; 2:50; Spurzheim, *Phrenology in Connexion*, 49.
53 Gall, *Fonctions du cerveau*, 1:334–6, 417–18.
54 Spurzheim, "Lectures," *The Lancet* 7 (1825): 137, 330–2, 361; *Manuel de phrénologie*,
67, 71; *Observations*, 340–1, 344–4, 355, 360–1; *Essai sur les principes*, 4; Cooter, *The Culture
of Popular Science*, 213.
55 Spurzheim, *Manuel de phrénologie*, 7–8.
56 Broussais, *Cours de phrénologie*, 780–1.

at large. More strikingly, he doubted that education was the most efficient means to improve the species. His high valuation of heritable traits anticipated late nineteenth-century attitudes toward degeneracy theory and eugenics, for he thought that by breeding "more good would be done to improve men, than has hitherto been done by all the institutions and by all the teaching of the present or past ages." He would forbid inbreeding among families in "classes softened by opulence" and prohibit marriage by "laws of hereditary descent" to screen out those who have "small proportions of the distinct attributes of humanity" – those with hereditary disease, kidney stones, tuberculosis, scrofula, gout, "the stone," or mental illness.[57]

Spurzheim also shared most phrenologists' confidence in expert judgment. He hoped phrenologists would judge the suitability of candidates for public trust. They could counsel a person with strong amative dispositions not to go into the priesthood, and a fearful young man not to embark upon a military career. Knowing innate dispositions, phrenologists could direct people toward appropriate professions.[58]

Only on the accumulation of wealth and on taxation issues was Spurzheim clearly more radical than Gall. Spurzheim by 1828 attacked primogeniture and even wondered whether an ideal society should have inheritance preserving family property. Though the Combes promoted self-help for British workers, Spurzheim dared hold the opinion that "legislators should favour the working classes as much as possible." In a distant future of natural morality and the reign of universal love, legislators could "fix a maximum of property and conditions on its acquisition." In an apparent plea for progressive or at least more effective taxation, "manufacturers should be obliged to lay out part of their gains in bettering the condition and adding to the comforts of their laborers."[59] Spurzheim disliked the Saint-Simonians, but his vision of society corresponded to their notions of an elitist meritocracy with justice for the most numerous and poorest class.

In fact, many French phrenologists would have less room for social justice and place more stress on Saint-Simonian functionalism. I have already mentioned the enthusiast for Saint-Simon, Bailly de Blois, who

57 Spurzheim, "Lectures," *The Lancet* 7 (1825): 328; *Essai sur les principes*, 43, 48–9, 65, 98–9, 157, 203, 215, 221; *Philosophical Catechism*, 26–7.

58 Spurzheim, *Essai sur les principes*, 186, 195.

59 Spurzheim, *Philosophical Catechism*, 95, 100–1, 104, 106; and Jean-Baptiste Sarlandière, review of Spurzheim's *Essai philosophique sur la nature morale et intellectuelle de l'homme* (1820) in *JSPP* 2 (1833): 339.

thought that in a post-revolutionary age, "peoples were no more fit to govern themselves wisely." In a society of equal rights, the talented ("social physiologists," in Saint-Simonian language, experts in the functioning of societies), deserved authorization as the "most capable to direct national interests."[60]

A WIDE SPECTRUM OF SOCIAL AND POLITICAL PRESCRIPTIONS

Along the political spectrum of phrenologists, some clearly had a commitment to social radicalism. The obscure Fourierist journalist Le Rousseau tried in 1847 to combine socialism and phrenology. He lambasted a society dominated by greed and hoped to see the reign of principles of association and solidarity in a society with abundance for the masses.[61] Yet this most politically radical statement could not avoid stressing a kind of inevitable organic inequality. In speaking of sons of peasants aspiring to careers in the Church, Le Rousseau remarked on the "disgraced class" of these rustic seminarists and the "organic imperfections of most of their parents." He continued, "all these heads are painful to look at, that's how defective they are in their shape." In a world of inequality of fact, each would play an assigned role with his or her dominant passions, in a more joyless version of Fourier's model commune, the phalanstery.[62]

The most militant document came from the physician and Academy of Medicine member who for a while edited the *Journal* of the Society, Jean-Baptiste Mège (1787–186?). In an almost unanimously approved manifesto supplementing the volume of 1834, he alleged that education and lifestyle "play more of a part in the actual manifestation of an organ than its innate predominance." Hence, despite the rarity of poetic genius or the ineluctable fate of the handicapped, repressing and diminishing troublesome faculties was almost always possible. Against prudent liberals or conservatives who feared education would only produce astute criminals, he advocated universal elementary instruction in skills and in morality. He also favoured central workshops for the unemployed: "each man incapable of earning his subsistence has the right to receive it from the state."[63]

60 Bailly de Blois, "De la physiologie," esp. 182–3, 189.
61 Le Rousseau, *Notions de phrénologie*, 14, 18, 21, 187–8.
62 Ibid., 87–8, 189–90, 273, 580–1.
63 [Mège], *Manifeste des principes*, 21, 27–9.

Mège in 1843 promoted other social welfare schemes within an over-all framework of economic liberalism. Colonization would be a safety valve against "abuses of the system of competition." The state, while maintaining inheritance and property, should also guarantee impover-ished children food, clothing, and education. He hoped to correct the worst injustices of the economic systems by mutual insurance plans, old age pensions, public works, and international commercial treaties to as-sure lower prices.[64] Mège clearly balked at the social workshop of Louis Blanc, a remedy he thought worse than the problem, and he claimed to prefer the liberalism of historians Jules Michelet and Edgar Quinet.[65]

With Mège and several other phrenologists, there seemed to be a clear understanding that organic inclinations could be of secondary im-portance to fulfillment of potential by education. The military physician and potential revolutionary Auguste Luchet (1806–72), secretary-general of the Society in 1837, wished to promote work for all citizens according to a philosophy that would be "useless for an idiotic great lord, but calls to all positions" the "shepherd with a wide forehead that education would have perfected."[66] The Fourierist Adrien Berbrugger had already in 1833 hoped for a social mechanism to place each individ-ual where he or she could "develop totally and choose freely the func-tion which corresponds to his penchants, faculties, and aptitudes."[67] The physician Adhémar Bérigny in 1837 explicitly used the Saint-Simonian slogan "from each capacity according to its works" in his course on "social physiology." However, Bérigny was more noncommit-tal on freedom of choice versus the role of the expert: "if each were placed conforming to his aptitudes or vocations, the arts and sciences would advance more rapidly."[68]

But such Romantic reformism did not drown out discordant notes about free choice of a social role, and these qualifications bring into question how much room for social mobility the phrenologists envis-aged for the typical French citizen. The popularizer Bruyères thought each person "could choose the occupation to which he feels drawn by his aptitude and taste," but he also believed most workers could not

---

64 Mège, *Avis aux patriotes*, 10, 16–17, 90–1.

65 Ibid., 38, 84–6; for his violent anti-clericalism, see Mège, *Des principes fondamentaux*, 14–16.

66 Auguste Luchet, "Rapport annuel du président," *La Phrénologie* 1, no. 17 supplément (20 sept 1837); on Luchet's radicalism, see Renneville, *Le Langage des crânes*, 261.

67 Adrien Berbrugger, *JSPP* 2 (1833): 312–14.

68 Adhémar Bérigny, "Physiologie sociale," *La Phrénologie* 1, no. 2 (20 avril 1837): 3.

develop their intelligence; consequently, the middle classes could benefit more from phrenological advice.[69] Some major exponents of phrenology were even less sanguine about potential educability. Casimir Broussais, a military physician as anti-clerical as his father, agreed with Gall that "only a very small number of the elect" have highly developed organs of reason. The majority needed to be satisfied with cultivating affections and good habits to overcome a milieu that called forth animal penchants.[70]

Gall's close friend, the Italian immigrant, ardent nationalist, and former Carbonaro revolutionary Giovanni Antonio Fossati (Jean-Antoine-Laurent; 1786–1874) vacillated between the models of a liberal and organic society.[71] President of the Phrenological Society from 1845 to 1848, he had predicted in 1841 an era of social reform with increased "well-being of workers" and re-assessment of the "great question of property."[72] But adjusting to the "needs of people" in a secular educational system meant one "finishes by choosing the most apt for each job," taking into account their organic predispositions.[73]

Despite impeccable progressive credentials, Fossati seemed to endorse the reign of the expert rather than democracy. In 1845 he insisted that the "reflective people," the natural aristocracy of talents, needed to organize themselves before organizing the working class. He hoped that phrenologists would help choose for public offices the men with the "indispensable moral qualities."[74] In 1839, citing Gall on the pitfalls of majority rule, he noted that elections turned out badly. The philosopher with phrenological knowledge had a duty to enlighten the masses.[75] Once again, organic Saint-Simonianism triumphed.

69 Bruyères, *La Phrénologie*, 302, 406, 450, 460, 477–8, 481.

70 Broussais, *Hygiène morale*, 251, 264–5; *cf* Renneville, *Le Langage des crânes*, 201–2.

71 On Fossati's career, see Renneville, *La Médecine du crime*, 1:358–61, 376.

72 Fossati, "Sur l'urgence de satisfaire à un besoin moral des peuples" (1841) in *Questions philosophiques*, 175–6, 180; "De l'organisation des intelligences" (1845) in ibid., 328–9.

73 Fossati, "De l'influence de la phrénologie sur les sciences, la littérature et les arts"(1828) in *Questions philosophiques*, 75–6; Fossati, *Manuel pratique*, 555–8; see his anti-clericalism in 1833 in *Questions philosophiques*, 86–7; *cf* the discourse of Casimir Broussais, 22 août 1831 published in *JSPP* 1 (1832): 75.

74 Fossati, *Questions philosophiques*, 323, 326, 329; Fossati, *Manuel pratique*, 8.

75 Fossati, "Du choix," (1839) in *Questions philosophiques*, 158; Fossati, *Questions philosophiques*, vii; Fossati, "De la mission du philosophe au XIXᵉ siècle" (1833) in *Questions philosophiques*, 80.

Already in 1836 the effective anti-phrenologist physician and spiritualist friend of Philippe Buchez, Laurent Cerise (1807–69), had concluded that phrenology legitimized a "natural aristocracy." This attitude would "tend to constitute races transmitting fatally by way of reproduction the organic conditions of their social superiority or inferiority." Fossati may not have intended this exaggeration, but Cerise aptly discerned the consequences of an organic, functionalist society with heritable innate dispositions.[76]

Another ex-Carbonaro physician was Jean-Baptiste Beunaiche de la Corbière (1801–78), a veteran of the Revolution of 1830 and president of the Phrenological Society in 1843–44. In 1833 he was an anti-clerical supporter of the "party of movement" under Louis-Philippe and, by 1842, an advocate of an enlarged, but not universal male, franchise.[77] He, too, seemed optimistic about the power of "hygiene, education, example, and institutions" to "dominate and direct the average natures ... the immense majority in the species."[78]

However, his speech of 1844 revealed a great fear of popular power. He thought that in helping to choose legislators and civil servants for a government, only phrenology "can truly give an equitable and natural portion to authority as well as democracy." He remembered Gall's scepticism in speaking of the "political and social necessity of a hierarchy" and the "madness of absolute moral and civil liberty."[79] In the post-revolutionary atmosphere of the empire in 1853, Beunaiche was frankly critical of the Republic, which "died of an organic vice of its constitution." Now he thought the inevitable democratic movement risked "ruining civilization and creating the shame and misfortune of humanity." He confessed his aversion for the "detestable cult of socialism and communism." The traditional values of religion, property, family, and Christian doctrine were compatible with phrenology.[80] Hence "indefinite" human perfectibility was not "unlimited."[81] So, even before 1848, Beunaiche was as much concerned about "authority" as about "democracy."

76 Cerise, *Exposé et examen critique*, 133, 139–40.
77 Delaunay, "Un Médecin," esp. 399–403, 405–8.
78 Beunaiche de la Corbière, *Discours de rentrée*, 6, 10, 12.
79 Beunaiche de la Corbière, *Discours de cloture*, 13, 25–6; Delaunay, "Un Médecin," 417.
80 Beunaiche de la Corbière, *De l'influence*, 49–52, 57, 60–1, 101–2, 138; *cf* Delaunay, "Un Médecin," 408.
81 Beunaiche de la Corbière, *De l'influence*, 62, 95, 101–2, 139.

At least three other adherents of phrenology approached the organic model even more closely. The Bonapartist deputy and former Saint-Simonian Emmanuel de Las Cases fils, son of the author of the famous *Mémorial de Saint-Hélène*, was vice-president, then president of the Society in 1832–33. In his presidential speech he recognized the need for a system of education to discern the particular talents of each person, and to allow the flowering of geniuses like Vaucanson, Buffon, and Lavoisier. But he said the "pyramid of intelligences" (an apex of a few great minds and a huge base of limited intelligence) resembled the pyramid of fortunes of the economists (a few wealthy, and a huge base of the impoverished). According to Las Cases, in democratic governments, "the dominant class is composed of too low a layer of the intellectual pyramid." So good intelligence must direct society, and phrenologists must find it. While Renneville interprets this statement as an attack on the imbecilic ruling elite of France, the alternative reading here sees a warning of the disadvantages of democracy.[82]

Similarly, Broussais's disciple Gaubert noted that in France the "elective system which demands that candidates offer themselves to the voters, does not use [the best capacities], and too often leaves societies to the malevolent talents." Like Las Cases, Gaubert saw another justification for an organic society and for a continued ranking of talents of different races.[83]

The most renowned partisan of an organic society was the elder Broussais, who was a ferocious anti-clerical, a republican, and critic of the Cousinian spiritual self, which he thought the resultant of brain organs.[84] Broussais converted to phrenology sometime between the death of Gall in 1828 and 1831, when he joined the Society. For Broussais, Gall's "theosophic" faculty was a deception to parry blows from the Church and a concession necessary to help maintain indispensable social hierarchy.[85]

For all his controversial political and religious opinions, he endorsed a hierarchical functionalism of aptitudes. He hoped to diagnose the abilities of children to "apply the great masses of the people to the work

---

82 Emmanuel de las Cases fils, "Les rapports entre la phrénologie et la politique" in *JSPP* 1 (1832–33): 137, 142; *cf* Renneville, *Le Langage des crânes*, 147–8 and Azouvi, "La phrénologie," 263.

83 Belhomme, "Compte-rendu des travaux," 78–9 summarizes Gaubert.

84 Braunstein, *Broussais et le matérialisme*, 155, 158–78; F.-J.-V. Broussais, *JSPP* 3 (1835): 23–5, and "Discours du 22 août 1835," *JSPP* 3 (1825): 380–404, esp. 396, 404; F.-J.-V. Broussais, "Mémoire sur l'association du physique et du moral," *JSPP* 3 (1835): 288–77.

85 Broussais, *Cours de phrénologie*, 657–9 on spiritual substance.

by which each of its members can best serve his family."[86] One must accustom people of slow intelligence and without leisure time to physical labour, and to inspire in them the habit of good actions both by precept and example.[87] He suggested that however diligent the attempt to acquire facility in any activity, no one could be distinguished in "an occupation for which he was not born" with already developed organs.[88]

Emile Debout, a former secretary of the Society and a prison physician at La Roquette, came closest to an explicit social criterion for assigning each individual a place. While he wanted all to "develop freely and to choose the function corresponding to inclinations, faculties, and aptitudes," he also spoke of a "necessary social hierarchy" that is the "result of endowed cerebral organization." To discern "the degree of cultivation to give to the intelligence" of a child, one looks at the "organization of the child" and "must take into account the social position of the parents."[89] Similarly, the Metz lecturer Henri Scoutetten admitted that education was less powerful where the contrary natural disposition was strong or cerebral organization faulty.[90] Therefore, society would be better if people followed their aptitudes on phrenologists' advice, rather than choosing an occupation by chance.

THE AMBIVALENCE OF FÉLIX VOISIN

Phrenologists rarely had opportunities to judge the capacities of substantial populations, but their remedial work in education and the prison system did occasionally allow some administrative discretion. One of the best illustrations of vacillation between cerebral determinism and the power of education occurred in the work of the alienist Félix Voisin. He was president of the Society in 1839–40 and collaborator with Dumoutier on a lecture series in the Athénée in 1841–42. Still another anti-clerical and anti-aristocratic liberal, in 1839 Voisin took aim at the avarice of the financial aristocracy, worse than the old nobility since "it sacrifices all to material interests."[91]

---

86 Broussais, "Discours du 22 août 1835," *JSPP* 3 (1835): 403.

87 Broussais in *JSSP* 3 (1835): "Considérations sur les rapports de la phrénologie avec la philosophie," 15–28; "Mémoire sur l'association du physique et du moral," 258–77; "Discours du 22 août 1835," 389–90, 396, 402–3; Broussais, *Cours de phrénologie*, 750–2, 836.

88 Broussais, "Lectures," *The Lancet* 2 (1835–36): 916–17.

89 Debout, *Esquisse de la phrénologie*, 78, 119.

90 Scoutetten, *Leçons de phrénologie*, 24–6.

91 Voisin, *De l'Homme animal*, 40, 86, 247, 405–6, 416.

For approximately ten years from 1832 he ran a specialized reform school in the suburb of Issy (at first in cooperation with another alienist, Jean-Pierre Falret) called an "orthophrenic establishment." The name implied correction of the mind, as orthopedic treatment corrects the position of the legs. A Paris police inspector expressed gratitude for this plan for "special education" of four categories of children: (1) slow learners, (2) spoiled, neglected, or harshly treated children who behaved badly, (3) willful, disorderly children, and (4) children at high risk of inheriting mental disorders or nervous disease.[92] Here Voisin announced that his objective was compensating for the neglect suffered by these unfortunate children.

Yet Voisin certainly believed in the accuracy of phrenological diagnosis and organic criteria for judgments on criminals. In an 1834 visit to the forced-labour gangs of Toulon, he thought he could identify the twenty-two rapists among the 350 inmates merely by the shape of their necks (prominent cerebella). In fact, he chose thirteen correctly, but, as critics pointed out, he misdiagnosed eighteen (nine incorrectly labeled, and nine not chosen).[93] This experience led Voisin to claim that two-thirds of criminals were "poorly born," with defective cerebral organs.[94]

At La Roquette detention centre for young criminals in Paris, Voisin worked with Debout on classifying them. Voisin also recognized that cerebral organization was only part of the story. Lack of educational opportunity and an unfavourable social milieu with child neglect, abandonment, and bad examples might lead to atrophy of moral and intellectual faculties. Therefore, he implored judges both to "measure criminals' heads" to classify them and also to recognize the need of neglected individuals for "a support in the outside world."[95]

Voisin hoped throughout his career to help individuals subordinate "animal" interests to the "human" faculties of benevolence and justice.

---

92 Voisin, "Application de la physiologie du cerveau à l'étude des enfans qui nécessitent une éducation spéciale," *JSPP* 1 (1832–33): 112–31, esp. 118, 122, 126–7, 131; "Etablissement orthophrénique," *JSPP* 2 (1833–34): 402–10; "Rapport au conseil général des hôpitaux, juin 1834," *JSSP* 3 (1835): 30, 185–200, esp. 200; see Lemercier's attack on the methods of this establishment as being as dangerous as astrology in Renneville, "De la régénération," 12.

93 Voisin, "Visite au bagne de Toulon," *JSPP* 3 (1835): 32–9.

94 Voisin, *Analyse de l'entendement humain*, 48–9, 93–121 and *Observations communiquées à l'Académie Royale de médecine ... Organisation cérébrale défectueuse de la plupart des criminels* (1838), supplément à *De l'Homme animal*, 1–7.

95 Voisin, *Observations*, supplément à *De l'Homme animal*, 7; on the children of the mentally disturbed, see Voisin, *Des causes morales*, 292; Debout, *Esquisse de la phrénologie*, 155–76.

Sceptical of utopian "indefinite perfectibility," he hoped to accomplish much on "eminently modifiable and perfectible" individuals by "custom, law, and social institutions."[96] The height of optimism was his Lamarckian hope that some "organic dispositions and faculties are in a relationship that may be transmitted by reproduction." Acquired dispositions might be heritable.[97]

As the sympathetic Bouillaud reported to the Academy of Medicine in 1841, after Voisin's diagnosis, the director of La Roquette confirmed Voisin's four behavioural classifications (including docility, intelligence, and work ethic) of the 500 inmates. Voisin then triumphantly exclaimed, "either I am a sorcerer or I have a science."[98] The Academy praised Voisin for his zeal but demanded further research on the problematic localization of faculties, and some members insisted that the director should have submitted his judgments in writing before Voisin's pronouncements.[99]

While Voisin did not openly mention phrenology even in his long, bizarre text (with a narrative as if by God) *Analysis of the Human understanding* in 1858 (a revision of an earlier work), he still used the mental faculty names of Gall and Spurzheim, "inscribed by God on our constitution." In the face of clerical or lay attacks on his profession, he was more confident than ever in the reign of the experts: "physicians, whatever one may say in high political circles, have more than enough reasons to place themselves as educators of peoples; it's truly they who know man in his root and essence."[100] By then the conservative atmosphere of the Second Empire had tamed the vestiges of his political radicalism. While he remained an advocate of welfare for the poor and a strong opponent of pure laissez-faire economics, he now cited Guizot favourably on the work ethic and the superiority of intellectual to manual labour. He denigrated the Fourierist pleasure principle and, against Proudhon, advocated the natural existence of property. He thought that his previous targets, the rich, might be guilty in their smug satisfaction, but the poor in revolutionary turmoil were not heroes.[101] He also reprinted his 1848 memoir against capital punishment that assessed its failure as a deterrent to those who are "poorly born." With overly energetic penchants and a weak moral

96 Voisin, *De l'Homme animal,* xxv, xxxii, 13–14, 39–40.

97 Ibid., 66.

98 Bouillaud, "Rapport sur le mémoire intitulé: Organisation cérébrale défectueuse de la plupart des criminels," *Bulletin de l'Académie Royale de médecine* 7 (1841–42): 149, 160.

99 Ibid., 163–6.

100 Voisin, *Analyse de l'entendement humain,* 24–5, 237, 242, 273.

101 Ibid., 241, 244, 247, 254, 273, 294–5.

sentiments, they would be "refractory to all modification" despite the efforts of their instructors.[102] Voisin remained poised in that delicate balance between animal, natural man, and educated humanity, never quite sure which faculties would triumph.

PHRENOLOGY AND PRISON REFORM

Certainly, phrenology called for a kind of Foucauldian exercise in authority and power – an arena in which to build and solidify its knowledge. Gall examined prison inmates and hospital patients, as well as crania of imbeciles, criminals, and suicides. With this background he envisaged applications of phrenology in moral philosophy, education, and criminology.[103] Voisin expressed the wish that physician-educators try to understand each person's "external relations, govern his passions, and trace for him the normal and regular use of his time and faculties."[104]

The socially necessary task was to diagnose, somewhat like the alienist, the incorrigible "idiot," "brute," or "insane" to suggest mitigation of responsibility or punishment. The alienist could define the taint of "monomania," a fixed idea excluding all others. For other patients, the phrenologist could help redirect destructive penchants such as the inclination to steal or murder. One homicidal individual controlled himself because he became a butcher, and another became a military chaplain so he could witness killing in battle.[105] Gall himself, unlike Voisin, favoured capital punishment and did not foresee rehabilitation of hardened criminals.[106]

Phrenological diagnosis and therapy never really reached expected dimensions in the French prison system.[107] Nevertheless, two promi-

102 Ibid., 351–2, 355, 363.

103 Gall, *Fonctions du cerveau*, 1:1 Prospectus and 1:5, 16; 6: 503.

104 Voisin, *Analyse de l'entendement humain*, 25.

105 Gall, *Fonctions du cerveau*, 1:325–31, 372 on "partial mania"; 2:444, 469–502; 5:219; 6:428; see Goldstein, *Console and Classify*, 152–5, 162–9, 256.

106 Gall, *Fonctions du cerveau*, 1:19, 344–5, 354, 368–70, 412, 426–7; 2:101–2, 107; 4:166; Spurzheim, *Manuel de phrénologie*, 70; see also Renneville, "Entre nature et culture," and Renneville, *La Médecine du crime*, 1:264, 298–303; see 362–8 for Benjamin Appert on classification; 419–67 for debates on criminal justice; see also Appert, *Bagnes, prisons et criminels*, 1:121, 128–9; 4:117–38, 297, 299, 302–3.

107 André Zysberg, "Politiques du bagne, 1820–1850" in Perrot, ed. *L'Impossible prison*, 165–207, esp. 168; Catherine Duprat, "Punir et guérir, en 1819, la prison des phlanthropes" in ibid., 64–122; *cf* O'Brien, *The Promise of Punishment* on work and education, 150–225.

nent prison physicians valued phrenology. The alienist Guillaume-Marie-André Ferrus (1784–1861) became head of Bicêtre in 1826 and later inspector-general of prison health services, despite his liberal politics. In his long examination of the prison system, he lamented that Gall's doctrines had "fallen into maddening discredit" and insisted that they never promoted irresponsibility for criminal acts. For him, classifying intellect and character was the key to a successful prison regime. A most important distinction, similar to the manuscript notes of Dumoutier on criminal crania, would be whether the criminals were "intelligent" or "degraded." He found a first category of the intelligent, who were incorrigible either by cerebral organization or ingrained bad examples. A second group, often abandoned or corrupted children, was less intelligent and morally weak. The third group had defective cerebral organization resulting in low intelligence. For most inmates lacking conscience and shame, Christian morality would be powerless, but one could speak to their interests.[108] A system of reward and punishment, work, religious instruction, and hygiene could attempt some moralization. For the intelligent and perverse, strict confinement to isolation cells might be necessary, while the morally vicious and limited needed only night-time confinement, and the totally inept could live in a dormitory and engage in collective work tasks.[109]

Probably the harshest prison physician dabbling in phrenology was the naval physician Hubert Lauvergne, a Legitimist and Catholic. In the forced-labour institution (*bagne*, which replaced the galleys) of Toulon, where inmates wore belt and chain and endured branding, he warmly received Voisin. Lauvergne was a great believer in the importance of the facial angle as depicted in ancient Greek and Egyptian sculpture.[110] He was convinced that at least 30 per cent of inmates had "half-brains," with natural penchants to theft and imitation. Cold, reflective murderers with large necks exemplified Gall's organs of combativeness and destructiveness. He also speculated the organ might be in the folds of the brain, not the protuberance, since over half of murderers had no apparent organ for carnivorous instinct.[111] While Voisin hoped for transmissible improvement, Lauvergne, in an early version

---

108 Ferrus, *Des prisonniers*, 164, 186–7, 189; for Dumoutier's manuscript, see AN AJ15 562.

109 Ferrus, *Des prisonniers*, 232.

110 Lauvergne, *Les forçats*, 33, 124.

111 Ibid., 43, 58, 69–70.

of degeneracy theory, feared harmful, heritable "organic transmuta-
tions" where the "superior brain does not dominate."[112]

Indeed Lauvergne had no time for "flaws of excess philanthropy" that
refused to recognize the permanence of the "social ladder," which could
be climbed only by "work, service, and love of the fatherland." The absence of morality and religion and the nefarious influences of materialism and romanticism brought forth serious crimes, such as rape,
prostitution, and child abandonment. In one respect, he found the
Saint-Simonians reasonable – that marriage needed remoralization.[113]

Lauvergne was a reformer in the sense that he advocated abolition of
the *bagnes*. As a whole, the phrenologists' association with prison reform
took place in the context of more liberal thinkers such as Benjamin Appert, Charles Lucas, and Prosper Lucas (1808–85). Every one of them
wished to classify prisoners according to their hereditary penchants. Appert and Prosper Lucas studied the degree of heredity involved in criminal dispositions and Charles Lucas was convinced the prison needed to
be more like a hospital or asylum.[114] The criminal code revision of 1832
reduced the number of crimes penalized by forced labour, and abolished branding on the shoulder. The prison reformers then worried
about the inefficiency of excessive punishment and about better programs to repress troublesome inclinations. In practice, phrenology in
the prison system remained more a matter of grandiose intentions than
an applied program.

CRITICISM OF PHRENOLOGY
AND DISARRAY OF PHRENOLOGISTS

Why did phrenology not develop into a template for a scientific physiological psychology? Perhaps the most important reason is the hostility of
some of the most illustrious of French scientists, both for philosophical
reasons and for phrenology's empirical shortcomings. Cuvier, the per-

112 Ibid., 165–6, 204.

113 Ibid., 172–3, 212, 239, 251.

114 Renneville, *La Médecine du crime*, 1:327–8, on Charles Lucas's 1827 study, *Du système
pénal et du système répressif*, and 332 for Prosper Lucas's study of heredity; see 419–67 for debates over the criminal law reform of 1832 and the relative role of legal experts and "alienists" in judgments of, for example, "homicidal monomania" of the 1820s or alienation with
free will; see also Goldstein, *Console and Classify*, 166–96 on legal-medical boundary disputes, and 276–321 on the new asylum law of 1838.

manent secretary of the Academy of Sciences, thought Gall a charlatan and dangerous materialist.[115] The second reason is the continuing internal disarray among phrenologists on the location and significance of brain organs. The renowned experimental physiologist Magendie found Gall unable to prove that the skull surface imaged the brain.[116]

Despite Bouillaud's efforts at confirming brain localization for speech, phrenologists themselves still disputed the number of brain organs and the techniques to measure them.[117] Vimont disdained others' models, while the military surgeon Jean-Baptiste Sarlandière (1787–1838) refuted Gall's explanation of the cerebellum and worried that protuberances, always difficult to isolate, might not reveal the extent of organ activity.[118] By 1835 Bailly de Blois thought that knowing the actions and behaviour of a person might be a necessary prerequisite for sound phrenological assessment.[119] The alienist and cardiologist of La Charité Hospital, Jacques-Etienne Belhomme (1800–85), in 1839 introduced further discord by contending that there were some kinds of "sympathetic madness" not in the brain itself. This seeming return to temperament theory seemed to be an "anti-phrenological idea" to his critics.[120]

In the 1830s and early 1840s, rapid-fire attacks by several leading physicians and physiologists helped undermine the successful diffusion of phrenology in the professional community. Louis-Francisque Lélut (1804–77), a physician at La Roquette, Bicêtre, and the Salpêtrière, performed cranial measurements on homicidal robbers that persuaded him that there was no correlation to lateral temporal areas of the

---

115 See Wegner, "Das Ringen um Anerkennung," esp. 49, 55–6; *JSPP* 3 (1835): 45; Napoleon to Las Cases in 1816, cited in Heintel, *Leben und Werk*, 30; Cuvier report reprinted in Gall and Spurzheim, *Recherches sur le système nerveux*, 1–2, 4.

116 Magendie, *Précis élémentaire de physiologie*, 1:138, 54–55; see also Lesch, *Science and Medicine in France*, 169–71, 185, 187, 261.

117 J.-B. Bouillaud, "Recherches cliniques propres à démontrer que la perte de la parole correspond à la lésion des lobules antérieures du cerveau, et à confirmer l'opinion de M. Gall sur le siège de l'organe du langage articulé" in *Archives générales de la médecine* 8 (1825): 25–45.

118 Vimont, *Traité de phrénologie*, 1:19, 34–5; *JSPP* 1 (1832): 49; see Renneville, *Le Langage des crânes*, 103–4; for Sarlandière, see *JSPP* 1 (1832–33): 155, 263–71, 313–4; Sarlandière, *Traité du système nerveux*, 240–1; see his same doubts in *La Phrénologie* 1, no. 25 (10 déc 1837): 1–2, and no. 34 (10 mars 1838): 2–3.

119 Lélut, *La Phrénologie*, 248–51 on Bailly; Bailly, "Sur l'utilité de la cranioscopie." *JSPP* 3 (1835): 289–91, 348.

120 Belhomme, *La Phrénologie* 3 (mai-juin 1839): 34–38.

brain.[121] By the 1850s he was convinced there were no distinct brain organs. He found phrenology materialistic, destructive of morality, and without anatomical or psychological justification.[122]

Lélut's salvos heralded more objections from the alienist François Leuret (1797–1881), who denied any correspondence between brain circumvolutions and mental faculties.[123] The permanent secretary of the Academy of Medicine, Frédéric Dubois d'Amiens, rejected Gall's premise that organ size, not quality, was most influential. He ridiculed the "triage of children, some to more abject and painful occupations, others to culture of science and arts." The only consequence of such a system would be the most complete fatalism, the end of morality and of belief in God.[124]

One of the most telling blows came from Marie-Jean-Pierre Flourens, who occupied the human anatomy chair (later the first anthropology chair) at the Muséum from 1832 and became permanent secretary of the Academy of Sciences the next year. By 1824, Flourens's experiments on the ablation of the cortex and cerebellum in pigeons indicated no loss of functioning with loss of surface parts of the brain. In addition, the cerebellum had no relation to sexual functioning, but coordinated voluntary motion.[125] Flourens's experiments were by no means conclusive, but he could argue Gall's faculties were names of imaginary organs. He also had the firm conviction of a "unified, free self," as in Bossuet and Descartes, which was the only basis of free will.[126] Once again, the condemnation of Gall was anatomical, psychological, and moral.

SIGNIFICANCE OF PHRENOLOGY

By mid-century the doubts about skull conformation to the cerebrum, the failure to locate distinct brain organs, and the ability of the brain to

121 Lélut, *De l'organe phrénologique*, 12, 15 on carnivores and plant-eaters; and "Examen comparatif de la longueur et de la largeur du crâne, chez les voleurs homicides," *Journal universel et hebdomadaire de médecine et chirurgie pratiques* 6 (1832): 49–67.

122 Lélut, *La Phrénologie*, vii, xvii, 36, 45, 71, 333–5, 345, 347–8, 350. His earlier and less harsh condemnations of phrenology appeared in *Qu'est-ce que la phrénologie?* and in *Rejet de l'organologie*, 1843.

123 Leuret, *Anatomie comparée*, 1: 327, 364–5, 367, 587–9 summary.

124 Dubois d'Amiens, *Philosophie médicale*, 1:122, 339–40, 343, 360–1.

125 Flourens, *Examen de la phrénologie*, 59–60; Clarke and Jacyna, *Nineteenth-Century Origins*, 249–56, 291–302; Shortland, "Courting the Cerebellum," 186; for Gall's objections, see *Fonctions du cerveau*, 3:400–5; 6:216, 224–5, 241, 384–8.

126 Flourens, *Examen de la phrénologie*, 17, 19, 23, 27, 35, 39, 48, 65, 94–5, 158.

regenerate despite lesions had swayed scientific opinion from phrenology.[127] Even Paul Broca's demonstration in 1861 of a centre of articulation of speech in the anterior lobe of the left hemisphere did not benefit phrenologists, since Broca deliberately distanced himself from phrenology.[128] Nevertheless, efforts at measuring brain and cranial size comprised a veritable long-term research program for the late nineteenth-century Société d'anthropologie de Paris.[129]

Phrenology could never locate internal brain organs correlated to the designated faculties, and therefore depended upon ever more dubious cranioscopic readings analogous to the profile readings of physiognomists.[130] The Foucauldian shift from external natural history to internal biological functionalism was therefore always incomplete. Disagreement about the organs themselves compounded the difficulty. Those who willingly combined phrenology with physiognomy did not balk at external readings, and even the most scrupulous phrenologists such as Voisin and sympathizers such as Ferrus would supplement cranial assessments with reading faces. At the same time, the leaven of religiosity and mysticism pervading physiognomy could not redeem phrenology. Despite vigorous denials from Gall onward, phrenology suffered the taint of alleged materialism and denial of moral responsibility.

Concepts of racial and gender hierarchy were pervasive in the surrounding culture, but physiognomists, through their appropriation of Cuvier's allegedly sound scientific measurement of facial angles, could consecrate invidious racial ranking. Gall and Spurzheim rejected simplistic facial angle indicators, but Spurzheim willingly ranked national characteristics. Dumoutier may have charitably received South American natives in Paris, but most French phrenologists believed that non-European, particularly "savage," peoples around the world had limited potential for development. While phrenologists thought European women had greater potential, their affectionate and maternal feminine nature marked them for domestic tasks. Even if women complemented men, they would not benefit from educational opportunity, occupational advancement, or full citizenship.

127 Broussais, *De la phrénologie humaine*, 3–4, 7–8.
128 Lantéri-Laura, *Histoire*, 183–90; see also ch. 6 of this book.
129 Blanckaert, "'L'anthropologie personnifiée,' Paul Broca et la biologie du genre humain" preface to Broca, *Mémoires d'anthropologie*; Harvey, "Races Specified, Evolution Transformed," 114–64; Williams, "The Science of Man," 95–109.
130 Cohen, "Functional MRI"; Raichle, "Modern Phrenology."

Phrenologists, like the Idéologues before them, promoted a view of secular and naturalistic self-improvement. The ambivalence between the unchangeable natural head shape and the exercise of faculties in education proved to be a great attraction for reformers of the moderate, liberal, and socialist persuasion, despite their other political differences. The naturalism of phrenology could attract ferocious anti-clericals like Broussais or Fossati. They expected Church authority to be diminished and belief in the spiritual soul to be eclipsed. There were only a few exceptional clerical supporters (abbé Frère, abbé Besnard) and the exceptional Catholic such as Lauvergne, while Bailly de Blois and Marchal de Calvi remained spiritualist by conviction.[131]

But the social significance of phrenology paralleled Saint-Simonian support for a functionalist meritocracy. For Gall, the majority would never contain their passions, and he never envisaged wholesale social or political reform. But even Gall believed education could help create for most people an artificial conscience. In arenas such as the prison, the expert found his diagnostic subjects and also a convenient place to practise his science. Spurzheim agreed with Gall that moral reform would be unlikely, and both he and Beunaiche hoped a kind of eugenics would be a more reliable means of improvement.

For some phrenologists, the meritocracy they envisaged meant hostility to privilege, even to the "financial aristocracy." Spurzheim and the Fourierists were profoundly disillusioned with the injustices of laissez-faire economics and the competitive society. The most progressive reformers among them could claim they would use education to promote both individual well-being and social harmony. Voisin's peak of optimism, perhaps shared by Le Rousseau, was that there were heritable moral characteristics and therefore possible improvement of the next generations.

On political issues, many phrenologists would expand the franchise, but few were true democrats. Most phrenologists certainly believed in representative government either through constitutional monarchy or a republic. All but a few had opposed the Bourbons, and after 1830 remained on the political left or Orléanist centre-left.[132] Yet they boosted the phrenologist-expert as a necessary adviser on assessing the necessarily unequal aptitudes of subjects. Mège, Luchet, Bérigny, and Berbrug-

---

131 See typical Catholic opposition in physician Debreyne in his *Pensées d'un croyant*, esp. 201–38; Renneville, *Le Langage des crânes*, 105–7, 270.

132 Renneville, *La Médecine du crime*, 1:375–6.

ger seemed to permit more scope for individual choice; others no less prominent in the Society, such as Broussais the elder and younger, Fossati, Beunaiche, Gaubert, and Debout warned against making misdirected choices without an expert. This very ambivalence between social order and political and religious change attracted many who were sensitive to the evils of industrialization, like Spurzheim himself, yet Fossati, Beunaiche, and Broussais stressed not the liberating opportunities of social mobility but rather the desirability of a natural aristocracy. Without even considering the issue of male domination, the result could easily be promotion of the existing hierarchical social order.

Both Saint-Simon and Auguste Comte used the defence mechanism of classification in their search for a social equilibrium that would terminate revolutions. Comte's positivist system honoured Gall by advocating the general principles of phrenology, although with a reduced number of eighteen faculties. His concept of social order in the positive polity certainly involved adjustment of individuals to their appropriate role in the "Great Being" of humanity.[133] The positivist organic model was, in its pure form, antagonistic to both social mobility and individual freedom.

In the asylum and prison, phrenologists would recognize those who deserved indulgence due to malformation. For others, the panacea of classification would assign rewards and punishments appropriate to individual deficiencies. Conservatives, of course, were scandalized that criminals might be exonerated on the basis of a speculatively envisaged malformation of their cranium.

When the Revolution of 1848 erupted, phrenologists failed to find wide acceptance of their doctrines. In the era of the last gasps of the Society that spring, Fossati presided over a Club des droits civiques, where he re-read his memoir on the need for phrenological advice to choose legislators. Voisin sent memoirs opposed to the death penalty to the Constituent Assembly.[134] But Beunaiche and Voisin were clearly disillusioned with revolution after the fact. Those who valued scientific classifications of personalities, especially of dangerous individuals, began to look toward the new degeneracy theory of Bénédict-Augustin Morel by the late 1850s. After 1876, they might turn to the new reading of "atavistic" criminal faces and bodies by Cesare Lombroso. Ultimately, the psychologist Alfred Binet's testing, transformed into IQ tests, would provide

133 Vernon, "The Political Self"; Haines, "The Inter-Relations."
134 Renneville, *Le Langage des crânes*, 279–80; Renneville, "De la régénération," 13.

a new means to sort and classify intelligences that in its original form did not permit biological determinism.[135]

Phrenologists assessed both individuals and peoples, but the geographic and ethnological societies took as their prime mission the analysis of human groups throughout the world. The geographers and ethnologists also assumed either that European guidance was needed to civilize these peoples or that Europeans must develop the wasted resources of the uncivilizable.

135 Cooter, *The Culture of Popular Science*, 259–70; Mucchielli, ed. *Histoire de la criminologie*; Renneville, "De la régénération," 7–19.

4

Human Geography, "Race," and Empire

Phrenology, invented by Gall, was a short-lived, always contested anticipation of techniques of modern personality psychology. Geography had
an ancient pedigree, with a disciplinary community already active in the
eighteenth century. Phrenology aspired to assess individual dispositions,
though its application to entire peoples emerged as a tendentious by-
product. Human geography, the observation of peoples in relation to
climate and landforms, had always been an integral component of
studying the earth.

In recent years historians of geography have recognized that the
description of climate, physical geography, and human inhabitants of a
region by European armchair geographers in the nineteenth century
often implied a search for market opportunities or territory to be
annexed.[1] There is even a consensus that late nineteenth-century
geographical societies were significant lobbyists for empire. British and
American scholars have been more likely to see ulterior motives of
French expansion even in the early Paris Geographical Society, which
was founded in 1821; the most thorough French study of the Society,
however, differentiates its early small group of "romantic notables" with
"purely intellectual, not utilitarian interests" from the large contingent
of business-oriented members who supported the imperial ventures of

---

1 On the links between geography and imperialism, see Livingstone, *The Geographical
Tradition*, esp. 216–59; Bell, Butlin, and Heffernan, eds. *Geography and Imperialism*, editors'
introduction, 1–12, and, on France, Heffernan, "The Spoils of War: The Société de Géographie de Paris and the French Empire, 1914–1919," 221–64.

the Third Republic.[2] This discussion will show that the Society from 1821 to 1848 had more than mere curiosity in the west African Sudan, the horn of east Africa, and the south Pacific. The search for commercial opportunities inexorably led to territorial ambition or the desire for economic domination.[3]

After a brief review of the commercial interests of the Society, the principal claim here is that Geographical Society members, with associated colleagues on their expeditions, helped construct an allegedly scientific racial hierarchy that formed a useful condition for imperial adventure. In this image some peoples were either culturally and socially retarded or organically deficient. From the eighteenth century onward, geographers and explorers developed the first "retardation" model – inevitable stages of development from savagery to civilization. The usual corollary was that climate and lifestyle shaped the emergence of "races" or human varieties, but that no group had a fixed moral or cultural capacity. Some phrenologists had clearly endorsed this latter view. Europeans would assist the maturation of peoples still apparently trapped in the childhood of the human species.[4]

Such an argument foreshadowed the ideology of assimilationism prominent throughout the nineteenth century in French imperial theory.[5] The French mission was to lead non-Europeans to civilization. By means of the French language, Christianity, its associated morality, and

2 Godlewska and Smith, eds. *Geography and Empire*, esp. Godlewska, "Napoleon's Geographers"; Heffernan, "The Science of Empire"; and Olivier Soubeyran, "Imperialism and Colonialism versus Disciplinarity in French Geography," 244–64; see Lejeune, *Les sociétés de géographie*, 15–17, 73–84 on the early society, a revised and condensed form of *Les sociétés de géographie en France dans le mouvement social et intellectuel du XIXe siècle*, Thèse Paris-X 1987 (Lille III: ARNT, 1988); McKay, "Colonialism"; for the early period, see Cohen, "Imperial Mirage" Cohen, *The French Encounter with Africans*, 161–78, 252–3, 264–5, 269; Taylor, "Nascent Expansionism"; for a contrary view on the relative purity of the explorer-scholar dialogue, see Surun, "De l'explorateur au géographe," and the 2000 doctoral thesis by Hélène Blais, "Les voyages français dans le Pacifique," summarized in *Bulletin de la Société française pour l'histoire des sciences de l'homme* n° 20 (autumne 2000): 58–61; on the composition, organization, and growth of the Society, see Fierro, *La Société*.

3 Guizot, *Mémoires*, 7:40–117, 467–71 on the Marquesas and Tahiti; Aldrich, *Greater France*, 94.

4 Meek, *Social Science*; Staum, *Minerva's Message*, 160–9; on the term "civilizing mission," Conklin, *A Mission to Civilize*, 1–23.

5 Betts, *Assimilation and Association*, 9–15 for definitions of assimilation and association; other accounts of French imperial ideology are in Murphy, *The Ideology of French Imperialism*; Betts, *Tricouleur*; Baumgart, *Imperialism*; Girardet, *L'Idée coloniale en France*; Meyer, Tarrade, Rey-Goldzeiger, and Thobié, *Histoire de la France coloniale*.

superior science and technology, the French would develop the intellectual and moral faculties of the colonized. Assimilationist policy ultimately stemmed from Enlightenment and Revolutionary universalist views of the perfectibility of all human beings. Its premises suggested that the French could turn non-Europeans into "overseas French." Even enthusiastic advocates of empire, who were only a minority among the politically aware French population, tended to articulate assimilationist views until the 1890s.

Yet long before participants in Colonial Congresses of the late 1880s or 1890s changed their assumptions, the emerging social sciences furnished a competing second model. Before 1848, Geographical Society and Ethnological Society members, like some of the phrenologists, propounded a theory of racial difference that always excluded some peoples from advanced artistic and scientific achievement. The pathbreaking study of Michael Adas has argued that belief in the superiority of European science and technology had overwhelming importance for images of non-European backwardness. He also asserts that racial theory based on physical differences had only a marginal impact on colonial policy before 1860. His study furnishes a much-needed corrective to explaining all exploitation by scientific racism alone.[6]

This discussion acknowledges the importance of theories of both cultural retardation and inherent organic difference. Geographers and ethnologists in the learned societies of the early nineteenth century often participated in government-sponsored expeditions where their theories provided intellectual justification for the colonialism that flourished later. Only the reserved policies of ministers such as François Guizot prevented further French expansion in the early nineteenth century.

Explorers and naval surgeons traveled the world using the Camper-Cuvier facial angle to measure indigenous faces and to discern allegedly lower intellectual capacity. At best, such an ungracious endowment implied an even more urgent need for European tutelage than did merely "retarded" civilizations. At worst, such low potential excused unimpeded European domination without a bad conscience. Such people could never hope to achieve civilization, or would take centuries to catch up. In its extreme form, the theory branded some human "races" as so divergent from the European norm that they could be considered distinct species.[7]

6 Adas, *Machines as the Measure of Men*, 274, 290–1.

7 Blanckaert, "Le système des races"; *Mémoires de la Société ethnologique de Paris*, 1 (1841) and 2 (1845).

Such arguments helped undermine the imperial policy of assimilationism, which flourished in the Third Republic after 1870. There was
no neat correspondence between assumptions about races and the rival
imperial doctrine of "associationism" that became more prevalent from
the 1890s. But the fundamental premise of associationism indeed
rested upon human inequality – the end of the egalitarian ideal.[8] As
junior "associates" of the French, colonized peoples could furnish labour for economic development and soldiers for military defence of
their own territory. Exploitation with no prospect of citizenship was the
logical corollary. In the sometimes coexisting evolutionist paradigm,
the prevailing model was the divergent paths of Europeans and non-
Europeans to civilization. French institutions would obviously be inap-
propriate for a colonized people slow to adapt. The theory of the
would-be psychologist and anthropologist Gustave Le Bon (1841–1931),
who in the 1880s postulated the inferior intellectual endowment of
non-Europeans, indeed had an impact upon some of the leading apos-
tles of associationism of the period from 1890 to 1910, the naval officers Léopold de Saussure and Jules Harmand.[9]

The emergence of associationism among colonial theorists and administrators never operated in pure binary opposition to assimilationism, and its triumph in discourse was indeed a tortuous one. For
practical reasons, even the ferocious General Thomas Bugeaud, who
subdued the Algerians in the 1840s, believed some form of preservation
of Arab institutions was a necessity. So did the naval officers who first established French rule in Cochinchina. After the advent of the Third Republic, there was a strong ideological resurgence of assimilationist
universalism, partly at the behest of Algerian colonists who resented the
military protection of Muslims from French property legislation. Within
two decades, the inherent problems of assimilation generated criticism
of the ideal. For one thing, Muslim resistance in Algeria and Indochina
and European fears of Muslim citizenship fostered a complete reap-
praisal of imposing French legal codes. For another, the necessity of a
protectorate in a region contested among European powers – Tunisia –
prevented the French from unilaterally attempting to transform that

8 Betts, *Assimilation and Association*, on the extreme racist psychologist Gustave Le Bon's
contested contributions to imperial theory, 59–89, and on the theory and inconsistent
practice of "association," 106–32.

9 Adas, *Machines as the Measure of Men*, 320–2.

society. In any case, after 1890 leading colonial policymakers gravitated to associationism, with racial theory an auxiliary to the problems of governance.[10]

True enough, the earlier racial theorists did not envisage the more tolerant side of associationism – that is, colonized peoples could not become French, but they should more freely retain their own customs and run their local affairs. The recall of Muslim judges in Algeria or of the recalcitrant mandarins in Indochina might be feasible where such relatively "advanced" structures already existed, and where there was an imperative to end French hostility to traditional elites.[11]

In the early Geographical Society, mildly benevolent attitudes indicating a perceived potential for civilization were apparent toward selected west African populations, Polynesians, and "half-civilized" Abyssinians. The geographers and explorers tended to view indigenous Australians and Melanesians as incorrigibly mired in a savage state, often on the basis of measurement of facial angles.

Scientific racism was not always the major motive for the imperial acquisition that often occurred for strategic or economic reasons, nor was every racist an advocate of empire.[12] There is no need to accept the extreme reductionism of Foucauldian power/knowledge frameworks to recognize the applicability of Edward Said's arguments about Orientalism. The geographers' discourse on racial theory created textual entities that concealed, while actually fostering, European hegemony.[13]

The Napoleonic scientific commission in Egypt, an important precedent for the Geographical Society, was a classic case of imaging the modern "Other" (Egyptians) as backward, barbaric, inauthentic, and without an informative voice.[14] The French geographers in Egypt helped originate the popular early nineteenth-century theme that the West was an active civilizing force, while the Orient was static and reactive. Other

---

10 For a thorough analysis of the distant origins of associationism in Algeria and Indochina, and a complex argument relating it to French sociological reformism at home and the end of evolutionism in ethnography, see the provocative thesis by Hoyt, "The Surfacing of the Primitive," esp. 284–99 on policies from 1840 to 1869, and 300–52 on the Third Republic; Hoyt, however, declines to see racial theory relating to administrative policy. On Algeria, see Ageron, *Modern Algeria*, 22–4, 33–4, 53–64 on early "native" policy.

11 For proponents of "association," see Betts, *Assimilation and Association*, 120–31.

12 On non-imperialist social Darwinists, Francis, "Anthropology and Social Darwinism."

13 Said, *Orientalism*, 3–5; among many critiques, Prakash, "Orientalism Now," 199–212.

14 Said, *Orientalism*, 42–3, 45, 85, 87.

theorists of imperialism such as Mary Louise Pratt have justifiably argued that the classification of others tended to naturalize European superiority. Non-Europeans rarely met European expectations for a work ethic deemed essential to civilization, while European commerce seemingly demonstrated the failure of indigenous cultures when European goods overwhelmed native crafts.[15]

THE COMMUNITY OF GEOGRAPHERS: VOLNEY, JOMARD, MALTE-BRUN

Before the full formulation of the discourse of the Geographical Society, a flourishing French geographic community was already increasingly implicated in government ventures – civil, military, and naval engineers, explorers in the Academy of Sciences, and cartographers in the Academy of Inscriptions. During the Revolution, there was also an unsuccessful effort to make geography into a more theoretical, less descriptive, social science in the short-lived Class of Moral and Political Sciences of the French National Institute.[16] The unrealized aspirations for a social-scientific geography stemmed partly from the brilliant, but far from comprehensive, correlation of "physical" and "political" states in the voyages and questionnaires of Constantin-François Volney.[17]

One of the most important founders of the Geographical Society was Edme-François Jomard (1777–1862), a military *ingénieur-géographe* who served in Napoleonic Egypt. As general editor of the twenty-two-volume *Description de l'Egypte* (1809–22), he coordinated the reports and commentaries of the expedition on ancient and modern Egypt.[18] Even as late as 1859, Jomard boasted of the French civilizing mission – carrying the treasure of French civilization to a "nation exhausted by oppression, fanaticism, and ignorance." Nearly fifty years earlier, in his essays on Egypt, he measured the facial angle of ancient Egyptian mummies

15 Pratt, *Imperial Eyes*, 1–2, 7, 32, 75–8.

16 Godlewska, *Geography Unbound*, 14–39; Staum, *Minerva's Message*, 154–71.

17 Godlewska, "Napoleonic Geography"; *Geography Unbound*, 204; Volney, *Voyage en Egypte et en Syrie*, 33–40, 198–214, 361–75, 401–5; Moravia, *Il pensiero degli Idéologues*, 645–71; Volney, *Questions de statistique*; Deneys, "Géographie, Histoire et Langue," esp. 85; Brahimi, "Volney chez les sauvages."

18 Godlewska, "Map, text, and image"; Mitchell, *Colonizing Egypt*; Laurens, et al., *L'Expédition d'Égypte*; for the cartographic fixation of Jomard, Godlewska, *Geography Unbound*, 129–47; Godlewska, "*Napoleon's Geographers*," 40; Godlewska, "Traditions, Crisis, and New Paradigms," esp. 209; Conklin, *A Mission to Civilize*, 18 on the Institut d'Égypte.

(77–78°) as evidence of their relationship to modern Arabs. The implication was that neither Coptic Abyssinians nor Africans had produced the ancient Egyptian civilization.[19]

Human geography was also for Jomard the summit of the entire science of geography. In his 1839 study of Arabia, he remarked, "ethnology is the science of geography itself seen as a whole and in its highest generality." It was "urgent to know thoroughly the degree of civilization of all races," both in physical constitution and cultures, to "have relations between them and us which are more certain and advantageous."[20]

Another significant founder of the Geographical Society was the Danish-born geographer Conrad Malte-Brun (1775–1826). Editor of the *Annales des voyages* from 1807, he supervised a clearinghouse for information on worldwide exploration. His eight-volume *Précis de géographie universelle* was one of the most widely popular textbooks of its age.[21] He, too, expressed the desire to "classify human races" by "corporeal nuances and languages," beliefs, and laws. He adopted the classic model of a progressive "march of civilization" (arts, sciences, laws) carrying the European torch to peoples in the depths of "savagery," "barbarism," or the "childhood of civilization."[22] This venture included Africans, who had a "disposition for civilization even if they were really inferior in intelligence."[23] In only one respect did the first edition of Malte-Brun suggest an interest in a new principle of racial hierarchy. He remarked that the Africans and particularly the blacks of Oceania had an "obtuse"(by which he meant "acute") facial angle, which suggested that the latter group occupied the "last rung of the ladder of the human species."[24] He therefore anticipated future explorers who wished to quantify either the retardation or organic deficiencies of peoples.

---

19 Dias, "Une science nouvelle," esp. 161, 165, 167–8, 170–1.

20 Jomard, *Études géographiques et historiques sur l'Arabie (1839)*, cited in Blanckaert, "'Story' et 'History' de l'ethnologie," 461; see also Dias, "Une science nouvelle," 161, 177 on the usage of "ethnography" or "geo-ethnography"; d'Avezac, BSG 2nd sér., 2 (1834): 280.

21 Godlewska, "Napoleon's Geographers," 42, 45; Godlewska, *Geography Unbound*, 103; Godlewska, "L'influence d'un homme."

22 Malte-Brun, *Précis de géographie universelle* 1 (1810): 2, 4; 2 (1812): 606, 610, 616.

23 Ibid., 2 (1812): 45, 549–50 on crania, 554–7 on racial types; 5 (1820): 30, 60–2; Ibid., 4 (1813): 675–6.

24 Ibid., 4 (1813): 251, 436.

THE PARIS GEOGRAPHICAL SOCIETY

Seven of the eight founding scholars of the Geographical Society were members of the historically oriented Academy of Inscriptions. These included the erudite Arabist, Persian, and Hindu culture student Louis-Mathieu Langlès (1763–1824), the Paris Faculty of Letters professor of ancient geography Jean-Denis Barbié du Bocage (1760–1825), and the curator of ancient Egyptian and other antiquities Jean-Antoine Letronne (1787–1848). Aside from Malte-Brun (who was not in the Academy) and Jomard, the eight principal founders also included Baron Charles-Athanase Walckenaer (1771–1852), successful textbook author, and the deputy director of the naval cartographic archive, Admiral Elisabeth-Paul-Edouard de Rossel (1765–1829).[25] Political luminaries or prestigious colleagues from kindred sciences often served as officers, but the all-important secretary-general of the central commission tended to be an armchair scholar such as Malte-Brun, who occupied this post between 1821 and 1826.

The rules of the Society announced its mission of "contributing to the progress of geography," "encouraging voyages to unknown countries," issuing questionnaires to travelers, establishing gold medals for voyages of discovery, prizes for solving other geographic questions, and publishing reports and correspondence with geographers all over the world.[26] Studies of Lejeune and Fierro have already established the composition of the membership. Distinguished members of the Royal Institute and its correspondents heavily weighted the ranks of the 217 all-male founders in 1821 (they constituted 11 per cent of the total – the Academy of Sciences contributed fifteen founders, Inscriptions ten, Fine Arts five).[27] The membership of the largely Parisian Society rose to 309 at its peak in 1829, followed by a gradual decline to 110 in 1848. Among the founders, about 8 per cent were political figures (deputies, peers, ministers), 15 per cent were national, department, or local government officials, nearly 10 per cent were army or civil engineers or officers, 10 per cent were lawyers or judges, 7.2 per cent teachers or men of letters, while only 3.5 per cent were bankers and merchants. A few founders later became members of the Phrenology Society (Mège, Las Cases), but

25 Fierro, *La Société de Géographie*, 7–8.

26 ASG, Société de Géographie, Règlement imprimé, Colis 65; see the list of founding members and officers in *BSG* 1 (1822): 10–24.

27 Godlewska, *Geography Unbound*, 130–5.

the geographers were largely a conservative, aristocratic elite (probably between 30 to 40 per cent were noble, judging by titles and the less reliable particle), who were pillars of the Restoration establishment.[28] By the 1840s noble participation had waned, while the percentage of high administrators and lower-level government employees increased. In the 1860s, the membership balance shifted toward a higher proportion of naval and military officers, foreign affairs and colonial officials, and more bankers and businessmen.[29]

THE COMMERCIAL AND COLONIAL IMPERATIVE

The erudite character of some founders did not, however, preclude interests in trade and expansion. Many of the active founders had important duties assigned and funded by the government. Naval officers charged with exploration and often with secret colonial reconnaissance missions, such as Louis-Claude Desaulces de Freycinet (1779–1842) and Jules-Sébastien-César Dumont d'Urville (1790–1842), were active members of the Society central commission.[30] Nor did the revolution of 1830 undermine a society tied to the Restoration establishment. King Louis-Philippe himself granted a modest annual subsidy to the Society in 1834, and members in the 1830s and 1840s followed very closely the Navy missions of exploration in Africa and the Pacific.[31]

Not only was there an implicit reliance on infrastructure and communication services supplied by the government, but even in its Prospectus of 1822 and in its appeal for royal recognition in 1824, the Paris Geographical Society underlined the "commercial and political advantages" of geographical study.[32] For at least three areas of the world – the west African Sudan, the horn of east Africa, and the south Pacific – Geographical Society members had a sustained interest in expanding French

28 For longitudinal and comparative study, see Fierro, *La Société de Géographie*, 271–2; I have computed my own figures from the list of founders in the *BSG*.

29 Lejeune estimated 34.6 per cent noble in *Les sociétés de géographie*, 27; see 25–8 for his long-term study.

30 ASG, MS in-4° 34, 1830, 1832 – Liste des présences, réunions de la commission centrale. For a parallel study of the relationship of the Royal Geographical Society (RGS) in Britain to imperial concerns, see Driver, *Geography Militant*, esp. 37–48; on RGS president Roderick Murchison, see the verdict of his biographer R. Stafford, quoted by Driver, 43: "By the late 1850s, the RGS more perfectly represented British expansionism in all its facets than any other institution of the nation."

31 Taylor, "Nascent Expansionism," 231*ff.*

32 ASG, Colis 26; AN F17 17201.

influence. Two of the most active founders, Malte-Brun and Walckenaer, were veritable enthusiasts for the western Sudan trade.[33] The supposedly fabulous wealth of Timbuktu and the Bambuk gold fields provided an incentive for expansion from French Senegalese coastal slave trading outposts. The Niger River trade tempted the French to control the Senegal River interior to forestall British expansion along the Gambia.

Baron Jacques-François Roger was an active correspondent of the Society while he was military governor of Senegal, and he remained an active member upon his return to France. Repeatedly he wrote to Jomard, the most committed Africanist in the Society, on the need in Senegal for "capitalists, especially industrious men, for France to count on another rich colony." In a telling equation of civilization and colonization, he hoped to "appreciate and facilitate the great enterprise, the colonization, that is, the civilization of a part of Africa."[34] Jomard himself envisaged that Africa "must endure in its turn modern civilization" by "paying its tribute to our industry," sending its "treasures, products, precious metals," and providing an asylum for the surplus active European population.[35] Such a sentiment anticipated by sixty years the views of economic imperialists in the heyday of the Third Republic.[36]

The most successful direct stimulus to exploration of west Africa was the Society prize contest that elicited in December 1824 a voyage to Timbuktu by a route closest to French African possessions.[37] Aside from questions on climate, natural history, the skin colour, face shape, and hair of inhabitants, language and customs, the Society expected the traveler to explore "usefulness for commercial industry." The minor government official René Caillié (1799–1838), acting on his own in Muslim disguise, completed a dramatic odyssey from the Guinea coast to Timbuktu and across the Sahara to Morocco in 1827–28. Though he found no wealth in Timbuktu, he parroted Jomard in declaring the need of Senegal for "new markets and relations in the interior of the continent" and the need for "new discoveries, new geographical knowledge" to "impose on distant populations the tribute of

33 Cohen, "Imperial Mirage," 420, 423; Walckenaer, *Recherches géographiques*, 44–5, 415.

34 *BSG* 2 (1824): 57–8; ASG, letter of 7 novembre 1824, Colis 19 and Colis 4 bis.

35 *BSG* 2 (1824) 239–40; *cf* Cohen, "Imperial Mirage," 424; see also ASG, Colis 19, letter of a négociant-droguiste, Laîné.

36 Betts, *Assimilation and Association*, 133–53.

37 AN F17 17201; *BSG* 2 (1824): 256 and 3 (1825): 44, 209–12; Lejeune, *Les sociétés de géographie*, 37–9 on this contest.

our industry."[38] At a Geographical Society assembly after his return, the Navy Minister and Society President Hyde de Neuville assured Caillié that "commerce will know how to take great advantage of the new route you have established."[39] Fifteen years later, the Geographical Society assisted naval officer Anne-Jean-Baptiste Raffenel, who became a member in 1846, in planning further exploration after he advocated a Niger River establishment to subdue the Fulani threat to Algeria.[40]

The French never had as significant a presence in the horn of east Africa as in the western Sudan, though they would acquire the port of Obock in 1862 and Djibouti in 1885. The ambitions of Egyptian viceroy Muhammad Ali (the would-be conqueror of Arabia and Syria) and strategic rivalry with the British (who moved into Aden in 1837) aroused great interest. The Geographical Society member and future Gold Medal winner Antoine d'Abbadie (1810–97) lobbied successfully for a consul and commercial agent in Massouah on the Red Sea coast.[41] The young naval officer and former Saint-Simonian sympathizer Charlemagne-Théophile Lefebvre (1811–60) pleaded directly with the Paris Geographical Society in 1838 to ask for government subsidies for his mission to Ethiopia: "I am sure a sign of interest that a learned society will have in my enterprise will increase the [Navy] Minister's good dispositions toward me."[42] The Agriculture and Commerce Minister Laurent Cunin-Gridaine in fact anticipated European migration to Abyssinia to help "fertilize the seeds of civilization, which it has in great number." Lefebvre hoped to obtain a coastal "port of call" for France on the Red Sea through the good offices of the Abyssinian ruler Oubié of Semien (Simen) province. Yet Foreign Minister François Guizot remained circumspect.[43] Even after disavowal by the government,

38 Caillié, *Voyage à Tombouctou*, 1:38–9, and Caillié, *Travels through Central Africa*, 1:286; 2:50, 56; Jomard, "Geographical Remarks and Inquiries" in Caillié, *Travels*, 2:336, 350–

39 *BSG* 13 (1830): 177.

40 ASG, Colis 3 bis, report of Jomard; AN F17 3000; Raffenel, *Voyage dans l'Afrique*, 32–3; *Nouveau voyage*, 1:Introduction, ii, 77; 2:57, 136 on Fulani; *NAV*, 5ᵉ sér., 4 (1845): 67, 211.

41 Aldrich, *Greater France* on Djibouti, 58–9; Malécot, *Les Voyageurs*, 8–9, 21, 29–31, 34, 43; Abbadie, *Douze ans dans la Haute*; for Jomard on Ethiopia, see *BSG* 2nd sér., 10 (1838): 145 and 2nd sér., 13 (1840): 280–90.

42 ASG, colis 3 bis; letter of 6 July 1838 in ASG, colis 21; see also AAE, Afrique 13, Abyssinie, 1. 1838–50, nᵒˢ 22, 37.

43 Inter-ministerial correspondence in AN Marine BB 1014; see also AAE Afrique 13, Abyssinie, 1. 1838–50, n. 39.

Lefebvre in 1845 sought European intervention to help Oubié unite a politically reformed Ethiopia to benefit French commerce.[44]

Concurrently, the adventurer Charles-Etienne-Xavier Rochet d'Héricourt, member of the Society by 1846 and co-winner of the exploration medal in 1847, attempted (unsuccessfully) to open a route from Somalia to the central Ethiopian province of Choa to enhance the security of Egypt. He had not only government backing but also encouragement from Society members Jomard, Marie-Armand-Pascal d'Avezac de Castera-Macaya (1799–1875), and Jean-Baptiste-Benoît Eyriès (1767–1846). In the elite, influential journal *Revue des deux mondes*, the economist and novelist Louis Reybaud welcomed Rochet's moves as a riposte to "English greed." He hoped for a French role in the division of the "spoils" of the decadent "Islamic empire in the Orient."[45]

Society members also commanded three of the largest Pacific expeditions of the Navy and Colonies ministry between 1822 and 1840. These investigations indirectly facilitated the proclamation in 1842 of a colony in the Marquesas and a protectorate in the Society Islands.[46] Freycinet's voyage (1817–20) preceded foundation of the Society, but his delayed publication, from 1825 to 1844, evoked later discussion. The Society sent him a letter suggesting how carefully he should describe the peoples of Brazil.[47] Freycinet's earlier private dispatches sought to interest the government in acquiring the Marianas from Spain as a penal colony.[48] Two other founding Society members, Louis-Isidore Duperrey (expedition of 1822–24) and Dumont d'Urville (expeditions of 1826–29 and 1837–40) pursued both imperial policy and ethnographic research. Duperrey, charged with investigating colonization of western Australia, recommended against a supply base in Tahiti since it would never be in the shipping lanes.[49] Dumont d'Urville found French private claims to northeast New Zealand dubious, but singled out the site of modern Auckland as the "only place in Polynesia where a consider-

44 Lefebvre, *Voyage en Abyssinie*, lxxviii–lxxix; on British geographers' interest in Abyssinia in 1867, see Driver, *Geography Militant*, 43–4. Driver also notes the heterogeneity of interests in the RGS, a caution equally applicable to any of the French societies.

45 Pleas in 1846 for ministerial subsidies in AN F173003B; AAE, Afrique 13, Abyssinie, 1. 1838–50, nos 116–40; Rochet d'Héricourt, *Voyage de la côte orientale*, 1:xiii, 367–9; Rochet d'Héricourt, *Second voyage*, 373–9; Malécot, *Les voyageurs*, 60–70; *Revue des deux mondes* (juillet 1841): 59–93, esp. 62, 93.

46 For government goals, see Guizot, *Mémoires*, 7:46, 467–71.

47 Letter to Freycinet of 11 October 1822 in ASG, Colis 26.

48 AN Marine BB4 998.

49 AN Marine BB4 1000; Guizot, *Mémoires*, 7:58; Faivre, *L'Expansion*, 245.

Portrait of Louis-Claude Desaulces de Freycinet
(1779–1842), Pacific explorer

able colony might be founded with some chance of success." Interestingly enough, he dismissed the Marquesas as commercially unprofitable and the Society Islands, including Tahiti, as already under British sway.[50] In these expeditions, political and commercial dimensions clearly complemented the scientific and ethnographic goals.[51]

Admiral Abel Aubert Dupetit-Thouars's seizure of the Marquesas and Tahiti in 1842 may have related more to strategic objectives of compensation for the British occupation of New Zealand in 1840 than to concerns of geographers. Nevertheless, Geographical Society members

50 Faivre, *L'Expansion*, 285–7; Dumont d'Urville, *Two Voyages to the South Seas*, 1:285 from AN Marine BB4 1002.

51 Navy Instructions to d'Urville, AN Marine BB4 1009 on whaling, commerce, shipping, and industrial markets; Guizot, *Mémoires*, 7:475; Faivre, *L'Expansion*, 465–93.

participated as Navy officers in plans for government expansion. They also purveyed the ethnographic assumptions needed for a worldwide French civilizing mission.[52]

CLASSIFYING PEOPLES:
WEST AND EAST AFRICANS

Strategic interests, rivalry with Britain, and local military or naval initiatives might in the end determine the actual annexation of territory. Yet the unshakeable belief in European superiority and racial hierarchy provided facile justification and a necessary condition for action, whatever the situation. The racial classification of naturalists among the Society members, such as Georges Cuvier and Jean-Baptiste-Maximilien Bory de Saint-Vincent, was essential reading for explorers' observations. In turn the journals of the naval surgeons on the Freycinet expedition, Jean-René-Constant Quoy (1790–1869) and J. Paul Gaimard, and on the Duperrey expedition, Geographical Society member René-Primevère Lesson (1794–1849) and Prosper Garnot (1794–1838), helped modify the classifiers' hierarchies. The graduated scale of physical features corresponding to mental faculties could construct an "other" fit for guidance and French tutelage or so remote from the European ideal as to be uncivilizable and meriting little benevolence.

Society questionnaires to explorers from 1823 to 1846 prominently included a concern for classifying races. Malte-Brun and Jomard attempted to elicit information from consuls on the Barbary coast about the facial angle of the Berbers. The Society asked Dumont d'Urville before his first voyage in 1826 for "ethno-geographic" research about the "particular races of Oceania." In 1846 Jomard insisted that Lefebvre report on the "physiognomy" of the "several distinct races" of the Nile region of Egypt and Ethiopia. He defined "race" as a "special population characterized by special forms and physiognomy."[53] The Society also stimulated the interest of authors such as Lesson with two prize contests – an unsuccessful exercise on the "origins of various peoples of the Great Ocean," their physical constitution, customs, and civil and religious institutions, and, in 1830, on the "origins of Asiatic Negroes."[54]

---

52 Taylor, "Nascent Expansionism."
53 ASG, Colis 3 bis, #43, questions of Jomard for Lefebvre, and *BSG* 3 (1825): 22.
54 *BSG* 1 (1822): 65; ASG, Colis 18 and Colis 65.

But the rich portrait of human variety is more evident in the works of individual members of the Society than in the issuance of collective questionnaires.

Between 1825 and 1836 the reviewers in the Geographical Society *Bulletin* seemed to have warmed to Bory's theories of racial classification based in part on the facial angle. Although in 1825 an anonymous commentator insisted, "let's recognize among men a single family," the enthusiastic ethnologist Pascal d'Avezac in 1836 called Bory "an ingenious and sagacious observer."[55]

Amid generally negative images of Africans, the more "advanced" peoples of west Africa seemed to justify some optimism about the effects of European guidance. Jomard remarked that the facial angle of the Senegalese Wolof was closer to that of Europeans, so perhaps they were not authentically "Negroes." Baron Roger stressed the courage, sensitivity, politeness, and hospitality of Senegal blacks.[56] The explorer and founding Geographical Society member Gaspard-Théodore Mollien thought that the Soninké of west Africa were polite enough to show that "these people have already made great progress in civilization."[57]

The explorer and Society member Raffenel detested the "insolence" of Africans who obstructed his voyage, but did not despair of Africans' potential for civilization.[58] In fact, so confident was he of west African capacities that he explicitly voiced support for an assimilationist imperial policy. He recommended that French policy "tend toward assimilation" with "occupation in common of territory" rather than American-style "destruction and resettlement," except where uncooperative peoples necessitated the use of force. Catholic missionaries, he hoped, would oppose Islam and help cultivate, at least with elementary education, the languishing intellectual faculties of west Africans.[59]

Yet the nagging doubt persisted that pure blacks had no truly accomplished achievements. One of the most contested questions in the Sudan was the nature of the nomadic, pastoral Fulani, who were lighter in colour and descended partly from Moors or Berbers. Raffenel thought them "the most advanced in civilization" with less acute facial angles,

55 *BSG* 4 (1825): 15–18; 2nd sér., 6 (1836): 281.

56 Roger, *BSG* 8 (1827): 355, and 10 (1828): 289.

57 Mollien, *Voyage*, 1:viii; 2:181–2; on Mollien, Caillié, and Raffenel, see also Cohen, *The French Encounter with Africans*, 252–3, 269.

58 Raffenel, *Second voyage*, extrait de la *Revue coloniale* (1849), 51.

59 Raffenel, *Voyage dans l'Afrique* 1:213; Raffenel, *Nouveau voyage*, 2:240, 266–7.

and Caillié confirmed their resemblance to European physiognomy with aquiline noses, oval shaped heads, and high foreheads.[60] The Saint-Simonian racial theorist and Society member Gustave d'Eichthal could not believe that they were truly black, since a physiognomically attractive, culturally advanced, and conquering people must be white, or possibly descended from ancient Malays.[61]

By 1839, the foundation of the Paris Ethnological Society (the subject of the next chapter) had heightened interest in the persistence of invariable racial types, as observed in facial angles, crania, head shapes, and, for some, phrenology. Geographical Society members who later joined the Ethnological Society, including d'Eichthal, Victor Courtet de l'Isle, Vivien de Saint-Martin, and d'Avezac, were more dubious about the possibility of civilizing and assimilating "true" Africans.[62]

The French image of Abyssinians (modern Ethiopians) differed fundamentally from their construction of west Africans in part because of the deeply rooted ancient Abyssinian Christian culture. Saint-Simonian influence among some explorers had stereotyped the portrait of an active Occident assisting a passive Orient to the final stage of civilization,[63] and d'Eichthal foresaw a special role for Abyssinians in the "approaching time of the wedding between Orient and Occident."[64]

In 1837 Jomard enthusiastically reviewed the exploration reports of ex-Saint-Simonians Edmond Combes and Maurice Tamisier about the importance of bringing Abyssinia into contact with the rest of the globe.[65] For a few years from 1839 to 1843, there were regular dispatches from French travelers in Abyssinia in the Geographical Soci-

---

60 On the Fulani, see Mollien, *Voyage*, 1:43, 149; 2:166, 181–2, 273, 289; Raffenel, *Voyage dans l'Afrique*, 263–4, 302; Raffenel, *Nouveau voyage*, 2:56; Caillié, *Travels through Central Africa*, 1:186, 222.

61 *BSG* 2nd sér., 14 (1840): 259, 265; d'Eichthal, *Lettres sur la race noire*, 147; d'Eichthal, "Histoire et origine des Foulahs ou fellas" in *MSEP*, t. 1.

62 Edwards, *Des caractères*, 14–16, 33, 45; on Lesson in Polynesia, 114–15n., 125; "Esquisse de l'état actuel de l'anthropologie," *MSEP* 1 (1841): 113, 121, 125; *MSEP*, *Bulletin* 1 (1841): vi–xv; Edwards, *Fragments d'un mémoire sur les Gaëls*; on Edwards, see Blanckaert, "On the Origins," esp. 34–41.

63 Emerit, *Les Saint-Simoniens*, 101–10; Reuillard, *Les Saint-Simoniens*, 81–2.

64 BA, Fonds d'Eichthal MS. 13759, letter to Enfantin, 14 janvier 1838; see Emerit, *Les Saint-Simoniens*, 100–14 and Enfantin, *Colonisation de l'Algérie* for Enfantin's own version of association of the French with Algerian local leaders and assimilation of Algerians through education and health measures.

65 Emerit, "Diplomates et Explorateurs"; Combes and Tamisier, *Voyages en Abyssinie*; see review by Jomard in *BSG* 2nd sér. 8 (1837): 337–71 and 9 (1838): 5–39.

ety Bulletin, including the preparations of naval officer Lefebvre and the explorer and devout Catholic d'Abbadie.[66] Jomard had also asked for a description of the "traits" and customs of the distinctive "races." Following the theories of Buffon and Blumenbach, Lefebvre's responses, partly intended for the Ethnological Society, insisted that skin colour was itself an insufficient indicator. Any skin colour, varying from olive to reddish-brown, could coexist with either very beautiful or apparently degenerate features.[67] He felt compelled to report that the black "Changallas" of the desert, with their narrow forehead and "acute facial angle," were "savages" cruel to foreigners.[68] The ruling Amhara elite (except for Oubié himself) were well proportioned with an open facial angle. Their cranial development reflected their superior faculties of perception and educability, albeit with less creativity than Europeans. The swashbuckling Arnauld d'Abbadie (brother of the gentle Antoine) later wished to stress that Christian Abyssinians, with "Arien" ancestors, had a developed forehead and open facial angle like the Caucasians, "more like Apollo than Hercules."[69] Similarly, Rochet, with the approval of Reybaud in the *Revue des deux mondes*, commented that the dark-skinned Somalis or Issas were not "Negro" since they had a large forehead, thin lips, and aquiline nose.[70] Facial features and head shape, as well as religion, could determine the ranking of peoples.

Lefebvre also remarked that the Oromo, or Gallas, had a highly developed occipital region of the cranium, showing a more instinctive, rather than intelligent, nature. Often the Galla were tricky and cruel,

66 On Lefebvre, *BSG* 2nd sér., 10 (1838): 32–8, and Jomard on Aubert in 145–6; on d'Abbadie, *BSG* 2nd sér., 11 (1839): 200–27, esp. 215; on Rochet d'Héricourt, *BSG* 2nd sér., 15 (1841): 96, 269.

67 See *BSG* 2nd sér., 14 (1840): 65–71, 129–46; questions of Jomard for Lefebvre in ASG, colis 3 bis; Lefebvre, *Voyage*, 3 (1846): 286–7; letter of 31 May 1839 in *MSEP, Bulletin* 1 (1840): xxvi, xxxvii, 2:liii, lxviii; Lefebvre and d'Abbadie corresponded closely with the Ethnological Society in hopes of distinguishing racial types in Abyssinia. Lefebvre presented two Abyssinians to the ethnologists in June 1840 and after his early reports was named a correspondent of the Society; *MSEP* 1:xxxvii–viii.

68 *BSG* 2nd sér., 14 (1840): 268; Lefebvre, *Voyage*, 3:289–99, esp. 293–4; *NAV* 5ᵉ sér., 1 (1845): 173 for Téours; 310–12 for head shapes of Axoum, Gondar; see his report to the Public Instruction Ministry on dimensions of crania taken in AN F17 2983 when appealing for a publication subsidy in 1844.

69 Lefebvre, *Voyage*, 1:vi, lvi; on Oubié 68; 3:293; Abbadie, *Douze ans de séjour*, 1:52–3, 109; 3:161–3.

70 Rochet, *Voyage de la côte orientale*, 1:115, 118; Reybaud in *Revue des deux mondes* (juillet 1841): 62, 74.

with horrible trophies of war, the private parts of their male enemies displayed at their doors.[71] Yet the more French explorers spent time among the Galla, the more they were willing to judge them handsome and intelligent.[72]

In the final analysis, religion was the all-important question in Abyssinia. Lefebvre, the explorer Louis-Rémy Aubert-Roche, Arnauld d'Abbadie, and Rochet d'Héricourt all agreed that the Christian religion and customs elicited the Ethiopian disposition to "attach themselves to European civilization rather than Oriental." France could thus foster this rebuilding of "linkages to the outside world." Ethiopians were like a stationary relic of a sixth-century European nation, just awaiting European commerce that would end isolation and decadence.[73]

The former Saint-Simonian Lefebvre even adopted a nineteenth-century version of the "clash of civilizations" thesis: in Ethiopia there was a struggle between Muslim civilization, "sterile and decrepit," and Christian civilization, capable of giving a "baptism of moral and intellectual regeneration."[74] If Lefebvre did not foresee outright annexation, he saw an imperative for France to assure European access by overcoming obstructive Muslim traders.[75] While the Geographical Society awarded him its exploration prize in 1843, and encouraged Rochet (a Society member in 1846), the absence of government adventurism in this region inhibited French expansion in Somalia and Ethiopia at that time.[76]

71 Lefebvre, *Voyage*, 3:290, 299.

72 Jomard, *BSG* 2nd sér., 7 (1837): 337–71, esp. 360–6 and 2nd sér., 8 (1837): 5–39, 302–21; 2nd sér., 12 (1839): 14; confirmation in Rochet d'Héricourt, *Second voyage*, 188–9; Antoine d'Abbadie in *BSG*, 2nd sér., 11 (1839): 216; Abbadie, *Douze ans de séjour*, 3:162–3 and Rochet on the Galla, *Voyage*, 1:174–5, 270, 276–7.

73 Lefebvre, AAE Afrique 13, Abyssinie, 1. 1838–50 no. 20, "Mémoire de Lefebvre sur l'Abyssinie"; Lefebvre, *Voyage* 1:lx, 187–8; Jomard's report in *BSG* 2nd sér., 10 (1838): 145 and Aubert-Roche in 2nd sér., 13 (1840): 290; Rochet d'Héricourt in ASG, Colis 18. See also Aubert-Roche's letter on how Ethiopia was the only black Christian nation in Africa in AAE, Afrique 13, Abyssinie, 1. 1838–50 no. 113, and Rochet d'Héricourt's boosterism in the same archive, no. 118, and in his publication, *Voyage* 1:274, 363.

74 Lefebvre, "Notice sur le commerce," in *Voyage en Abyssinie, Relation historique* 2:24; Emerit, "Les explorateurs," 99–100; cf Rochet d'Héricourt, *Voyage de la côte orientale*, 1:274–5.

75 Abbadie, *Douze ans dans la Haute*, 81; Abbadie, *L'Abyssinie et le roi Théodore*, 16, 19.

76 See the enthusiastic report of Roux de Rochelle for a Geographical Society commission including Jomard and Walckenaer as members in *BSG* 3rd sér., 5 (1846): 284.

OBSERVING WOMEN

Studies of the curious relationship between theories of racial and gender inferiority avow that all deviations from the European male norm, whether white women or black men, could become analogous. Theorists might consider blacks feminine, and read into women's bodies the same alleged deficiencies as with blacks (in brain size, for example). Or, alternatively, the deviant label applied to both might reflect anxieties about "control" of sexuality or "control" in the simplest sense of domination in the household.[77]

In the accounts of explorers here considered, the status of women often signaled the degree of civilization attributed to a people. Heavy manual agricultural labour or brutal treatment of women was sufficient to label a group barbaric. For René Caillié, there was "less dignity of human nature" as women were "more enslaved."[78] In Abyssinia Lefebvre commented favourably on the independent private households of noblewomen, which matched European expectations more than in other "Oriental" countries.[79] Freycinet saw as a sign of primitivism the alleged treatment of Australian aboriginal women as beasts of burden.[80] There was little effort at understanding other cultures; rather, there was revulsion at the apparent absence in indigenous males of the stereotypical politeness and delicacy approved for European interaction with middle- and upper-class European women.

Most of the time, however, the blatantly voyeuristic remarks treated women as objects for aesthetic ranking or moralizing by the European male. Gaspard-Théodore Mollien found African women passionate and sensual, an attribute sometimes associated with all Africans.[81] Caillié reproved the Moors for so preferring large women that they force-fed them milk.[82] Rochet lyrically celebrated the "noble demeanor" and "reddest lips in the world" of Amhara women, from a civilization "well above bar-

---

77 See most notably Stepan, "Race and Gender," 261–77 and Schiebinger, *Nature's Body*, esp. 143–84; Schiebinger, ibid., 144, 147, 163–72 contends that women were rarely compared across racial lines, but nineteenth-century accounts offer counterexamples; on the Hottentot Venus and control of sexuality, see Sander Gilman, "Black Bodies, White Bodies" in Gates, ed. *"Race," Writing, and Difference*, 223–61.

78 Caillié, *Travels through Central Africa*, 2:61.

79 Lefebvre, *Voyage*, 3:223.

80 Freycinet, *Voyage autour du Monde*, 2, part 2:717, 732, 736.

81 Mollien, *Voyage*, 1:91, 98, 290–1.

82 Caillié, *Travels through Central Africa*, 1:61, 67, 458 on Timbuktu; see excerpts in BSG 13 (1830): 101–14 and 149–62.

barians."[83] To Dumont d'Urville, the women of Tonga could be models for artists.[84] Explorers also categorized women by the welcome they extended to the sailors. Dumont d'Urville generally disdained Melanesians because of the paradox that the "blacks, whose women in general are very ugly, are the only ones whose men folk are so strict about keeping their womenfolk, married or otherwise, from the gaze of Europeans."[85]

Considering the fabled charms of Tahiti and the Marquesas in eighteenth-century accounts, early nineteenth-century explorers were disenchanted in their denigration of Polynesians. Lesson found Tahitian women "generally ugly," and Garnot agreed there were "no more Venuses in Tahiti, despite some seductive eyes."[86] Both were particularly repelled by the masculine-looking New Zealand women, with their copper skin colour and fish and seal smell – proof enough of the "philanthropists' fictions of the man of nature."[87]

Melanesian women further disappointed European observers; hence Lesson insisted that the women in New Guinea were "disgraced by nature."[88] He found the "repulsive, half-lidded women" of Australia "an immense distance from the Vénus de Médicis."[89] Dumont's phrenologist Dumoutier found Tasmanian women "even more hideous than their men. After suckling one or two children, they appear more like harpies or furies than human creatures."[90]

Two somewhat contradictory views emerge from the observations of south Pacific women. The first is an essentialist cliché, as in Lesson's comment that the women of Port Jackson, Australia, "as everywhere else, are essentially women, that is, mobile, impressionable, and loquacious."[91] A surgeon on the Dumont d'Urville voyage, Jacques-Bernard Hombron, also thought women less affected by distinctive climates, somewhat counteracting eighteenth-century comments that climate affected "malleable" women more than men. However, there was also an

83 Rochet d'Héricourt, *Voyage* 1 (1841): 174, 270–2.

84 Dumont d'Urville, *Voyage de la corvette*, 4:229, 232.

85 Dumont d'Urville, *Two Voyages to the South Seas*, 1:150.

86 Lesson, *Voyage autour du Monde*, 2:239, 287, 361; Garnot, "De l'Homme."

87 Lesson, *Voyage autour du Monde*, 2:283, 287, 312, 325 (on man of nature).

88 Ibid., 3:129.

89 Duperrey, *Voyage autour du Monde*, 1ère partie *Zoologie*, 106–8; Lesson, *Voyage autour du Monde*, 2:274–7.

90 Dumoutier, *Journal*, 191 on Samoans, 434r on Tasmanians.

91 Lesson, *Voyage autour du Monde*, 2:294.

anti-essentialist insight in Hombron's work – that "civilization" created the "delicate and feminine."[92]

Women for some observers were essentially women all over the world – subject to all the disabilities that female nature implied. But an important component of the "ignoble savage" view applied equally to men and women of "backward races": women as the graceful, ornamental beings that European men expected could only exist in civilization, not even in the supposed erotic paradise of Polynesia.

FACIAL ANGLES AND PHRENOLOGY IN OCEANIA AND AUSTRALIA

While religious affinity loomed large in Ethiopia, the questions of racial status and amenability to civilization in Oceania led to even more frequent measurement by explorers of facial angles or crania. Society founder Freycinet instructed his officers to assess the variety of races by "the proportions of their head, cranium, jaws, arms, and legs, and the size of their facial angle." His surgeons and naturalists, Quoy and Gaimard, reported their findings to the Academy of Sciences in 1823.[93] The "miserable, malnourished, weak" New Hollanders, or Australians, most frequently exhibited the most acute facial angles, as low as 74°, though there were variations up to 80°.[94] The dark-skinned, curly-haired "Papuans" on Rawak and Waigiou Islands with a facial angle of 75° were actually a hybrid people with African physiognomy and hair on a Malay body.[95] The allegedly more advanced Hawaiians, with larger angles between 76.2° and 79.5°, were more intelligent. Yet even Polynesians' cultural retardation was still obvious in their practice of infanticide and the prostitution of wives to strangers for trifles.[96]

The commander Freycinet displayed sympathy for the Australians' plight, even though they were "miserable beings." Since they were intelligent enough to track enemies in sand and grass, they were uncivilizable by choice. Europeans, including atrociously behaving convicts, had "destroyed the inhabitants' essential means of subsistence" and were

92 Hombron, *Voyage au Pôle Sud*, 2:273; see also Schiebinger, *Nature's Body*, 126.

93 See the personal dossier of Gaimard in AN AJ15 574.

94 Freycinet, *Voyage autour du Monde*, 2, part 2:709; for Freycinet's model questionnaire, see the Journal de Raillard in AN 5JJ 68, fol. 38.

95 Freycinet, *Voyage autour du Monde, Zoologie*, 4–6 and *Zoologie* 2, part 1:47–9 for facial angle.

96 Ibid., 2, part 2:574, 586–7.

trying to change them too quickly.[97] By contrast, the ferocious, vigorous, and honour-bound New Zealanders had a "favourable disposition to receive the benefits of Christianity, and civilization which is the consequence." Religion and commerce would induce them to abandon their ferocity for civilized habits.[98] Freycinet was more tolerant than those who merely maligned aboriginals, but he remained committed to diffusing Christianity and commerce in the Pacific. The measurement of facial angles by his crew, however nuanced by remarks on culture, served to maintain concepts of racial hierarchy.

Pacific islanders did not fare well either when Quoy and Gaimard in 1823 tested Gall's mapping of moral dispositions. The surgeons discerned circumspection, suspicion, an "innate drive to steal," and a "carnivorous instinct" that indicated a "penchant to murder" among the Papuans. The observations were somewhat "favourable to the doctrines of Dr Gall." But they thought the faculties of Papuans "only need to be exercised and developed to make them hold a distinguished rank among the numerous varieties of the human species."[99] Even the pessimistic Gall approved their conclusion about Papuans' educability.[100] But Broussais in 1836 illustrated once again the ambivalence of phrenology. He cited Gaimard to argue that the Australians had hardly any language and that they lacked the necessary organs for becoming civilized.[101] Garnot, on the voyage of Duperrey of 1822–24, also retained his respect for phrenology. In a dictionary later edited by Bory, among others, he praised Gall's theory of cranial protuberances correlated to the development of moral and intellectual faculties.[102]

Lesson accepted the unity of the species, but was more pessimistic than Quoy and Gaimard on the educability of Pacific peoples, or even their ability to survive European contact. On the surface the "Oceanic" (Polynesian) islanders were, with the Malays, closer to Europeans in the "Hindu-Caucasic" race. Yet these peoples' manners showed "perfidy,

97 Ibid., 2, part 2:717, 742, 894, 902, 905–7.

98 Ibid., 2, part 2:911, 915–16.

99 Freycinet, *Voyage autour du Monde*, 1:9–11; Quoy and Gaimard read their memoir to the Royal Academy of Sciences on 5 May 1823; *cf* Renneville, "Un Terrain phrénologique," 92–4.

100 Gall, *Fonctions du cerveau*, 5:420–8.

101 Broussais, *Cours de phrénologie*, 790, 794.

102 Duperrey, *Voyage autour du Monde*, 1ère partie *Zoologie*, 115–16; see Renneville, "Un Terrain phrénologique," 96 for Garnot's remarks in Duperrey, *Zoologie* 2 (1830): 507–22; on Gall, see Garnot, "De l'Homme," extrait 27.

vengefulness, and bad faith." The Caroline, Marianas, and Philippine islanders were Mongolic, with advanced craftsmanship bespeaking civilized ancestry. The least favoured group of Pacific island peoples were
branches of the third "black" race, including the "Cafro-Madécasse" (related to southeast African and Madagascar peoples), Papuans (Malay-
black hybrids), the Tasmanians, and the true Papuans of the Solomon
Islands and coastal New Guinea. All displayed the domination of instinctive faculties and hateful passions with a lack of modesty and of the
arts.[103] With facial angles between 67° and 70°, there was no prognosis
that they could be civilized.[104] For Lesson, Australians appeared in the
second branch of the "black race," with interior New Guinea islanders
in the primitive "Alfourou" category. With their alleged ferocity, impov-
erishment, profound ignorance, and lack of moral faculties, "culture
cannot emerge where organs for it are lacking by a long succession of
deficient beings."[105]

Garnot's somewhat different measurements of the facial angle in fact
gave an average of 64.3° for the true Papuans and 65.6° for the hybrid
Papuans of Waigiou Island northwest of New Guinea, with highly developed "parietal" bumps on the cranium. While the ferocious Alfourous
measured 67°, equal to the more "advanced" New Zealanders, their crania
showed predominant instincts and their jaws "sufficiently prolonged to be
comparable to the profile of an orangutan."[106] The relatively small differences in facial angle demonstrated the actual difficulty of establishing reliable measurement for the purposes of determining a racial hierarchy.[107]

Even the graceful bearing of Polynesians could not save them from
Lesson's disapproval. Tahitians were "big children," with their native
physiognomy disfigured by new habits from Anglican missionaries.
Their now decadent "nautical architecture" testified to their inferior
"degree of civilization."[108] The best that could be said about licentious,

103 Lesson, *Oeuvres complètes*, 3:1; Lesson, *Voyage autour du Monde*, 2:36, 39–40, 54.

104 Lesson, "Considérations générales sur les Îles du Grand-Océan, et sur les variétés
de l'espèce humaine qui les habitent," 36–41, 51–8, 67, 70, 73–6, 89, 100–1 in Duperrey,
Voyage autour du Monde 1, 1ère partie Zoologie: 1–117; this portion was read to the Société
d'histoire naturelle in 1825. For the facial angle in Buffon, 3:69, and 3:72 on their hideous-
ness and ferocity.

105 Duperrey, *Voyage autour du Monde*, 106–8; Lesson, *Voyage autour du Monde*, 2:274–7.

106 For Garnot's measurements, see Duperrey, *Voyage autour du Monde*, 1:114–17.

107 Blanckaert, "Méthode des moyennes," esp. 217–18 on suspicion of statistical craniometry.

108 Lesson, *Compléments de Buffon*, 2:199, 205, 209, 240–1, 247, 251, 267; also *Voyage
autour du Monde*.

Portrait of chiefs of Tahiti and New Guinea natives from Louis-Isidore Duperrey, *Voyage autour du monde ... sur la corvette* La Coquille

ill-mannered New Zealanders was that they had a form of worship, government, and some fine arts. As Bory pointed out, so-called savages might be as advanced as many French peasants and even more religious and poetic.[109] Yet, even in this pre-Darwinian era, Lesson thought contact with Europeans inexorably meant that the "indigenous race must disappear."[110]

DUMONT D'URVILLE

Perhaps the most sensitive and fascinating observer among the Geographical Society members commanding Pacific expeditions was the intrepid admiral Dumont d'Urville. Despite his dour temperament, he displayed great empathy for cultures in the process of destruction. Still, Dumont reinforced the idea that certain peoples were civilizable, and possibly more apt candidates for colonization, while others were beyond redemption. He also employed as naturalist the famous phrenologist Dumoutier, who undertook elaborate innovative measures to reproduce the cranial form of many peoples. Dumont was a very active member of the Geographical Society whenever he returned from his voyages. He became president in 1841, shortly before his tragic death in a spectacular railway accidental fire,[111] and his reports appeared regularly in the Society's *Bulletin*, as well as in journals for the cultural elite such as the *Revue des deux mondes*.[112]

Before Dumont's first voyage on the *Astrolabe* in 1826–29, Jomard had prepared questions for him urging "ethno-geographical research on races, customs, languages, religions and cults" and about the success of Christian missionaries.[113] The Navy Ministry had also asked him explicitly to investigate the path of savage peoples in "leaving their primitive sentiment to come closer to a perfect state of civilization."[114]

109 Lesson, *Compléments de Buffon*, 2:250–1, 301–2.

110 Lesson, *Voyage autour du Monde*, 1:427–8.

111 For biography, see Vergniol, *Dumont d'Urville*; Guillon, *Dumont d'Urville*, as well as two doctoral theses to which I have not had access: Christian Couturaud, "Le troisième voyage de circumnavigation de J.S.C. Dumont d'Urville 1837–1840," thèse inédite de l'Université de Provence, Aix-en-Provence, 1986 and France Herjean de Briançon, "Le Voyage de l'Astrolabe sous le commandement du capitaine de frégate Dumont d'Urville 1826–1829," Paris-IV, 1994.

112 Renneville, "Un Terrain phrénologique," 96.

113 ASG, colis 3 bis.

114 Dumont d'Urville, *Voyage de la corvette*, 1:lxii.

Portrait of Jules-Sébastien-César Dumont d'Urville (1790–1842),
Pacific explorer and classifier of Oceanic peoples

Anthropologists still debate the fruitfulness of making physical and cultural distinctions between Melanesians and Polynesians.[115] By the end of
1831, Dumont had already deduced from his first voyage that there were
three distinct races in Oceania. The two major branches differed "both in
their moral and physical qualities." The yellow-olive straight-haired group
resembling Europeans were probably the conquerors, whom he called
"Polynesians" and later ranged in the Mongolic race. Their established gov-
ernmental and religious institutions showed great potential for development.

115 Thomas, "The Force of Ethnology."

Dumont expressed genuine admiration for the noble dignity of the warrior culture of New Zealand, "worthy of occupying one of the first ranks in the ladder of savage nations, in physical respects as well as in bravura, confidence and intelligence."[116] While the Maori angered easily, their warriors enslaved only prisoners of war or criminals, and cannibalized only those killed in combat.[117] Like Freycinet, he thought they would make "rapid progress toward civilized life" under European tutelage or under a native "genius."[118] The anti-clerical Dumont worried that Tahitians in their present state of subjection to missionaries were undergoing a "return to barbarism, not a progress of civilization."[119] But on the whole Hawaiians, Tahitians, and Tongans had made the most advances among the Polynesians.

On the small, lower islands of the north Pacific was a second, distinct branch of the Polynesians, the darker brown "Micronesians" of the Gilberts, Marshalls, Carolines, and Marianas. Unlike the Polynesians, their language seemed related to Tagalog of the Filipinos; they had no religious taboo, and chewed betel nuts rather than drinking kava. The dark-brown or black, frizzy-haired "true native'" race, an African branch, were the "Melanesians" (after Bory's "Melanian" species). With "irregular forms and deformed extremities," they were less "perfected" than Polynesians.[120] They, too, had languages unrelated to the Polynesians and no kava ceremony.

Dumont's sojourn in Australia convinced him that the English were correct when they "totally renounced the hope of bringing the nations of New South Wales to a state of civilization."[121] On Australia and Tasmania were Melanesians "closest to the brute," with no form of government or regularly established religion, no housing or land cultivation.[122] He predicted aboriginal extinction (realized in Tasmania) by "maladies or excesses." As with Lesson, civilization

---

116 Dumont d'Urville, Rapport au ministre de la Marine (1826–27), AN BB4 1002.

117 Dumont d'Urville, *Voyage de la corvette*, 2:397, 415, 474.

118 AN Marine BB4 1002; Dumont d'Urville, *Voyage de la corvette*, 2 (1830–35): 394, 413, 415, 474, and Dumont d'Urville, *Two Voyages to the South Seas*, 1:99 (Citation).

119 *BSG* 12 (1829): 6; *BSG* 14 (1830): 159, 163 and 2nd sér., 20 (1843): 91; Dumont d'Urville, *Two Voyages to the South Seas*, 2:359–60, 530; Dumont d'Urville, *Voyage au Pôle Sud*, 5:63, 79, 83.

120 Dumont d'Urville, "Sur les Iles du Grand Océan," *BSG* 17 (1832): 1–21, esp. 3–4, 6, 11.

121 Dumont, *Voyage de la corvette*, 1:395, 410, 470, 521; *Two Voyages to the South Seas*, 1:150 and *Voyage de la corvette* 4:579.

122 Dumont d'Urville, *Two Voyages to the South Seas*, 2:387.

would prove incompatible with the savage state, leaving the man of nature to obey or perish.[123]

Tense confrontations with the islanders of Vanikoro led Dumont to assert, "like all members of the black race of Oceania, these peoples are disgustingly lazy, stupid, savage, and greedy, and without any good qualities or virtues that I know of."[124] He received applause from the Geographical Society assembly and the president, Navy Minister Hyde de Neuville, in 1829 when he commented on the need to intimidate "with the terror of arms" these "miserable and disgusting people."[125]

For Dumont, it was clear that "nature did not endow the three races in an equal manner in moral matters, and one would say that nature wished, in each of these races, to set quite different limits to the intellectual faculties of man." It was a law of nature that the blacks always obeyed the yellow races, or disappeared, while both black and yellow races always obeyed the whites. On re-reading Bory and Cuvier, he shared Cuvier's position that there were three great races in humanity, with Malays and Americans in the yellow race and Papuans in the black race Unlike polygenists, Dumont refused to speculate on multiple creations of human races or different human species.[126]

THE IMPACT OF DUMONT'S VOYAGE: DUMOUTIER AND PHRENOLOGY

Publications associated with Dumont's second expedition spawned several new theoretical variants of racial hierarchy. After being converted by the London phrenologist James Deville, Dumont took to the Pacific in 1837 Pierre-Marie-Alexandre Dumoutier, the artist-anatomist known for his work for the Phrenological Society of Paris and his phrenological museum.[127] Dumoutier would join both the Geographical Society and the new Ethnological Society. The elder Broussais on behalf of the Phre-

123 Ibid., 1:56, 84, 90, 188–9; 2:387–8, 405; Dumont d'Urville, *Voyage de la corvette*, 1:396–8, 521; 5 (1830–35): 95–6; for a critique of essentializing cultural distinctions between Polynesians and Melanesians, see Thomas, "The Force of Ethnology," 30–1 on Dumont.

124 Dumont d'Urville, *Two Voyages to the South Seas*, 1:219, 236.

125 *BSG* 12 (1829): 261, 264.

126 *BSG* 17 (1832): 19–21; the gradations of obedience of black to yellow and white races had also been a principle of Edwards: see *Des caractères*, 18; *cf* Blanckaert, "On the Origins," 36; Dumont d'Urville et al., *Histoire générale des Voyages*, 1:vii–ix.

127 For Deville's report, see Dumont d'Urville, *Two Voyages to the South Seas*, 2:564–5; on Dumoutier, see Renneville, "Un Terrain phrénologique," 98.

nological Society deliberately asked Dumoutier to try a new procedure of moulding native heads and faces to reproduce shapes precisely without artistic prejudice. In fact Dumoutier reaped an amazing harvest of fifty-one busts and fifty-one crania on this enterprise.[128] On return to Toulon, the press described some 4,000 visitors marveling at the display.[129]

Dumoutier had commented favourably on the Charrua band of Uruguay in Paris and was kindly disposed to Patagonians encountered on the voyage, but virtually his only favourable comments on Melanesians and Oceanic blacks referred to the Fijians. He thought the phrenological theory of "independence of [cerebral] faculties of man" justified their obvious love of children amid a "barbarous and cannibalistic" society. The Fijians also had superior memory, and despite their intellectual and cultural backwardness, they limited passions to natural needs.[130]

But most other comments in the journal and to the Ethnological Society denigrated blacks. Like the eighteenth-century naturalist Daubenton, Dumoutier still believed that the "occipital cavity" of blacks was recessed toward the rear of the head, and that they therefore resembled animals. The "crude, hideous traits" of most Tasmanians, more like New Guineans or Mozambicans than Australians, "recalled those of the Negro closest to animal nature." Haitians returned to their African fetishes.[131] The Papuans of New Caledonia showed, like "almost all these dark-skinned peoples, a marked predominance of instinctive [and perceptive faculties for food-gathering] over intelligence and moral faculties."[132] Dumoutier, like the more open-minded phrenologists, championed at least limited civilizability for Australians, who would "acquire desires and excite faculties necessary to make them industrious" in the company of civilized people.[133] Dumoutier was no more impressed with the Tahitians than Dumont had been,[134] but even the

128 Renneville, "Un Terrain phrénologique," 105 and *Le Langage des crânes*, 25–6, 235–7.

129 *BSG* 2nd sér., 16 (1841): 436–9 and 441 on Serres' report to the Academy of Sciences.

130 Renneville, "Un Terrain phrénologique," 101–10 on Uruguayan Charruas and Dumoutier; on Fijians, see Dumoutier, Journal, 181, 212r, 216r, 219r, 231r and v.

131 Ibid., fols 132, 211, 212r, 283r, 335v, 433v, 436, 441, 444; *MSEP* 2:lv; *NAV* 5ᵉ sér., 10 (1847): 378; 11 (1847): 237–8; *BSEP* 1 (1846): 102; 2 (1847): 173, 288; *cf* Renneville, "Un Terrain phrénologique," 92–4.

132 Dumoutier, Journal, fol. 436, 441–7.

133 Ibid., 335v, 341v, 348r.

134 Ibid., fol. 58.

miserable population of New Zealand might not be incapable of making some progress and acquiring more wealth.[135]

The year following Dumont's death, Dumoutier read his phrenological sketch on the Marquesas to the Ethnological Society. It appeared in print first as part of the study of the islands by the hydrographic engineer Clément-Adrien Vincendon-Dumoulin.[136] Dumoutier could not resist the observation that the posterior, instinctive part of the brain among Marquesas natives was more highly developed than their intellectual faculties. Cerebellar development also proved their fabled erotic instincts. Upper occipital prominence showed their love of family, while the women demonstrated friendship and devotion. Like the Papuans, they were unreflective, though with some moral and religious sentiment.[137]

Even in the manuscript notes, Dumoutier scorned the "pride and vanity" on Hiva Oa that led the indigenous people to be ready to "take the upper hand and to assume they are our equals." Particularly remarkable in the journal was Dumoutier's scandalized reaction to the "saturnalia" when nude Marquesan women boarded ship. He reproved the "lubricious dances of the night and their insatiable enjoyment," the greed of their husbands who prostituted them, and the egotism and brutality of the sailors in exploiting them. As usual, there was ample commentary on the "pleasant figures" of the women and their "well-placed bust."[138]

Dumoutier concluded his published sketch by labeling the Marquesans "big children" (a term Lesson already used for the Tahitians). Yet, he observed that a different social state, more developed than the childhood of their society, could enhance the activity of cerebral organs. As of now, however, the Marquesans, "incorrigible thieves and murderers," felt little need for improvement that could lead them to the "pleasures of the honourable life of civilized man."[139]

Dumoutier did not close off development and civilizability for these Polynesians, or even for the Australians. But his low estimate of blacks

135 Ibid., 464.
136 Vincendon-Dumoulin, *Iles marquises*, 334; Dumoutier's "Notice phrénologique et ethnologique sur les naturels de l'archipel Nouka-Hiva" is on 292–304 and also appeared later as an extract; the reading to the Ethnological Society was recorded in *MSEP* 2 (1845): xxxiv; his first report to the Society was in *MSEP* 2 (1845) November, xv.
137 Dumoutier, "Notice," in Vincendon-Dumoulin, *Îles marquises*, 292–3, 298, 300–1.
138 Ibid., 298, Dumoutier, Journal, 139–140, 143, 147, 169.
139 Dumoutier, "Notice," in Vincendon-Dumoulin, *Îles marquises*, 302–4; for Lesson on Tahitians, see *Voyage autour du Monde*, 1:238. Renneville believes that Dumoutier may not have written the passages deriding Marquesas islanders.

reeked of conventional prejudice. The populations of Oceania were instinctive, unreflective peoples, and therefore unlikely to reach a European level of accomplishment.

Dumoutier's plaster casts won great praise in the Academy of Sciences from the holder of the anthropology chair in the Muséum national d'histoire naturelle, Etienne-Renaud-Augustin Serres (1786–1868). Serres speculated that the diversity of the Pacific populations might demonstrate different species of humanity, rather than just diverse races or types, and zoologists would be tempted to classify them as a genus or family.[140] For Serres, a species was determined by the "existence of certain differentiating characteristics transmitted by generation." Among other quirks, he offered the opinion (or rationalization of a real situation in slavery) that union of a black man and white woman tended to be infertile because of the disproportion of organs, while the converse was not true.[141]

Apart from his atlas of heads, Dumoutier declined to continue work on the anthropological volumes of the Dumont voyage. Consequently, three polygenists, the surgeon Jacques-Bernard Hombron, the assistant surgeon and younger brother of the second ship commander, Honoré Jacquinot (a member of the Ethnological Society by 1846), and the entomologist Emile Blanchard provided the text. Here the slide from monogenism to polygenism and against any potential assimilation of these peoples is distinctly observable.

Hombron, who joined the Ethnological Society in 1847, believed in invariable fixed human species with several different centres of creation. He thought inferior species, such as the "Eskimos" and "Pecherais" (Fuegians) were destined for elimination. Blacks did not degenerate because of climate, but had an immutable nature incapable of brain development.[142] Head characteristics, such as beauty of face and elevation of forehead, were far more important than skin colour.[143] In approaching the civilizability of peoples, it would be "necessary to keep track of the degree of elevation in the human series." Clearly, Melanesians would be difficult to civilize. Polynesians were more educable and

---

140 Serres, "Rapport"; summary in *BSG* 2nd sér., 16 (1841): 436–9, 441; on Serres see Blanckaert, "La Création."

141 Serres, Rapport, 644–8, 653–4.

142 Hombron, *Voyage au Pôle Sud*, 1:98, 104, 351, 359, 361, 379, 384–5, 395; on Gall, see 401.

143 Ibid., 1:133, 139, 143, 166, 351, 353–4, 359; on Caucasians, see 369, 371; see also Renneville, "Un Terrain phrénologique," 121–3.

morally advanced, but even New Zealanders were so amoral and unreflective that they would "kill their friends in a moment for a trifle."[144]

Jacquinot, a naval surgeon who also joined the Ethnological Society
by 1847, unhesitatingly proclaimed his belief in three separate species
(Caucasic, the "Negro," and Mongol), with four or five races in each.
The "most degraded" Africans "oppose an invincible obstacle to the theory of the unity of species." The criteria of shape and thickness of crania
(insufficient in themselves), skeletal form, and Camper's angle (especially for Caucasian and Negro) were important when related to traits of
face, skin colour, and hair.[145] For Jacquinot, like Edwards, primordial
types not dependent on climate, such as the Jews, persisted everywhere.[146] While perceiving the fallacy of over-reliance on the facial angle, Jacquinot was concerned about racial purity. He recognized that
slavery created the opportunity for undesirable racial mixing by "shame-
ful exploitation."[147]

Emile Blanchard's text to accompany Dumoutier's atlas of busts and
crania appeared only in 1854. He, too, believed that three distinct,
invariable species of humanity were created in the countries where
they were presently observed as natives.[148] Like Jacquinot, he thought
climate produced no racial change, and interbreeding was naturally
repugnant.[149] While proclaiming his opposition to slavery, he also believed blacks to be inferior. New Hollanders (Australians) were at the
lower limit of humanity.[150] The facial angle could be a key indicator.
The Australians rejected civilization, and even Tahitians progressed little because they lacked a work ethic or business sense. They were just
"not organized ever to offer an example of civilization."[151] Equality does
not exist among humans, and with a malformed cranium, "there will be
never be men of genius or talent as European society understand
them." However, Blanchard was more a racist than an avid imperialist,
since he agreed that the strongest and most intelligent, like the Europeans, should not molest or destroy the weakest and least intelligent.[152]

144 Hombron, *Voyage au Pôle Sud*, 281, 289, 302.
145 Dumont, *Pôle Sud*, 2:36, 144; Jacquinot, *Études*, 25, 66, 74, 81, 94, 104–5, 126, 175.
146 Jacquinot, *Études*, 32, 36, 43, 96.
147 Ibid., 66, 81, 94; on ensemble of traits, 144.
148 Blanchard, *Voyage au Pôle Sud*, 19, 256–60.
149 Ibid., 30, 33.
150 Ibid., 48, 128.
151 Ibid., 48, 70, 74, 84, 101; on facial angle, 230–1.
152 Ibid., 204–5, 256, 260.

The publications stemming from the Dumont expedition therefore demonstrated a general trend in the 1840s and 1850s toward polygenism and the importance of innate endowment of peoples, even though the phrenologist Dumoutier advocated as much educability as peoples could absorb. For all the nuances in the explorers in the Geographical Society, including Dumont's sensitivity to the accomplishments of New Zealanders and Freycinet's empathy for Australians, they still believed some races were either uncivilizable or forever fated to rank below the European in the racial hierarchy. The consequence was that these peoples were ripe for exploitation.

THE SYNERGY OF RACIAL INEQUALITY AND IMPERIALISM

The members of the Geographical Society considered here show, by the late 1830s and 1840s, either a polygenism postulating unequal potential for human development or a monogenism in which racial characteristics are difficult to modify. By 1839, when the physician William-Frédéric Edwards founded the Ethnological Society, there was a cross-fertilization of racial theory between the two societies. Edwards convinced d'Eichthal to become an active member of the Ethnological Society. The ex-Saint-Simonian Victor Courtet de l'Isle had been a member of the Geographical Society when he constructed his rigid endorsement of inequality of racial endowment from 1835 onward.[153] The next chapter details his contributions to debates in the Ethnological Society.

The youngest founding member and later secretary-general of the Geographical Society, Louis Vivien de Saint-Martin, also became an adherent of polygenism. In 1849 Vivien even suggested a merger of the Geographical and Ethnological Societies, but the majority, led by Jomard and Walckenaer, rejected the proposal.[154] A third case of cross-fertilization between the Geographical and Ethnological Societies was the student of Africa, d'Avezac, who as secretary-general of the Geographical Society helped introduce Bory's doctrines and also contributed important memoirs to the Ethnological Society.[155]

153 Courtet de l'Isle, *Mémoire sur les races humaines extrait du Journal de l'Institut historique* 2–4, 13 (citation); *Au congrès*, 8, 10, 15 (citations); *La science politique*, 12–13, 20–5, 48–51, 56–7, 89, 98, 136, 232; Boissel, *Victor Courtet*, 44–5, 65–6, 89, 146–7.
154 Fierro, *La Société de Géographie*, 35–6.
155 d'Avezac, *Histoire et description*, 17–19, 24.

There always were counter-currents in the Geographical Society that refused to accept indelible racial traits. The great explorer Alexander von Humboldt, president of the Society in 1844–45, lent his prestige to the view of the unity of the species. Distinct types were illusory, given the "numerous gradations of skin colour and cranial structure." Some Africans were lighter than the Tamils of south India, and so-called "Negro" traits of hair and physiognomy were not always present together. "We reject," concluded Humboldt, "by a necessary consequence the desolating distinction of superior and inferior races."[156]

But for active adherents like Vivien, who were in the majority, the moral unity of the species did not mean physical unity.The eighteenth-century idea of stages of development culminating in civilization never completely disappeared. Any people thought to be civilizable could be brought into the inexorable march of history, under the proper guidance. Strategic interests often dictated the degree of enthusiasm for such intervention. While inferior Oceanic blacks might be both the easiest to dominate but also the most hostile, the more advanced Polynesians were ostensibly more likely to accept foreign guidance.

Most of Polynesia was not of great commercial or geopolitical value compared to the British prizes of Australia and New Zealand. Certainly, the early explorers did not recommend the colonization of the Marquesas and Tahiti, partly because Tahiti at least seemed already in the British sphere. Yet the civilizing mission and concepts of racial inferiority could furnish a rationale underlying the justification that Admiral Dupetit-Thouars used in his 1842 ventures: the Polynesians would be a "people easy to lead." The government, however reluctant to become embroiled with Britain, approved the principles of "religious and judicial action for moralization and civilization of the natives." In his confidential instructions, however, the Navy minister left no illusions about the mission – force would be used to repress hostility.

In neither archipelago did the indigenous population passively accept French domination. More "civilizable" peoples did not necessarily prove docile. In Tahiti, there were at least three years of raids against the French after the quarrel with the English Protestant missionary George Pritchard, and the Marquesas, temporarily a penal colony, remained

---

156 *NAV* 5ᵉ sér., 7 (1846): 114, 116, 119; Godlewska, *Geography Unbound*, 235–65 suggests that Humboldt also never succeeded in gaining disciples in France for his sophisticated model of a theoretical geographical science.

turbulent until the 1880s.[157] Notably, though, the French established a protectorate over Tahiti at first, as if to imply that the Tahitians were "advanced" enough to play some role in their own government. When the French search for a penal colony resulted in the seizure of New Caledonia by Admiral Febvier-Despointes in 1853, they cared little for the aspirations or even subsistence needs of the indigenous population. The inferiority of the "Melanesian" New Caledonians, whether presumed to be inherently racial or cultural (at the stage of savagery), was an underlying presumption in all of the French actions depriving the indigenous "Kanak" of their lands.[158]

Though Dumont d'Urville had advised against colonizing hostile peoples, the expected commercial and strategic value of west Africa outweighed this caution. The ultimate push for annexation rested on the military efforts of leaders such as General Louis-Léon-César Faidherbe against the stubborn Muslim chieftains of the Tukulor empire radiating out from the Niger valley.[159] The mirage of Timbuktu had dissipated, but there was still the lure of the western Sudan and the ferocity of the Moors to be contained. The constant efforts to gain routes from Senegal to Algeria or across the Sahara preceded the final French military ventures. The French commercial inroads into east Africa bore fruit only with the gradual annexation of Djibouti. In Ethiopia racial ideology was masked by the alleged kinship in religion and culture marking an ancient but stationary civilization, but Geographical Society discussion of expeditions to Ethiopia nevertheless manifested the desire to classify peoples by facial angle, which helped boost the favourable view of the Christian elite.

Edwards and the Ethnological Society promoted notions of different centres of creation, if not outright polygenism. They perpetuated interest in cranial form as much as in customs, since it was important for measuring brain capacity and limits to intelligence. Phrenology, as interpreted by Dumoutier, could be ambivalent on the educability of peoples and still believe in a single species, but, as interpreted by Broussais, it could also reinforce an indelible racial hierarchy. The more classification, the more there was a tendency to make invidious comparisons in which certain peoples were deemed uncivilizable or civilizable only with

157 Guizot, *Mémoires*, 7:83–4, 478–85, 493; Faivre, *L'Expansion*, 462–95.

158 See, for example, Alice Bullard, "Becoming Savage?" and her recent publication, *Exile to Paradise*, esp. 30–66.

159 Bathily, "La conquête française."

European intervention. The alleged disparities within the human species, combined with commercial or strategic motivations, provided a
synergy between theories of race and projects of empire. In this fashion
scientific studies of ethno-geographers gave aid and comfort to French
expansion even before the heyday of imperialism and the distinctive
Third Republic version of the civilizing mission.

Among the several types of imperialism in the later era differentiated by Michael Heffernan, the varieties promoted the most by geographical societies were the cultural and the economic. They wished
France to demonstrate its cultural vitality by subjugating and assimilating colonized areas. Other members sought commercial opportunities. Heffernan justifiably concluded that, despite the different forms
of imperialism, geography was to a large extent a "science of empire."
Geographers provided practical knowledge for those planning colonial ventures, and scholars helped justify and advance government
objectives.[160]

It would be a facile assumption to conclude that the early Paris society
was indifferent to colonization because it lacked a numerous commercial membership or the incentive of expansionist government policies.
The promotion of racial hierarchy could justify spreading the benefits
of civilization or exploiting the resources of inferior peoples. This ideology did not propel annexation of Pacific islands, but it provided a necessary foundation. Otherwise, the usually cited motives of the 1870s were
already in evidence – commerce, spreading Christianity, spreading European arts and industry, and strategic rivalry with the British.[161]

The republican "civilizing mission" that assumed French superiority
and the duty to remake "primitive cultures" could prevail in modified
form during the Restoration and July Monarchy.[162] Before the Third
Republic, governments were less secular and less committed to univer-
salizing the principles of 1789, nor were they then in a position to
speak extensively of the development of resources or provision of hygiene (with the exception of Algeria). The French simply did not as
yet control sufficient territory or deploy a sufficient number of skilled
agents or health officers to have a policy of economic development
(*mise en valeur*).

160 Heffernan, "The Science of Empire," 102–5, 105–8, 92, 114; see also Lejeune, *Les
sociétés de géographie*, 172.
161 On the shift after 1900 in west Africa from assimilation to association due to its
practical difficulties in a large area, see Conklin, *A Mission to Civilize*, 142–212.
162 Ibid., 1–2.

But even in the early nineteenth century, the French articulated a kind of civilizing mission, as in the assimilation of some west Africans and the integration of Christian Abyssinians in the European economy. Some Pacific explorers hoped for the civilizability of the Polynesians and some at least the limited educability of the Melanesians, while others had severe doubts about whether the Pacific islanders could or would ever wish to be civilized.

By mid-century, rigid hierarchical monogenism and rigid polygenism foreshadowed the harsher forms of imperial associationist policy. While few theorists had the contempt for non-Europeans of Gustave Le Bon, the associationists of the turn of the century could have found ample arguments for inequality in the literature stemming from the Dumont expedition. Otherwise, associationists triumphed for practical reasons, such as the resistance of the indigenous population of Algeria and Indochina. Conklin has shown that the problems of applying assimilation in west Africa, including the potential promotion of rebellion, as well as less tolerant views in France itself, virtually eliminated assimilationist policy after World War I. The fundamental paradox she discusses – exploitation of the colonized amid an ideology of spreading democracy or the benefits of civilization – was already evident in the earlier theories of geographers, phrenologists, and ethnologists. Classifying some peoples as uncivilizable already made them liable to domination, liable to be used as not quite equal human resources.

5

Ethnology and the Civilizability
of "Races"

While there were few common members among the Société phrénologique de Paris and the Société ethnologique de Paris (SEP), the early
effort by phrenologists such as Spurzheim to found a Société anthropologique in 1832 displayed a kindred approach to a science of humankind.[1] Both societies sought holistic explanations for the unique nature
of human faculties as compared to merely "animal" faculties. Both
placed great importance on the physiological and anatomical constitution of individuals. Both also wished to differentiate human varieties by
mental capacities deriving from physical make-up. Phrenology accented
the individual, but produced invidious distinctions among races as a by-
product. Ethnology was motivated by the study of peculiarities of each
kind of human being. The relations between geography and ethnology
were somewhat more straightforward. Many members of the Paris Geographical Society interested in explorers' descriptions of peoples joined
the Ethnological Society. The continuing debate about the civilizability
of diverse peoples became complicated by doubts concerning the membership of all peoples in a single humankind.

EARLY ANTHROPOLOGICAL INSTITUTIONS

Early uses of words such as anthropology and ethnology raise the common question of whether a field of study can exist before the terminol-

---

1 Renneville, *La Médecine du crime*, 1:485. Dumoutier, the sculptor David d'Angers, and
the alienist Achille-Louis Foville were among the few common members of the Phrenological Society and Ethnological Society; David d'Angers also figured in the short-lived Anthropological Society of Spurzheim and Edwards.

ogy that names it. From our retrospective and anachronistic viewpoint, any systematic traveler's report describing the appearance and customs of peoples, any philosophical reflection on human capacity, any comparative natural history relating humans and animals could qualify as potential anthropology in the eighteenth century. One of the most useful classical studies of French "anthropology" in the eighteenth century includes discussion of the philosophers Denis Diderot, Jean-Jacques Rousseau, Claude-Adrien Helvétius, and Voltaire. More commonly, candidates for the designation "proto-anthropologist" include those students of natural history who studied the human species, even if it was not their principal endeavour, such as Georges-Louis Leclerc, comte de Buffon and Georges Cuvier. Later naturalists such as Pierre Flourens designated Buffon as the forerunner of anthropology.[2] Finally, those who analysed variety within the species, such as the Göttingen physician Johann Friedrich Blumenbach, seem to have anticipated the concerns of subsequent anthropologists and ethnologists.[3]

In Latin treatises of the seventeenth century, in the curriculum of German universities, and in the French usage of Swiss theologian Alexandre-César Chavannes in 1788, "anthropology" referred to both "anatomical" and "psychological" studies. Even in this cultural context, so different from the present, there was a rudimentary distinction between a kind of physical and a kind of cultural anthropology.[4] Around 1800 the Idéologue circle created an impetus to establish both medical and philosophical components of a "science of man." Following the terminology of German university lecturers Ernst Platner and Immanuel Kant, the Idéologue physician P.-J.-G. Cabanis employed "anthropology" in 1804 as a synonym for a science of physical-mental relations including "ethics, analysis of ideas, and physiology." As related in the second chapter, Cabanis's occasional disciple Louis-Jacques Moreau de la Sarthe had previously in 1801 divided anthropology into "physical" and "moral" branches.[5]

2 Blanckaert, "Buffon and the Natural History of Man," esp. on how Flourens praised Buffon's study of human varieties, 20.

3 Duchet, *Anthropologie et histoire*; on the role of Buffon as founder see also Paul Topinard's discussion of 1883, cited in Nathalie Richard, "Rituels d'instauration et constitution des identités disciplinaires; les lieux de mémoire de l'anthropologie (1859–1900)" in Blanckaert, *Les politiques de l'anthropologie*, 340–1.

4 Blanckaert, "L'anthropologie en France," esp. 16–17, 21.

5 Cabanis, *Oeuvres philosophiques* 2:77 and in the 1805 preface to the *Rapports*, in *Oeuvres philosophiques* 1:126; for Moreau de la Sarthe, *La Décade philosophique* (20 prairial an IX): 458–9; Gusdorf, *Dieu, la nature, l'homme*, 405–8, 417–23; Moravia, *La scienza dell'uomo*, 75–80, 214–15 and *Il pensiero degli Idéologues*, 574–84.

The picturesque, but almost indefinable, first anthropological society in France has attracted considerable commentary. At the time of an ambitious, government-sponsored exploration of Australian waters by Captain Nicolas Baudin, a group of scholars headed by the educational theorist Louis-François Jauffret employed the term "anthropology" in the memoirs of the Société des Observateurs de l'Homme (1799–1804).[6] They represented an effort to bridge various areas of study, including natural history (the famous botanist A.-L. Jussieu was president), medicine, study of language, Orientalism, history, and exploration. The Society, in its brief, generally ill-documented life, produced several important treatises, including Jauffret's "Introduction to the Memoirs," his plea for an anthropological museum, and his lectures (mostly lost) on the "natural history of man" encompassing hygiene and anatomy. There were also several significant studies, such as Philippe Pinel's assessment of the "wild child" of the Aveyron, and other commentaries on the Chinese man Tchong-a-Sam. Composed specifically for the Baudin crew were the classic work "on the observation of savage peoples" by the increasingly rebellious Idéologue Joseph-Marie Degérando, the parallel instructions on collecting crania by Cuvier, and the brief "observations on anthropology" by the young naturalist who actually traveled with Baudin, François Péron.[7]

The most recent research has substantively revised former views that the Society was somehow an organ of Idéologue purposes or that it shared Idéologue conceptions of "anthropology." Jauffret wished both to avoid the notion that physiology and comparative anatomy were the sole foundations of anthropology and to avert confusion with any underlying materialism. In fact, the predominant group in the Society, including the famous instructor of the deaf-mute, abbé Sicard, was a conservative, somewhat anti-republican coterie who had little in common with Idéologue political inclinations. Their appeal to freely interpret the natural history of Buffon as a physical-moral dualism appears to

6 Copans and Jamin, eds. *Aux origines*; Baudin, *The Journal*; Horner, *The French Reconnaissance*; Faivre, *L'Expansion* and "Les idéologues," 3–15; Bonnemains, Forsyth, and Smith, eds. *Baudin in Australian Waters*; Stocking, "French Anthropology in 1800"; on Jauffret's plagiarism of the German philosopher Christoph Meiners, see Rupp-Eisenreich, "The 'Société des Observateurs de l'Homme,'" 5–11 and "Des choses occultes," esp. 134–5.

7 Degérando, *The Observation of Savage Peoples*, 1–58; Péron, *Observations sur l'anthropologie*, reprinted in Copans and Jamin, *Aux origines*, 177–86; G. Cuvier, "Note instructive sur les recherches à faire relativement aux différences anatomiques des diverses races d'homme," also in Copans and Jamin, 171–6.

have been a consensus-building step against rigid disciplinary specialization and against the predominance of medicine. For other members, the legacy of Buffon was a direct challenge to the materialism and transformism of the Idéologues.[8] In any case the Society, for all its brief patronage by leading scientific figures and its attempts at popularization, languished in internal conflict and broke apart by 1804.

The terms "ethnology" and "ethnography" also originated in the German-speaking world. In 1771–72 August Ludwig Schlözer of the University of Göttingen used "ethnography" as a synonym for Völkerkunde (all peoples) or Volkskunde (one people) in a universal history of peoples of the globe, including accounts of travelers and comparative linguistics. Eleven years later the historian of public law Adam Kollar employed "Ethnologie" or "Ethnologia" in a Latin work to denote a descriptive, historical study of the origins, language, and customs of peoples. The Italian linguist Adrien Balbi in 1826 published in France an *Atlas ethnographique du globe* equating ethnography with a classification of all peoples in language families.[9] He followed Blumenbach in asserting that there were five major human varieties in a single species and attacked early believers in several distinct species, such as the physician Antoine Desmoulins (1796–1828). However, Balbi left himself open to charges of contradiction by speculating on distinct origins for these varieties.[10] Before mid-century, "ethnologists" and "ethnographers" would rely less on language and culture and more on differentiation of physical types. On the French scene culturally oriented "ethnographers" became remarkably distinct from physically oriented "anthropologists" only after 1859.[11]

The primary research and educational establishment for the life sciences in France, the Muséum national d'histoire naturelle, provided the other major institutional foundation for the study of anthropology. From 1832 the famous nerve physiologist and opponent of Gall, Pierre Flourens, occupied the human anatomy chair and included the "natural history of man," while discussing after 1836 the "natural history of races."[12] Flourens's research on the skin pigments of different races made him doubt that climate could alter human varieties. Nominally a believer in the unity of the species, he opposed all transformism of the

---

8 Chappey, "Les sociétés savantes"; his doctoral thesis, "La Société des Observateurs de l'Homme"; Chappey, "L'Anthropologie et l'histoire naturelle," esp. 52–3.

9 Godlewska, *Geography Unbound*, 224.

10 Balbi, *Introduction à l'Atlas ethnographique*, xvii, lxv, lxxxi.

11 Vermeulen, "Origins and institutionalization," esp. 50–5.

12 Blanckaert, "La Création."

kind advocated by Jean-Baptiste de Lamarck. He thought that that the three major "races" were fixed and determined types. In fact, as Blanck-aert points out, his monogenism was tenuous enough that pillars of the Paris Ethnological Society such as Gustave d'Eichthal cited him to justify polygenism.[13]

In 1838 the Muséum professors retitled the chair "human anatomy and natural history of races" and recommended appointment of the naturalist Etienne-Renaud-Augustin Serres. Throughout the following decades, Serres conceptualized a hierarchy of races measured by the position of the navel and umbilical cord in embryos of various human varieties. By mid-century he believed that non-whites were animal-like imperfect beings, with limited potential according to their particular nature.[14] Only in 1855 was there an officially titled "anthropology" chair, occupied by the leading monogenist naturalist and former Ethnology Society member Jean-Louis-Armand Quatrefages de Bréau (1810–92).

The saga of institutionalization of French anthropology must surely highlight the Muséum. There also needs to be a more conspicuous place for the learned society, which attracted over 300 members, including distinguished foreigners, during the decade from 1839 to 1848. The foundation of the Paris Ethnological Society was part of a movement of interest throughout Europe and North America in the varieties of non-Europeans (no doubt sparked by controversies over slavery and, in the British case, colonization) that included the foundation of the American Ethnological Society in New York in 1842 and the London Ethnological Society in 1843.[15]

Compared with the Société d'anthropologie founded by Paul Broca (1824–1880) in 1859, the ethnologists appear much less intellectually coherent. Unlike the anthropologists, they left no enduring legacies such as a journal, laboratory, and a school. But Broca himself, for apparently political reasons, neglected the significance of the SEP.[16] In 1859, the government subjected the fledgling anthropological society to police surveillance. Any subject risking implications of materialism or any

13 Ibid., 92, 96, 99.
14 Ibid., 100, 104, 111; Serres was particularly indebted to the English theorist Charles Hamilton Smith.
15 Stocking, *Victorian Anthropology*, 48.
16 Nathalie Richard has also discussed disciplinary reasons for presenting anthropology as more general and inclusive than ethnology in Richard, "Rituels d'instauration et constitution des identités disciplinaires; les lieux de mémoire de l'anthropologie, 1859–1900" in Claude Blanckaert, *Les politiques de l'anthropologie*, 337–63.

politicized matter had to be avoided. Broca knew that the passions of the slave emancipation debate of the late 1840s had affected statements by the vocal anti-slavery members of the earlier society, and in his view, they intruded "risky speculation" into the objective terrain of science. A scholarly account of the Ethnological Society similarly concludes that the anti-slavery impetus even handicapped the Society's contributions to anthropology. Hence, politicization harmed science.[17]

In this and the following chapter, we will illustrate first how, despite these claims, the discourse on the "perfectibility of races" between the two societies was almost a seamless web. Second, contrary to Broca's denials, the ethnologists discussed critical issues that remained central to anthropology after 1859. These issues were the very same articulated by Broca – the place of humanity in nature, the differences of humans from the animal kingdom, the nature of species, the diversity within humankind, including the place of various races, and the supposed physical indicators of intelligence.[18] In fact, the physical features and constitution of peoples occupied an unusually prominent place, given the expectation that "ethnology" would investigate language and culture. Third, just as Fourierist phrenologists could subscribe to racial hierarchy, the racial theory of the SEP does not fall on a predictable progressive-conservative axis. Fourth, we shall show the significant influence of Saint-Simonianism, with its ambivalent consequences concerning the function of different races.

Among the ethnologists there were at least three positions on the spectrum of racial theory. At one extreme was the belief called polygenism by the "American school" after 1857 – separate creation for each race, conceived as distinct species. Within the SEP, polygenists were quite diverse – political conservatives, colonial slaveholders, timid Orléanist liberals, and functionalist and organicist Saint-Simonians. In the centre of the spectrum were the more moderate naturalists and physicians who still assumed a graded hierarchy of races, but at least nominally supported the unity of the species (monogenism). Finally, there

17 Broca, *Mémoires de la Société d'Anthropologie de Paris* 3 (1868–69): cx–cxiv; Williams, "The Science of Man," 55–67 and 74–123 on Broca; Schiller, *Broca*; Gould, *The Mismeasure of Man*, 114–40; on the Anthropology Society of Paris, Harvey, "Races Specified, Evolution Transformed."

18 For a summary on the SEP, Brissonnet, "La Société"; on the culturally and linguistically oriented post-1859 Société d'ethnographie, Williams, "The Science of Man," 130–75; Lacombe, "Essai sur les origins"; Stocking, "Qu'est-ce qui est en jeu dans un nom?"; see also Blanckaert, "La Création."

were the egalitarians – one vocal atheist, progressive republican allied with a correspondent sympathetic to Christianity and with a Saint-Simonian who no longer accepted an organic society.[19]

THE RISE OF POLYGENIST RACIAL THEORY

If polygenism was thinkable from the 1820s, the decline of belief in climate-induced change was an important motivation. When Lamarck argued for the transformation of species, the possibly unintended materialist implication was that nature, without Divine intervention, could achieve such change. Powerful and religious naturalists such as Cuvier reacted to the threat of materialism by questioning the variability of species. For him, there were two essential aspects of defining a species: (1) anatomical – morphological resemblance of offspring to parents and common descent; and (2) physiological – the ability to breed continually through succeeding generations. "Hereditary conformations" of varieties produced by "accidental causes" such as climate could not have great impact, since species were essentially fixed. All varieties of humans produced fertile offspring, and were therefore essentially one species, albeit with a marked hierarchy among the races. Pacific exploration provided more evidence for this view. If the Pacific climate were a consistent determining factor, Polynesians and Melanesians would not differ so much in skin colour and facial features.[20]

Virey and Bory de Saint-Vincent, the racial theorists discussed in chapter 2, had great influence on the SEP. Both believed in different species rather than mere varieties within humankind and used the facial

19 For a survey of racial theory in early nineteenth-century France, see Blanckaert, "Le système des races"; Blanckaert "Monogénisme et polygénisme"; for British parallels, Stocking, *Victorian Anthropology*; for the pioneering survey of French racial theory, Cohen, *The French Encounter with Africans*; see also "The Species Problem" in Haller, *Outcasts from Evolution*, 69–94, who mentions Quatrefages and Bory.

20 On the changing species concept, see Phillip Sloan, "From Logical Universals to Historical Individuals" in Atran, ed. *Histoire du concept d'espèce*, 102–40 and Jean-Louis Fischer, "Espèce et hybrides," also in Atran 253–68; for the early Cuvier, see *Tableau élémentaire*, 10; Cuvier, *Le Règne animal*, 1 : 98; Blanckaert, "On the Origins," esp. 29. Cohen, *The French Encounter with Africans*, 85–95, 213 also notes the characteristic nineteenth-century shift to biological endowment of race from the eighteenth-century optimism about development of all savage peoples, despite the few anti-clerical eighteenth-century polygenists; his interpretation that the new emphasis on race is attributable to the shift to biological explanations is also valuable, although materialism in and of itself, as with the Idéologues, did not necessarily result in racism; see also Cohen, "French Racism and its African Impact."

angle as a marker. Both could be considered politically progressive, since Bory was a deist, possibly an atheist, with a tinge of republicanism and Virey a centre-left liberal deputy in the 1830s. For that matter, both professed to be against slavery by the 1820s, though in 1803 Virey had not hesitated to proclaim slavery the eternal destiny of "Negroes."[21] In addition, there was still another anti-Bourbon anti-clerical racial theorist, Cuvier's rather disgruntled assistant, Desmoulins. In France, he was among the first to develop the concept of separate creation of human races conceived as distinct species.[22]

Perhaps the most important single document in the prehistory of the SEP was the essay on the permanence of types (a word evading definition of species, race, and variety) of the Society's founder, the physician and son of a Jamaica planter, William-Frédéric Edwards (1777–1842). Edwards's inspiration came from the historian Amédée Thierry's study of the lineage of Gauls and Franks. This issue stirred political passions in France because some propagandists for noble privilege preferred to trace their ancestry to the conquering Franks who subjugated the Celtic (Gaul) populace. Any denigration of the role of the Franks was definitely a "bourgeois," rather than aristocratic, viewpoint. Edwards consequently became interested in observing not just the skin colour but the "forms and proportions of the head and traits of the face" of various French and European regional populations.[23]

Edwards's primary contention was that the "forces tending to conserve the original type" of ancient peoples preserved their physical characteristics in modern peoples. Once again the naval surgeon Lesson's publications on Oceania helped persuade Edwards that the Pacific climate did not change "types." Nor did he find convincing James Cowles Prichard's hypothesis that "stage of civilization" changed the type, since Europeans were stable in the colonies. Edwards also thought Jews were the same all over the world. Supporting evidence came from the study

21 Virey, *Histoire naturelle* (1800) 1:124, 138–40; Virey, *Histoire naturelle* (1824) 1:249, 408, 429, 438; 2:56, 72, 106–7. Jacques Léonard, "Pour situer Virey," in Bénichou and Blanckaert, eds. *Julien-Joseph Virey*, 17–22; Blanckaert, "1800–Le moment 'naturaliste,'" esp. 120; Cohen, *The French Encounter with Africans*, 98, 214, 233; Bory de Saint-Vincent, *L'Homme*, 1:48, 68, 71, 80, and 2:52, 114–15; Rôle, *Un destin hors série*; Blanckaert, "On the Origins," 31–3; Pietro Corsi, "Julien Joseph Virey, le premier critique de Lamarck" in Atran, ed. *Histoire du concept d'espèce*, 181–92, esp. 188.

22 Desmoulins, *Histoire naturelle des races humaines*, 193–4, 335.

23 Edwards, "Esquisse de l'état actuel de l'anthropologie," MSEP 1:124–5; Blanckaert, "On the Origins," esp. 44–5; Williams, *The Physical and the Moral*, 224–8; see also Augstein, "Aspects of philology and racial theory."

of his Scottish physician friend, Robert Knox, who claimed that the sculpted portraits of Ethiopians, Persians, and Jews on an Egyptian tomb in London strongly resembled their modern counterparts.[24]

If climate could not affect type, only crossbreeding could produce major transformations. Characteristically, when there was a small group of conquerors, like the Franks, the traits of the larger indigenous population prevailed. The conquerors predominated only if they settled in conquered areas, as did the Saxons in England, or if the conquered fled, as did the "savage" North Americans. Hence, types tended toward permanence. Besides, when interbreeding races resembled each other, the stronger type tended to win out. In France, the Franks were only a small foreign source, while two indigenous Celtic types – the Gaels and the Cymris – could still be observed. Only when types were quite diverse, as in the case of whites and blacks, were there intermediate métis or mulattos. As with Bory, there was an analogy between the lower classes and savages, since neither group participates in civilization.[25]

As Thierry contended, the first indigenous type was the aboriginal Galls or Gaels (Caesar's Gauls, also found in Wales and Brittany). They were short, round-headed, round-chinned, and dark-haired, with wide foreheads. Observers in northern and eastern France could still see the taller, long-headed, lighter-haired Cymris (or Kimris; true Celts, not Germans) from the area that became Belgium. They had elevated foreheads and salient chins, and tended to displace the weaker type of the Galls.[26]

Shortly after establishing the Paris Ethnological Society, Edwards's definition of both "physical" and "metaphysical" components of "anthropology" followed previous usage and even anticipated Broca's later reflections, for anthropology was first of all the study of human nature in general and secondly the study of human variety.[27] Edwards praised the pioneers of research into physical-mental relationships such as Cabanis and Gall. Despite his emphasis on head shape, he had to admit that phrenology was "not yet a science" since it could not marshal the "scientific proof" of statistics commanding conviction. For someone

24 Edwards, *Des caractères*, 9, 11–15, 19.

25 Ibid., 21, 26–30, 35–7, 42, 126–7.

26 Ibid., 62–8 on Galls and Cimris, 114–15n., 126–7; see also his posthumously published *De l'influence réciproque des races*, 8, 32; Young, *Colonial Desire*, 14, 79–80.

27 Edwards, "Esquisse de l'état actuel de l'anthropologie" *MSEP* 1:109–28; Broca in his Encyclopedia article "Anthropologie" (1866) defined the place of man in nature as a third type of anthropology.

who inspired hierarchical racial theory, Edwards was not an extremist. His endorsement of Virey was lukewarm, since he saw no great innovation in Virey compared to Blumenbach. Edwards also found that Victor Courtet de l'Isle (1813–67), the most vocal polygenist of the Society, "went too far" with his contention that "beautiful" races were the most intelligent.[28]

FOUNDATION OF THE SEP

In Britain a member of Parliament and anti-slavery crusader, Thomas Fowell Buxton, established in 1835 a Parliamentary Select Committee on Aborigines with a view to safeguarding these peoples from extinction. Shortly thereafter, in 1837, Buxton's friend, the Quaker physician and anatomy professor Thomas Hodgkin, founded the British Aborigines Protection Society for the "civil freedom and the moral improvement" of aboriginals. Using "Ab Uno Sanguine" (From One Blood) as their motto, they hoped to improve conditions for the "Kaffirs" of the Cape, the Maori in New Zealand, the freed slaves of the West Indies, and North American Indians. No doubt this effort meant Christian missionary work, if not direct annexation of territory by Europeans. The members subsequently became a study group that prefigured the London Ethnological Society. Hodgkin traveled to France to persuade Edwards to establish an equivalent society.[29]

While Edwards had expressed concern for the plight of North American natives, the French group decided that their principal purpose was scientific, rather than philanthropic or humanitarian. In 1839 they stated their mission: to probe the "physical organization, intellectual and moral character, languages and historical traditions" of the "human races." They would further establish through collections of portraits and objects the "degree of intelligence and culture which distinguishes diverse peoples."[30] Article 6 of their internal regulations provided that the "Society, while pursuing its scientific purpose, will not neglect any means to contribute to improving (as much as possible) the fate of aboriginal peoples." In 1844, however, after Edwards's death, a member asked for a letter to the new American Ethnological Society expressing

28 Ibid., 113, 118–19.
29 Gallagher, "Fowell Buxton," esp. 40; Stocking, *Victorian Anthropology*, 241–2 and "What's in a name?"; Curtin, *The Image of Africa*, 2:329–32; Driver, *Geography Militant*, 75–6.
30 *MSEP* 1:i, iii, iv; "Instruction générale adressée aux voyageurs," vi–xv.

"philanthropy for native Americans." A committee of the Society replied that this would be "subsidiary to the scientific purpose of the society."[31]

The instructions for explorers and travelers prepared for the Society by Edwards, the student of Africa and Arabia, Noël Desvergers (1805–67), and the topographer of Tyre, Jules, comte de Bertou, included recommendations to draw front and side views of the heads of peoples, to assess the proportions of the body and their physical strength, and to procure crania to help distinguish "pure types from mixtures."[32] The consequence is that so many members spent so much time on physical characteristics. Following Edwards's priorities, language was the next most important key to the development of "type." The bulk of the questionnaire concerned a comprehensive investigation of geographic surroundings, individual and family life, childrearing, rituals, education, diet, clothing, occupations, means of subsistence, social customs, law, mythology, and relations with other peoples.[33] In 1847 there were three sections of the society: (1) the physical study of peoples, (2) historical and linguistic study, and (3) moral and political questions, but the practical consequences of this division have been difficult to trace.[34]

The small group of sixteen founders included eight members of the Institute (Edwards; historian Jules Michelet from the Academy of Moral and Political Sciences; zoologist Henri Milne-Edwards [1800–85], who was W.-F. Edwards's own brother; Flourens from the Academy of Sciences; sculptor David d'Angers from the Academy of Fine Arts; and ancient geographer Jean-Antoine Letronne; historical cartographer and medievalist viscount M.-F. de Santarem [1791–1856]; and the Hindi linguist J.-H.-S.-V. Garcin de Tassy [1794–1878], all three from the Academy of Inscriptions). Ultimately, at least fourteen Institute members would join the Society. The sixty-seven adherents of the early months were largely geographers, naturalists, linguists, and historians. At least twenty-two came from the existing Paris Geographical Society (including Africanist d'Avezac, Letronne, Canary Islands expert Sabin Berthelot, Santarem, botanist and explorer of South America Alcide d'Orbigny [1802–57]. Eighteen honorary members in 1844 included illustrious foreign personalities such as the British Lord Brougham, while twelve corresponding members were explorers or scholars posted to foreign

31 *MSEP* 2 (1845): lix.
32 *MSEP* 1:vi–vii.
33 *MSEP*, 1:vi–xv.
34 *NAV* 5ᵉ sér., 10 (avril 1847).

sites. The "elected foreigners" were renowned scholars such as William Lawrence and James Cowles Prichard, as well as kindred spirits such as Hodgkin and Buxton. Of about ninety known occupations on various membership lists, the largest single category of twenty is physicians (less overwhelmingly predominant than among the phrenologists), while nine others made careers in the sciences as naturalists or botanists. Seventeen were scholars, librarians, or men of letters, and ten more were teachers. There was a smattering of artists (six), diplomats (four), and military or naval officers (five). Practically no lawyers joined, but several bankers (seven) had connections with prominent members. In the years before 1848, the Society raised funds by encouraging educated laymen to join, such as the ex-Saint-Simonian banker Olinde Rodrigues-Henriques and the ex-Saint-Simonian turned liberal economist Michel Chevalier (1806–79). By 1848 there were over 200 adherents to the SEP. The Society managed to publish memoirs and a bulletin sporadically, though it never truly prospered.

Among the most active members were, from the existing Geographical Society, the Africanist Marie-Armand-Pascal d'Avezac, the linguist and scholarly geographer Louis Vivien de Saint-Martin (1802–97), and the Saint-Simonian banker, Gustave d'Eichthal. Besides Milne-Edwards, there was the eminent naturalist Isidore Geoffroy Saint-Hilaire (1805–61). Other active officers included Charles Lenormant (1802–59), historian at the Sorbonne until 1846, and the historian/librarian Alfred Maury (1817–92). The SEP was also the vehicle for the review of geographic explorations discussed in the previous chapter – of west Africa by Raffenel, of Ethiopia by Lefebvre, and of the Pacific by Dumoutier.

PHYSICAL AND CULTURAL INVESTIGATIONS OF THE SEP

The great influence of Edwards's permanence of types model explicitly affected the research of the botanist Sabin Berthelot in 1842–44 on the Guanches, or aboriginal Canary islanders. Though they endured Roman, "barbarian," and Spanish conquests, Guanche customs and chronicles from isolated areas revealed to Berthelot that they preserved their identity from distant antiquity. Their physiognomy, confirmed by mummies found in the grottoes, resembled Berber types from nearby Morocco. Language affinities bolstered this relationship. Like Edwards, Berthelot used cranial descriptions but not phrenology. He directly cited Edwards on the need to examine physiognomy and on the effects of isolation on preserving traits.[35]

Given the French conquest of coastal Algeria and the war raging in the interior, French relations with the Islamic inhabitants of North Africa absorbed the interest of several members of the Society. The construction of a separate Berber identity proceeded apace within the SEP and supported French imperial objectives.[36] Political radicals did not scruple to endorse the French imperial role. An officer of the Society, Fourierist, and future radical deputy, Pascal Duprat, wrote for Pierre Leroux's *La Revue indépendante*. Duprat insisted on distinguishing Berbers, ancient Libyans originating in India, from Arabs. While less focused on the facial angle, Duprat thought this indomitable mountain people, little affected by their many conquerors, was a beautiful race meriting a French alliance.[37] Since Berber merchants wished to trade with the French, an expedition against them would be a strategic error. Alienating Algerian Berbers would hinder the predestined role of France to exert influence among Moroccan Berbers.

Raymond Thomassy (1810–63), another Fourierist who wrote for *La démocratie pacifique* in 1846, sent memoirs to the Society on Muslim-Christian relations in North Africa.[38] Thomassy curiously combined sympathy for both Islam and French imperial aspirations. He hoped for civilian French emigration behind a military safety cordon so that France could carry out its "civilizing ascendancy on Muslim races." "The Orient," he continued, "is in effect henceforth destined to European colonization."[39] Thomassy praised the Muslim missionaries in Africa, since they abolished fetishism, human sacrifice, and created a better morality in the family. Yet the French had to face the reality that Muslims would not accept them.[40] A surgeon with the army in Africa, Dr Lacger, communicated a much more negative stereotypical descrip-

35 *MSEP* 1:146–7, 191, 229–31; *MSEP* 2:124–5, 143.

36 Thomson, "Bory de Saint-Vincent."

37 Lorcin, *Imperial Identities*, 50, 149–53 on Duprat; see also Harvey, *"Almost a Man of Genius,"* 48–52; Duprat, "Peuples anciens et modernes du Maroc et du rôle de la France dans l'Afrique occidentale," *La Revue indépendante* 16 (1844): 54–73; "Expédition contre les Kabyles ou Berbers de l'Algérie," *La Revue indépendante* 17 (25 mars 1845); and *Essai historique*, 5, 9; Gustave d'Eichthal seems to have labeled Duprat as unreliable: see BA, Fonds d'Eichthal, 13751/56.

38 *MSEP* 1:xlv, xlviii.

39 Thomassy, *De la colonisation*, 1, 9.

40 Thomassy, *Le Maroc et ses caravanes*, 6–7, 61.

tion of depraved Algerians who indulged in polygamy and abandoned sick children without reproof from Muslim leaders.[41]

Descriptions of other cultures in the SEP vacillated between exoticism oblivious to empathy and the Orientalist culture of contempt. The noted travel writer Théodore Pavie's memoir from Bombay on the Parsees favorably commented on their pleasant appearance and European tastes. He also sensationalized their attachment to a religion that approved exposure of cadavers to vultures.[42] Similarly, the former physician to the prince of Lahore, a Dr Benet, found that Sikhs so resembled Europeans that they might descend from the army of Alexander the Great. But he devoted his essay to denigrating their predilection for astrology, arranged marriages, polygamy, and funeral pyres for widows – all in all, the "most barbarous fanaticism."[43] The same contempt for the non-European surfaced in the work of the traveler Isidore Löwenstern, who reported from Mexico on the "thieving, stupid, crafty" Mexican Indians and the depravity of mixed-race peoples.[44]

The influence of Balbi's linguistic ethnography, combined with the work of German scholars such as Friedrich Schlegel and August Schlegel (a foreign member of the Society) and the German Orientalist Julius Heinrich Klaproth (1783–1835), provoked a lively cottage industry relating linguistic and ethnic kinship. Ultimately, this approach stimulated the rise of the "Aryan" theory of racial descent that would have such an unfortunate future. Duprat himself used the term "Arian" for the ancient Phoenicians of North Africa – disdaining a Semitic ancestry for them, in keeping with his general hostility to the Jews of North Africa.[45]

Another proponent of the "Aryan" theory was the Austrian-born, aging army officer Captain Troyer, who had been aide-de-camp to the British East India Company governor-general Lord William Bentinck and who devoted his retirement to Sanskrit scholarship.[46] His ethnological sketch of the peoples of India (available only in the minutes, not in full text) classified lighter-skinned groups as "Iranians" or "Ariens," Caucasians who crossed the Hindu Kush Mountains into the Punjab. Following his colleague, the historian Charles Lenormant, he thought that India west of the Indus was an "Indo-Scythic" population

41 *MSEP* 1:xliv; see Lorcin, "Imperialism, Colonial Identity, and Race," 662.
42 *MSEP* 1:244, 248.
43 *MSEP* 1:284.
44 *MSEP* 2 (1845): xxvii.
45 *BSEP* 2 (1847): 177–8.
46 Eckstein, *Lettres inédites de baron d'Eckstein*, 140–1.

area. In the south of India in the Deccan arose a distinct civilization of inferior, darker-skinned peoples.[47]

The assistant secretary Gustave d'Eichthal speculated wildly about linguistic kinships, based on the idea that identity of language syntax, if not vocabulary, might mean racial identity.[48] He devoted inordinate efforts to finding resemblances of vocabulary among Polynesian, African, Coptic, and American languages. He was convinced that Polynesia was a veritable wellspring of ancient civilizations. Hence, if there were Malaysian peoples of Madagascar, Polynesia was a likely source. The Madagascar tribes in turn were relatives of ancient Egyptian and Mandingo (Malinke) peoples. The lighter-skinned Foulah (Fulani or Fulbe) of the Sudan seemed to have Malay affinities in language, customs, and Islamic religion. They might have come from Malaysia via Madagascar. For d'Eichthal, Islam was as much a civilizing influence as for Thomassy: Islam improved the fate of aboriginal peoples and initiated them into Biblical doctrines.

D'Eichthal believed that even American Indian languages such as Carib and Algonquin had resemblances to Coptic, west African, and Polynesian languages. If North Americans could not under present conditions have populated Polynesia because of prevailing winds and currents, he wondered if the earth might have been different in the past to allow for that possibility. Moreover, the blacks of the South Pacific of Vanikoro seemed to resemble Africans, and Dumont d'Urville found Egyptian sphinx-like artifacts in New Guinea.[49]

VARIETIES OF SAINT-SIMONIANISM

The SEP discussion of 1847 on the "appropriate relations between the black and white races" crystallized the many issues concerning racial hierarchy and the nature of the human species that fascinated anthropologists all through the century. The Saint-Simonian legacy affected three participants: d'Eichthal, Rodrigues, and Courtet de l'Isle. Arising in part from d'Eichthal's own organic, functionalist Saint-Simonian convic-

47 A brief reference is available in *MSEP* 2 (1845): liii–iv, lvi, and lix; for the early history of the Aryan concept, see Poliakov, *The Aryan Myth.*

48 *MSEP* 2 (1845): xl–xlii.

49 D'Eichthal, "Histoire et origine des Foulahs, ou Fellans," in *MSEP* 1:1–300 and separate edition (1856), 105, 118, 138, 142, 155–7, 162 and "Études sur l'histoire primitive des races océaniennes et américaines," *MSEP* 2:151–309; also in separate edition (1845), 18, 40, 43, 105, 121.

tions, the extended forum enabled Society members to offer opinions on the distance between humans and apes, the rank of the races, the consequences of intermarriage, and the fertility of hybrids as an indicator of unity of the species.[50]

The introductory chapter has already outlined the functionalist, organic society advocated by Saint-Simon and derived from the physiology of Bichat. After Saint-Simon's death, the Saint-Simonian circle generated more egalitarian and more functionalist wings, both of which surfaced in the Ethnological Society. Saint-Amand Bazard, one of the two Saint-Simonian leaders, argued in *Le Producteur* in 1826 that the capacities of intellect, muscular prowess, and nervous sensitivity were independent of climate or racial ancestry.[51] Rodrigues endorsed this viewpoint in the SEP. Rodrigues's family was so close to the d'Eichthals that the father of Olindes taught Gustave d'Eichthal bookkeeping. A tireless advocate in the 1840s of mutual aid societies, easy credit, and profit sharing for workers, Rodrigues also invoked Olympe de Gouges in an appeal for citizenship for women.[52] In the 1847 discussion he firmly postulated that all human races had an "equal aptitude for civilization in suitable circumstances," just as some day "women will one day conquer equality without any restriction."[53] The naturalist Milne-Edwards strongly rebuked this expression of sentiment for lacking a scientific basis.

A second Saint-Simonian, d'Eichthal, found solace for his own conflicted personality and problems of identity in a functionalist organic version of racial hierarchy.[54] Of Jewish origin, d'Eichthal had converted to Roman Catholicism before coming under the spell of the secular

50 Aspects of this discussion, in particular the opposition between Schoelcher and Courtet, as well as d'Eichthal's black/feminine analogy, appear in the article of Seymour Drescher, "The Ending of the Slave Trade," 433–42 (reprinted in *From Slavery to Freedom*, 275–311); Drescher's context is primarily whether abolitionism helped mitigate racism, as he believes, or whether it hardly staunched the hostility, as James Walvin contends in *Black and White: The Negro and English Society, 1555–1945* (London: Allen Lane, 1973). Drescher tends to see Schoelcher as an isolated dissident and to overlook the potential connection between abolitionism and imperialism.

51 *Le Producteur* 4 (1826): 417–18.

52 Rodrigues, *Projet de constitution* and *Organisation du travail*; Fondation Dosne-Thiers, Fonds d'Eichthal: Rodrigues undated letter to Leroux, and d'Eichthal [1851], "Projet de notice sur Olinde Rodrigues," Carton IV/R2; see also correspondence in BA, Fonds d'Eichthal, MS. 14719; d'Allemagne, *Les Saint-Simoniens*, 42.

53 *NAV*, 5ᵉ sér., 10 (avril-juin 1847): 386–7; *BSEP* 2 (1847): 96–7.

54 For identity conflicts, BA, Fonds d'Eichthal, MS. 14720, fols 3, 8; and for Enfantin as Jesus, see d'Allemagne, *Les Saint-Simoniens*, 264–5.

religion of the Saint-Simonians. One inspiration came from the vision of the Saint-Simonian leader Enfantin – a union of the spiritual, static, feminine Orient with the materialistic but active Occident. In 1832 d'Eichthal read about a material embodiment of Enfantin's scheme – Michel Chevalier's article about the "Mediterranean system," a vision of a "peaceful crusade" of European civilization. There would be a "marriage-bed" of Occident and Orient by railways, harbours, and port development along the Mediterranean. In this fashion Europe would "push civilization ahead of itself" and "lift up the half-buried Orient."[55]

The next year d'Eichthal's letters to Enfantin enthused about the French civilization of Algeria and recommended Virey as the "first to my knowledge who has divided the human genus into two species, black and white, making only subdivisions of the other races." In 1838 he prepared a questionnaire to assist Enfantin's projected ethnographic survey of blacks in Algeria.[56] In letters of 1839 to Enfantin (misdated in the manuscript but identifiable due to references to Fowell Buxton's publications and Tocqueville's report on abolition of slavery), d'Eichthal revealed some of the deepest sources of his thinking. Steeped in the work of French Orientalists Abel de Rémusat and Samuel Ustazade Silvestre de Sacy, of German Orientalists August Schlegel and Klaproth, d'Eichthal asserted that Bory treated Virey too lightly. On the contrary, d'Eichthal esteemed the "work of Virey on blacks quite superior to the rest of his work; at least the physiological demonstration of the *black-woman* emerges clearly from it." Milne-Edwards, among others, had assured d'Eichthal that the "phrenology of blacks agrees with this formula that the lower posterior parts of heads of blacks develop as with women."

Virey's feminization of blacks also could justify European intervention in Africa. The French expeditions to Egypt and to Algeria followed the principle of the "need to civilize Africa," or at least to give blacks the "relative civilization to which they are susceptible," family decency and

55 Chevalier, *Religion Saint-Simonienne*, 119, 137, 145; d'Eichthal cites Chevalier in Fondation Dosne-Thiers, Fonds d'Eichthal, Carton IV/R6, fols 5–6.

56 BA, Fonds Enfantin, MS. 7839/14, letter of d'Eichthal to Enfantin, 24 oct. 1833; Fonds d'Eichthal, MS. 13759, letter to Enfantin, 14 janv. 1838; see also d'Eichthal's recommendation of Virey to Urbain, 16 oct. 1839, in MS. 13741/23; d'Eichthal's notes on Algiers blacks in Fonds Enfantin, MS. 7839/12 and Fonds d'Eichthal, 13741/37; Enfantin, *Colonisation de l'Algérie*; on Enfantin and Urbain, see Emerit, *Les Saint-Simoniens en Algérie*.

good morals. Hence, the union of Europe and Africa would produce a greater degree of civilization for the world.[57]

Recruited by Edwards in 1840 at a Geographical Society meeting, d'Eichthal became assistant secretary of the SEP in 1841–46 and secretary in 1846–52.[58] In 1839 he published letters to his Saint-Simonian friend Ismaïl Urbain (partly read to the SEP in 1841), a Guyanese mulatto convert to Islam. Here he publicized his images of the white race as masculine, the blacks as feminine.[59] The corollary was that blacks did not have "political" or "scientific" intelligence as yet, but had developed faculties of the heart, affection, and feeling. Whites could help teach them greater respect for women in the family. D'Eichthal also did not reject intermarriage, but rather idealized the mulatto as expressing the best qualities of both races.[60]

In an 1843 review of the early English anthropologist James Cowles Prichard, d'Eichthal solidified his views of distinctiveness of races. Prichard's religious orthodoxy attributed racial differences to climate and external agents rather than to "typical differences of races or crossing."[61] D'Eichthal's attraction for polygenism grew when he met the Egyptologist George R. Gliddon. The famed American craniologist Samuel George Morton had obtained skulls from Gliddon for investigating ancient Egyptians. By 1844, at a time when Morton was already communicating with the SEP, d'Eichthal had read Morton's *Crania aegyptica*, which ordered races by cranial capacity.[62]

D'Eichthal was the principal animator of the Society's discussion in April to July 1847 of "what part is reserved to each of the white and black races in the common work" of humanity, "in proportion to its

57 BA, Fonds Enfantin, MS. 7839/14 (letter misdated 1833); the most likely sources for d'Eichthal's conflation of the black and the feminine are in Virey, *De la femme*, 173, 182, and Virey, *Histoire naturelle* (1824), 2:31–73, where both blacks and women are considered affectionate and childlike, not reflective.

58 BA, Fonds d'Eichthal, MS. 13741/23; Ratcliffe and Chaloner, "Gustave d'Eichthal."

59 D'Eichthal, *Lettres sur la race noire*, 14, 60; MSEP 2 (1845), xvi; see also Cohen, *The French Encounter with Africans*, 236–7; d'Eichthal shows the limits of Saint-Simonian images of women, despite women's workers' circles and Enfantin's celebrated search for a female Messiah; Burke, "Thomas Ismail Urbain (1812–84)."

60 D'Eichthal, *Lettres sur la race noire*, 60, 67.

61 D'Eichthal, "Histoire et origine des Foulahs, ou Fellans," MSEP 1:127, 131, 139, 142, 162; MSEP (1845): xxxvii–xxxix.

62 BA, Fonds d'Eichthal, MS. 13750/170 on Morton, 13750/211 on Gliddon; see also BSEP 1 (1846): 52 for Morton on the "red race."

moral and physical qualities." Against the background of petitions to the Chamber to abolish slavery, the Society asked what should be the new "mode of association between the races?" D'Eichthal himself offered a hypothesis: many blacks, including Oceanians and Australians as well as Africans, were in a "primitive state" with no sciences, no systematic religion, no developed fine arts, literature, or administration. If abandoned, they would have no "civilizing initiative of their own." However, the Tocqueville commission for the Chamber of Deputies on abolition of slavery in 1839 had arrived at the conclusion that west African coastal peoples had a "relative civilization." Contact with Europeans was not therefore fruitless for purposes of education.[63] Ethnology, according to d'Eichthal, here "works to combine itself with social science, politics, and touches religion itself." The crucial question was whether blacks were inherently an inferior species or modifiable by circumstances. As with the role of women in society, absolute equality might be impossible, but women have a "role of the same importance [as men] in the organization of the couple." Similarly, the "happy and benevolent dispositions" of blacks designated them for a special role in the new peaceful age.[64]

The third Saint-Simonian, Courtet, was a more hard-line polygenist than d'Eichthal.[65] Courtet succeeded d'Eichthal as assistant secretary of the Society and even rented them a meeting hall in 1847.[66] Citing Virey, Bory, Desmoulins, and Edwards, Courtet considered racial types virtually synonymous with species. Phrenology might discern permanent cranial features of each race in their "gradual and providential" hierarchy. The Egyptian monuments revealed a ruling white race far back in recorded history. Since blacks were transitional to the orangutan and could not develop their intellectual aptitudes, slavery seemed predestined for them.[67] In 1838, Courtet facilely adopted Christoph Meiners's old idea that the allegedly most beautiful races were the most intelligent.[68] Nevertheless, in Gallic-Germanic France, Courtet advocated a society with wider property ownership through easy credit and social

63 *BSEP* 2 (1847): 94.

64 Vivien de Saint-Martin, ed. *NAV* 5ᵉ sér. 10 (1847): 102, 226–35, especially 229–32, 239–40; 380–1 on Tocqueville; see also *BSEP* 2 (1847): 64–73, 90–1, 94 on Tocqueville.

65 Boissel, *Victor Courtet*; Cohen, *The French Encounter with Africans*, 214–16, 237.

66 BA, Fonds d'Eichthal, MS. 13751/16

67 Courtet de l'Isle, *Mémoire*, 4, 9, 13; *Au congrès*, 5, 8, 10, 18, 22.

68 Courtet de l'Isle, *La science politique*, x–xi, 20, 48, 53–6, 224, 232–3, 314; Edwards, "Esquisse," *MSEP* 1:120–1.

mobility. Indeed, in a letter to d'Eichthal, Courtet complained that his political opponents labeled him both a communist and a reactionary. Among Europeans, rigid castes were unwarranted, since racial mixing and education would lead to greater equality.[69] In June 1846, Courtet warned d'Eichthal that ideas of racial equality in general could lead to an undesirable "fusion of races." He rejected the analogy with women, since women were intellectually equal to men, while "the intelligence of the Negro is not apt to rival that of the white in any specialty."[70]

EGALITARIANISM VERSUS RACIAL HIERARCHY – EVIDENCE OF EGYPTIAN MONUMENTS

To help clarify the terms of the SEP discussion, the physician François Lallemand, a recent adherent of the Society, tried to enumerate alleged "Negro" characteristics, including the shape and proportions of legs, arms, and back, which excluded some darker-skinned Africans such as Abyssinians and Gallas.[71] A commission selected in May 1847 then examined the general issues, although almost all were believers in black inferiority – the *rapporteur* d'Eichthal, the geographers Vivien and d'Avezac, the naturalists Milne-Edwards and Quatrefages, the phrenologist Dumoutier, and the conservative baron and enthusiast for Aryan India Ferdinand d'Eckstein. In his report, d'Eichthal modified the usual model of stages of civilization from hunting to pastoral to agricultural peoples. He asserted that in Africa the pastoral, even nomadic peoples such as the Foulah were closer to whites, while agricultural west African blacks failed even to domesticate animals. Yet their rudimentary civilization clearly showed the "most important human faculties," far above the animal world. D'Eichthal as usual tended to define civilizability by moral qualities, and recognized that despotism and customs such as human sacrifice contributed to "barbarism." But northern or Islamic influence explained the advanced agricultural and commercial

---

69 Courtet de l'Isle, *Programme de réformes*, 6–7, 12; BA, Fonds d'Eichthal, MS. 13751/65; Courtet de l'Isle, *La science politique*, 89, 98, 232, 314, 322, 328, 357–9, 362–3. Courtet was clearly less pessimistic than Gobineau, but should not be considered an advocate of general miscegenation; for analogies to Courtet and the use of phrenology in a "democratic" and "socialist" view of the ascendancy of the Gauls within France, see Rignol, "Anthropologie et progrès," esp. 175.

70 BA, Fonds d'Eichthal, MS. 13750/250, Correspondance, 13 juin 1846; 13750/265, 14 juillet 1846.

71 *NAV* 5ᵉ sér., 11 (1847): 69; *BSEP* 2 (1847): 101, 103.

development of the Foulah, while they still lacked the scientific elements essential to true European-style civilization.[72]

This conclusion inspired the two major polarized statements of the
debate from two sons of the commercial bourgeoisie – the egalitarian
credo of the staunch republican, social democrat, and abolitionist Victor
Schoelcher (1804–93; a member of the SEP from April 1846), and the
response by Courtet.[73] In 1842 Schoelcher's bitter satire on the racial
theorists asserted that they had "very little brains themselves to build, on
the more or less acute facial angle, petty philosophical theories which
tend to refuse [blacks] approximately all intelligence." From his travels
in the West Indies, he reported that physicians there mocked the unten-
able speculations of Bory and Virey about the physical attributes of
blacks. On the other hand, pro-slavery planters also, when defending
Bory and Virey, conveniently forgot that, by the 1820s, both had condemned slavery.[74]

A tour of the Nile valley in 1845 gave Schoelcher more ammunition
for his arguments that blacks produced a civilization. Citing Herodotus
and recent explorers, Schoelcher maintained that Nubian Meroe (now
in the Sudan) generated Egyptian civilization, and that ancient Egyptians themselves were all or partly black while manifestly equal in intellect to "whites." The mid-nineteenth century already had its "out of
Africa" debates on the influence of Egypt on Greece – a kind of "battle
of the monuments." Schoelcher, too, invoked the royal tombs at Gizeh
and the Thebes sculptures of Amenophis III to claim that statues and reliefs of high-ranking figures had African features, while their image of
the "savages" was the blue-eyed European.[75]

In 1846 the Catholic conservative president of the SEP, Charles Lenormant, challenged Schoelcher's interpretation and in January 1847,
Courtet offered his own rebuttal. Both argued that a white Scythic (Hyk-
sos) people conquered Egypt. Courtet believed that whites even inhab-

72 *NAV* 5ᵉ sér., 11 (1847): 68–86, esp. 70–3, 84 (or *BSEP* 2 (1847): 105–21).

73 On Schoelcher, see Alexandre-Debray, *Victor Schoelcher*, 36–8; Schmidt, *Victor Schoelcher et l'abolition* and *Victor Schoelcher en son temps*, 1–12; Schoelcher, *Histoire de l'escla-vage*; Cohen, *The French Encounter with Africans*, 196–7.

74 Schoelcher, *Des colonies françaises*, 139–41, 144–5; for the debate on Egyptian (pre-sumed black) influence on Greece, see Bernal, *Black Athena*, and Lefkowitz and Rogers, eds. *Black Athena Revisited*; the question of "white" versus "black" Egyptians in some ways antici-pates the "Afrocentrism" debates on the importance of African contributions to civilization (in this case Egyptian).

75 Schoelcher, *L'Égypte en 1845*, 269–71, 275, 280, 283, 288.

ited Ethiopian Meroe. To Lenormant Egyptians were "Japetic," that is, the same race as Europeans, while Courtet found them Indo-Germanic or Indo-Semitic – in any case "Arian" – on the basis of physical features, not language. Morton's recent study of the crania and facial angles of Egyptian mummies, which classified only 8 per cent as black, supported the argument that Egyptian civilization was Asiatic, not Nubian.[76] Courtet also used Lenormant's antiquities collection, where the tomb of Mnepthtah (Merenptah?) I and other sites depicted upper-class Egyptians with lighter skin colour than lower-class or conquered blacks.[77]

In the SEP discussion of 11 June 1847, Schoelcher gave a trenchant response to the SEP commission report. He assumed the "equality of all members of the great human family, whatever their sex, the colour of their epidermis, and the nature of their hair." No scientific evidence proclaimed the relative inferiority of one race. Besides Meroe, Africans constructed the great Niger valley mosques, and many explorers reported favourably on west African aptitudes. If a contemporary of the ancient Celts and Gauls had prejudged them as savages incapable of civilization, he clearly would have been mistaken. Blacks were no more uneducable than French peasants.[78]

Schoelcher's mockery of anthropology enabled Courtet to pose as a scientist who dealt in facts, not sentimentality. For Courtet, climatic theories of human diversity could not explain the disparity of Polynesians and Melanesians in the same climate. Nor could an admittedly favourable climate explain the "primitive" status of Hottentots and Australians.[79]

But now Courtet had an ingenious reply to Schoelcher's examples of the achievements of Ethiopians, southeast African Caffirs, Foulah, and Mandingo. None of these peoples was "Negro," and in fact each was higher than the "Negro" on the great ladder of being. The genuine Negroes, as in Benin, the Makua of Mozambique, and the Bushmen, were

76 Lenormant, *Cours d'histoire ancienne*, 292, 322; *BSEP* 1 (1846): 109, 113, 116; see also Blanckaert, "L'esclavage des Noirs," esp. 402.

77 For d'Eichthal's hopes for Courtet's speech, BA, Fonds d'Eichthal, MS. 14719, fol. 55v; *BSEP* 2 (1847): 5–22, especially 14–17; also *NAV* 5ᵉ sér., 10 (1847): 299–318; *NAV* 5ᵉ sér., 9 (1847): 326–67.

78 Schoelcher, *NAV* 5ᵉ sér, 11 (1847): 228–36, esp. 228–30, or *BSEP* 2 (1847): 151–64, esp. 155–6, 160; Baron Roger in the Geographical Society had also used the comparison with peasants.

79 Courtet de l'Isle, *Tableau ethnographique*, republication of speech on 1–30; original in *NAV* 5ᵉ sér., 11 (juillet-sept 1847): 363–86, esp. 364–70; in *BSEP* 2 (1847): 181–206, esp. 181, 185–90.

truly backward. D'Avezac immediately objected that with such defini-
tions one could practically eliminate the classification of Negro. But
Courtet conceded in conclusion that if blacks were to be emancipated,
Europeans should guide them and settle among them.[80]

MONOGENISTS (SECULAR AND RELIGIOUS)
AND POLYGENISTS IN THE SEP

Among non-Saint-Simonian Society members, we may discern three
groups – the Christian monogenists, the hierarchical monogenist geographers and naturalists (both secular and religious), and the polygenist
colonial delegates and geographers. Other than Schoelcher and Rodrigues, the potential egalitarians in the Society did not directly participate in the discussion of 1847 but had intervened earlier either as
orthodox Christians or supporters of Prichard's orthodox natural history. One largely reticent possible ally in the discussion was the explorer
of South America for the Muséum, Alcide d'Orbigny. In the SEP meetings he asserted only that blacks seemed less likely of enlightenment
than American Indians, but that blacks might change in the Americas.
His major work on South American Indians revealed belief in the relative equality of "primitive" man. Among the naturalists he alone was so
open-minded regarding non-Europeans.[81]

A somewhat active participant was the Christian monogenist François
Eusèbe de Salle (also written de Salles), a onetime physician turned
army interpreter and modern Oriental language instructor in Marseille.
D'Avezac and Garcin de Tassy read excerpts that de Salle sent to the Society in 1843 on "ethnographic philology" that attacked Desmoulins's
anti-Biblical polygenism. In a kind of anticipation of the "lumpers" versus "splitters" typology of taxonomists, de Salle astutely remarked that
naturalists seek pretexts to divide the species while moralists assert the
unity of all humans. Staunchly anti-materialist and politically conservative, his stray comments on revolutions indicated a propensity for the

---

80 *NAV* 5ᵉ sér., 11 (juillet-sept 1847): 374–85 or *BSEP* 2: 199–204; for d'Avezac, see
NAV 5ᵉ sér., 11 (juillet-sept 1847): 390–1 or *BSEP* 2: 204–11. Disputes over definitions of
"Negro" led to a second commission, which apparently never reported, including Milne-
Edwards, d'Orbigny, d'Avezac, Quatrefages, Dumoutier, polygenist naval surgeon Honoré
Jacquinot, Lallemand, the physician Denonville, surgeons Blandin, Suquet, and Dumar-
quay, medical student Lebret, and the sculptor Cumberworth; see *BSEP* 2 (1847): 212.

81 d'Orbigny, *L'Homme Américain*, 129, 133, 144n., 170–1, 221.

Masonic plot theory of 1789 and a lament that 1848 elevated equality above liberty.[82]

De Salle strikingly believed that polygenism promoted exploitation. The "partisans of the right of the strongest" benefited from finding "several physically unequal castes." Such a conclusion "in itself makes these castes unequal in aptitudes and rights." Thus, the "legitimacy of their slavery could be definitively demonstrated," and similar arguments could apply to the European conquest of the Mongols, foreshadowed by the opium wars. In North America, whites repressed those natives "who cannot assimilate to be like the colonists" or they "exterminate whoever resists." Instead, de Salle believed in climatic causes for diversity of races and in the moral educability of all.[83] As far as the testimony of Egyptian monuments was concerned, de Salle doubted they were old enough to prove the permanence of types. Like d'Eichthal and unlike Courtet, he also thought mixed races were beautiful and vigorous, not degenerate.[84]

The former physician, local historian, and school inspector from Bourges, C.-Claude Pierquin de Gembloux, is more difficult to classify, as he had published a work clearly arranging the races in a Chain of Being. He included particularly egregious comments, such as "Negroes are more talented as imitators rather than having an aptitude for the abstract sciences." He also relegated Hottentots and Bushmen to a level close to the orangutan. But he responded to Bory de Saint-Vincent's use of the facial angle with a critical letter to the Society that stated that all humans were equally intelligent and doubted that "genius consistently depends on a more or less open facial angle." Moreover, belief in distinct species was only a gratuitous contradiction of the Bible. It appears his Christian commitment impelled him at least to consider favourably equality of intellectual potential.[85]

The Africanist Marie-Armand-Pascal d'Avezac, a former secretary of the Société de géographie, was a hierarchical monogenist. He produced the most in-depth cultural survey ever done by the SEP by interviewing a Brazilian slave of Yebu origin (from what is now southeastern Nigeria). D'Avezac respected the man sufficiently to remark that his "facial angle doesn't seem to me extremely acute." Still, he had "little intelligence," though, along with the stereotype, he was blessed with a "gentle moral

82 *MSEP* 2 (1845): xxxix–xl; de Salle, *Histoire générale*, 89, 312–16, 351.

83 de Salle, *Histoire générale*, 32–4, 82, 179, 184, 205–9, 268, 297–8.

84 Ibid., 182, 216, 259, 273.

85 Pierquin de Gembloux, *Traité de la Folie des animaux* 1:165, 221, 240, and *Lettre au général Bory de Vincent*, 35, 38–40.

character" and some industrious habits. In an illustration of Edward Said's contention that European Orientalists constructed their own image of others, d'Avezac did not allow the African an authentic voice. D'Avezac rearranged and edited the replies to his questions, though he claimed to have tried to avoid undue influence on the responses. Sections of the memoir included discussion of the language, marriage customs and po-lygamy, circumcision, divorce, funeral practices, means of subsistence, housing, and occupations of the Yebu. In commenting on the religion, he admitted that "fetishism was less primitive than we think" and allowed no human sacrifices. It was "less opposed than one admits to the adoption of the dogmas of a purer religion." The government was at least a tempered monarchy with a council of elders and judges.[86]

Despite this relative empathy for the Yebu people, d'Avezac elsewhere eagerly adopted a theory of the British naturalist William Swainson (1789–1855) that the white race was the norm, the Mongol a sub-type, and the "Ethiopic" race an aberrant form. Blacks were always destined to be "mediocre or nil."[87] In the geographers' periodical, he publicized sympathetically Bory's polygenism and Courtet's early papers. In the 1847 discussion d'Avezac also affirmed that Africans had never had a real civilization, and that races such as the Foulah and Negro had always been enslaved.[88]

The hierarchical monogenist naturalists used the supposed objectivity of science to question the evidence for Biblical monogenism. Particularly fascinating for them was the issue of whether colonial-born West Indian blacks were superior, and if so, whether because of climatic influence or interbreeding. This general biological issue had important implications for European adaptability to colonization.[89] In the 1847 discussion, Milne-Edwards, Dumoutier, and Quatrefages urged more study to sort out the influences of climate and interbreeding.[90] If crossing were more sig-nificant, then so-called pure blacks had less adaptability. The previous chapter has already explicated the position of Dumoutier, an active partic-ipant in the discussion, and remarked on the membership of polygenists Jacquinot and Hombron in the Society by 1847.

86 D'Avezac, "Notice sur le pays et le peuple des Yébous en Afrique," *MSEP* 2, part 2: 1–103, especially 9, 45–6, 84–9.

87 D'Avezac, *Histoire et description*, 23–5.

88 *BSG*, 2ᵉ sér., 6 (1836): 280–1; *BSEP* 2 (1847): 128–31.

89 Osborne, *Nature, the exotic, and the science of French colonialism*.

90 *NAV* 5ᵉ sér., 10 (1847): 238, 377–8, 386–7 and 11 (1847): 237–8; *BSEP* 2 (1847): 96, 173.

Milne-Edwards's popular natural history school text (co-authored with Achille Comte) announced a single human species, with the Caucasic race most civilized, but provided a caricatural portrait of an ape-like African and simplistically correlated shape of forehead to brain size. First published in 1833 for use in collèges and école normales primaires, this work went through at least eight editions (twenty-six separate cahiers) in 1876 and may have been consulted by thousands of students![91] While in 1840 Milne-Edwards had seemed sceptical about relating intelligence to the facial angle or cranial capacity, by 1880 he again assumed the utility of the angle and concluded that "Negro inferiority is so well known there is no need to prove it."[92]

The most fascinating naturalist and teacher of zoology who bridged membership in the SEP with the Société d'Anthropologie was Quatrefages, a protégé of Milne-Edwards and, by 1855, the Muséum professor of anthropology. Although only an occasional participant in the discussion of 1847, his staunch monogenism counteracted his early revulsion for blacks.[93] Born into a Protestant family like Broca, the mature Quatrefages was more like a Voltairian deist. The important difference was that religious belief was for him a distinctive and presumably praiseworthy human attribute.[94] In an article of 1843 for the *Revue des deux mondes*, he did not hesitate to label the "African Negro" as an "intellectual monstrosity."[95] By early 1847, in a private letter to d'Eichthal, Quatrefages was ready to admit possible improvement of "inferior races": "if I believed in the multiplicity of species, I would despair of those whose present inferiority cannot be denied."[96] In the SEP discussion, Quatrefages still doubted whether blacks were capable of spontaneous civilization. However, in contrast to Courtet's interpretation of permanent racial types in the fashion of Edwards, Quatrefages firmly differentiated a "species" from a "race." A species is the "collection of beings descending from common parents," which Quatrefages would always believe to be fixed. A "race" was a product of

91 Milne-Edwards and Comte, *Cahiers d'histoire naturelle*, 23, 29.

92 Milne-Edwards, *Éléments de zoologie*, 1:200, 202, and *Leçons sur la physiologie*, 185.

93 Hamy, "Vie et travaux de M. de Quatrefages"; Hervé et de Quatrefages, "Armand de Quatrefages de Bréau"; Cartailhac, *Notice sur A. de Quatrefages*.

94 Quatrefages, *Souvenirs d'un naturaliste*, from "L'Archipel de Chausey," 1 May 1842, 30.

95 Quatrefages, "Le Floride," *Revue des deux mondes* 2nd sér., 1 (1 mars 1843), 733–73, esp. 755–6, 758–60; see Blanckaert, "Le système des races," 25.

96 BA, Fonds d'Eichthal, MS. 13751/1, undated but early in 1847.

climatically induced change – "descendants of the same species with transmissible characteristics of individual variety ... caused by the action of the milieu."[97]

At the firmly polygenist extreme of the discussion, along with the Saint-Simonian Courtet, were the colonial council delegates in the SEP, de Reiset from Guadeloupe and Dejean de la Bâtie from Réunion (Bourbon Island). De Reiset insisted that the "races were created at different times in different places." African agriculture was unsophisticated, pastoral peoples were uncivilized, and only white guidance, or racial crossing, as in the colonies, could improve blacks.[98] The conservative baron d'Eckstein also argued that blacks never had a civilization. Contrary to Schoelcher's example of the improvement of Gauls, Gauls had already been civilized, so there was no analogy to the potential of blacks.[99]

Perhaps the most distinctly polygenist participant after Courtet was the former Geographical Society secretary Louis Vivien de Saint-Martin. His support for Casimir-Périer in 1841 and nostalgia for Guizot in the 1870s revealed his social conservatism.[100] As editor of the periodical *Nouvelles annales des voyages* in the 1840s, Vivien made sure to include a section on "ethnology," which reported faithfully the activities of the SEP. In the discussion of 1847, Vivien, too, insisted that whites brought "Aryan" civilization to Europe while blacks could not civilize themselves.[101] In lectures beginning in 1843 he suggested to the SEP the likelihood of a "certain number of foyers of creation" for human races, since there was a "diversity of centres of creation for organized beings in general." The "unity of the species," he continued, "was a dogma to be questioned," since no influence of climate or regimen would be sufficient to produce the disparities separating the black and European. In 1847 Vivien repeated that the known facts could not make conceivable how a single couple could be ancestors of such distinct races. The He-

97 *NAV* 5ᵉ sér., 10 (1847): 378, 386; *NAV* 5ᵉ sér., 11 (1847): 237; *NAV* 5ᵉ sér., 12 (1847): 119–20; *BSEP* 2 (1847): 85–90, 96, 173, 238.

98 *NAV* 5ᵉ sér., 10 (1847): 376, 381; *NAV* 5ᵉ sér., 11 (1847): 86–7, 91; *BSEP* 2 (1847): 85, 92, 121, 126; on the Guadeloupe delegates' proposals for a Fourierist associationist community on very onerous terms for freed slaves, see Jennings, *French Anti-Slavery*, 248–9.

99 On d'Eckstein, see Eckstein *Lettres inédites de baron d'Eckstein*; *NAV* 5ᵉ sér., 10 (1847): 386; *BSEP* 2 (1847): 95.

100 Vivien de Saint-Martin, *Histoire générale de la Révolution française*, 1:3, 97, 112; 2:440; ASG MS. in-4° 12, Vivien de Saint-Martin "Études d'histoire générale," t. 1: 11–14; t. 7, 271, 285.

101 *NAV* 5ᵉ sér., 12 (1847): 124–5; *BSEP* 2 (1847): 242.

brew professor and Islamicist at the Theology Faculty of the Sorbonne, abbé Jean-Joseph-Léandre Bargès, countered that if the unity of the species were uncertain, why should the members not rely on Biblical tradition? D'Avezac insisted on the freedom of scholars to question tradition.

Vivien exemplified the trend away from linguistic classification. Unlike Edwards and d'Eichthal, he found physical differences far more important.[102] Siberia had similar ethnic groups speaking many languages, while North American natives had many languages despite their physical similarities. Anthropology was principally concerned, he said, with the "physical or natural viewpoint of man." Such considerations, however, did not spell the death knell for the Aryan theory. In the 1840s Vivien preferred terms such as "Hindu-Celtic" or "Indo-Germanic" to Caucasian, since the Caucasus was a place of migration rather than origins. He prefigured the full acceptance of the Aryan theory in his later manuscripts by labeling the Medes of the Near East "Ariennes" or "Iraniennes" and suggesting that the Aral Sea was an important point of origin of Europeans.[103]

REPORT OF THE 1847 DISCUSSION AND THE
DECLINE OF THE SOCIETY

In early July 1847, the SEP Commission presented its concluding report.[104] Not surprisingly, d'Eichthal reproved Schoelcher for the dogma of absolute equality. This conclusion would destroy ethnology, which was about the "classification of races according to their characteristic differences."[105] The misuse of anatomy was no reason to reject it. The commission agreed with Courtet that the admitted accomplishments of peoples such as the Galla, Foulah, and Caffir would not support Schoelcher's egalitarianism since these groups were not "Negro." Moreover,

102 *MSEP* 2 (1845): xxxvii–viii, xli, 46–75; also published separately, *Recherches sur l'histoire de l'anthropologie*, 9, 11, 16, 20; see his manuscript fully endorsing the primacy of Aryans in ASG, MS in-4° 12, Vivien de Saint-Martin; on Humboldt, see *NAV* 5ᵉ sér., 7 (1846): 357 and 8 (1846): 228; *BSEP* 1 (1846): 81. Arthur de Gobineau, little known among ethnologists and anthropologists, would soon once again insist on a corresponding hierarchy of race and language, while Abel Hovelacque would take an intermediate position between Broca's physicalism and Ernest Renan's linguistic emphasis; see Desmet, "Abel Hovelacque," 55.

103 Vivien de Saint-Martin, *Recherches sur les populations primitives*, 1:13, 95, 170, 189; read to the SEP in 1846.

104 *NAV* 5ᵉ sér., 12 (1847): 102–16; *BSEP* 2 (1847): 218–33.

105 *NAV* 5ᵉ sér., 12 (1847): 104; *BSEP* 2 (1847): 221.

Schoelcher's examples of commercially and agriculturally advanced peoples all benefited from Arab or Islamic contact. However, the commission disapproved Courtet's association of intellectual capacity with beauty of physical type, as well as his redefinition of the category of "Negro." Thinking of his friend Isidore Geoffroy Saint-Hilaire (who nevertheless was a monogenist), d'Eichthal argued that naturalists now believed in parallel series of organisms, not one single Great Chain.[106] This belief would be easily compatible with post-Darwinian polygenism later in the Society of Anthropology.

In the spirit of scholarly concord, which formed the ethos of so many learned societies, d'Eichthal tried to reconcile the conclusions of the two opponents. Schoelcher acknowledged a need for European education of blacks to "propagate our civilization," so he was implicitly denying absolute equality. Courtet realized that freed blacks would need help from Europeans and might be educable. Therefore, both saw the need of whites to assist blacks in a paternal fashion.

On the monument question, the commission sided with Courtet – blacks did not civilize Egypt. In a nineteenth-century "not out of Africa" argument, they argued that Egypt was less influential on Greece than Herodotus and others had claimed.[107] On the whole, then, the conclusions of the SEP dovetailed well with the viewpoint of the geographers. Since less developed races would need tutelage even if they could be improved by contact, Europeans would have good reason to intervene to civilize them. And those classified as a different species would be implicitly limited, at least in their intellectual potential, whatever their moral perfectibility. Europeans could treat them as incorrigible, and with the benevolence of superior beings.

Even before the Revolution of 1848, d'Eichthal reported that falling attendance at Society meetings induced him to consider resigning as secretary.[108] No doubt the Revolution disrupted the Society, though the achievement of slave emancipation in April 1848, partly through the efforts of Schoelcher himself as a deputy minister in the new republican government, may not have been the reason for the falling attendance. Rodrigues was preoccupied with mobilizing credit, Courtet became distracted with electoral politics, while d'Eichthal recruited Geoffroy, Urbain, and Lenormant for a "religious democracy" discus-

---

106 *NAV* 5ᵉ sér., 12 (1847): 105, 108, 112; *BSEP* 2 (1847): 223, 226, 230.
107 *NAV* 5ᵉ sér., 12 (1847): 113–16; *BSEP* 2 (1847): 232–3.
108 BA, Fonds d'Eichthal, MS. 14720, 9v and 25.

sion group.[109] In January 1849, Quatrefages, Vivien, and d'Orbigny were attending d'Eichthal's meetings on European "re-organization," including Italian unification. After Vivien failed to persuade the Paris Geographical Society to merge with the SEP in 1849, the ethnologists came under pressure for reasons not entirely clear from Louis-Napoleon Bonaparte's government, and stopped meeting in 1850. A plan to promote a statistical study of the ethnology of the French never materialized until the anthropologists' prize contest of 1873. D'Eichthal's correspondence mentioned a desire to revive the Society (with Lenormant, d'Orbigny, Quatrefages, d'Avezac, Maury, and Lamartine, plus the physicians Robin and Follin). By 1859, Broca and the linguist Léon de Rosny had respectively founded the Anthropology and Ethnography societies.[110] The Anthropology Society refused a merger effort from the few remaining Ethnological Society members in 1860, but in 1873 finally accepted the SEP treasury and surviving documents.[111]

FRENCH ETHNOLOGY AND AMERICAN POLYGENISM

Stephen Jay Gould has elaborately dissected the voluntary or involuntary biases of Morton in his famous series of cranial measurements of native American and Egyptian remains.[112] Late in 1847, there was a sign of the symbiotic relationship of the SEP with Morton and the "American" school. Morton proclaimed limited degrees of fertility of hybrids according to the proximity of the species, and Isidore Geoffroy Saint-Hilaire accepted a similar view, though only for animal, non-human species. Other SEP members thereby concluded that human interracial fertile marriages did not prove a single species. D'Eichthal trumpeted a justification of Edwards's idea that proximate races might produce offspring close to the stronger of the original races, while distant races would produce mixed offspring.[113]

109 Ibid., MS. 13751/76, fols 15, 19–21.
110 Ibid., MS. 13751/339, fol. 50v; Lacombe, "Essai sur les origines."
111 Musée de l'Homme, Archives de la Société d'Anthropologie de Paris, M1 1745, letter of Vaïsse to Quatrefages, and M1 1660, letter of d'Eichthal; for the 1850 meeting see the unnumbered bundle "Société d'ethnologie."
112 Gould, *The Mismeasure of Man*, 82–101.
113 On Morton, see Jean-Louis Fischer, "Espèce et hybrides," 255 in Atran, ed. *Histoire du concept d'espèce*; *NAV* 5ᵉ sér., 12 (1847): 356; *BSEP* 2 (1847): 260; for the implications of French anthropological views on the slavery debate in the United States, see Forest, "De l'abolitionnisme."

In 1855 d'Eichthal reviewed for the Geographical Society the work of Morton's American polygenist disciples, Josiah Nott, an Alabama physician and defender of slavery, and George R. Gliddon. He disapproved their prejudices against blacks, but agreed with their "ethnological opinions" concerning an "essential inferiority of the black, in scientific capabilities," compensated by the "sympathetic faculties" of blacks.[114]

Meanwhile, Nott and Gliddon repeatedly employed the findings of French theorists and SEP members along with Morton and British authors.[115] In 1844 Nott cited Virey in his plea for the "Caucasian" nature of Egyptian mummies. The illustrations of the massive *Types of Mankind* (1854) collection employed plates from Courtet and the Dumoutier anthropological atlas. Nott's introduction extensively discussed W.-F. Edwards's idea that the primitive diversity of racial types is permanent. The authors also cited the polygenist naval surgeon from the Dumont d'Urville expedition, Honoré Jacquinot. The American school accepted d'Eichthal on the Foulah as a distinct type from the Negro.[116] In their second major work in 1857, they were delighted at d'Eichthal's remark to Schoelcher that there would be no ethnology if there were no racial distinctions.[117]

Like Lenormant, Nott and Gliddon made reference to the Egyptian statue at the Theban temple at Karnak from the nineteenth dynasty of Menepthah I with the god Horus conducting four groups of different races. They could thus allege that blacks with the identical cranial shape had had the same "benighted fate" for 5,000 years. While the SEP was far from their only source, their attitudes on perfectibility were similar to the those of SEP commission – blacks were susceptible only of a limited degree of improvement, and, when freed without white contacts, might relapse into barbarism.[118]

In the context of this militant polygenism of 1854–57, the new anthropology professor Quatrefages accepted a version of black per-

---

114 *BSG* 4th sér., 9 (1855): 53–65, esp. 64–5; Blanckaert, "L'Esclavage des Noirs," 394–5.

115 Stanton, *The Leopard's Spots*; Horsman, *Josiah Nott of Mobile*; Blanckaert, "L'Esclavage des Noirs," 391–417; Forest, "De l'abolitionnisme."

116 Josiah Nott, "Two Lectures on the Natural History of the Caucasian and Negro Races" (Mobile, 1844), reprinted in Faust, ed. *The Ideology of Slavery?*, 206–38; Nott and Gliddon, *Types of Mankind*, 49–52, 62; on Edwards, 89–105.

117 Nott and Gliddon, *Indigenous Races of the Earth*, 404.

118 Nott and Gliddon, *Types of Mankind*, 85, 95–6, 188–9, 196, 422–3, 465; see also Lenormant, *Musée des Antiquités Egyptiennes*, Planche VII Thèbes, planche 10, nos. 17 and 19.

fectibility. Like Broca, Quatrefages had the self-image of scrupulous scientific neutrality untouched by political and religious contamination.[119] By 1856, he clearly wished, along with his colleague Isidore Geoffroy Saint-Hilaire, to preclude speculation about races or species intermediate between apes and humans. For Quatrefages there was a separate human kingdom, later defined by the unique characteristics of morality and religiosity.[120]

SIGNIFICANCE OF THE SEP

Broca's deliberate eclipse of the SEP debates attempted to brand them as unjustly politicized and narrow in their conception of anthropology.[121] True enough, the motivations of the SEP egalitarians Schoelcher and Rodrigues stemmed from their anti-slavery passion and, later, sympathy for the colonized.[122] Yet even before anthropologists accepted as authentic the discovery of human fossil remains, the SEP had considered problems that Broca thought fundamental. They sought to situate humans in nature. In ordering the races, species, or types, they commented on whether "inferior" non-Europeans could be considered transitional to forms of "animality" such as the orangutan or higher apes. Courtet insisted on this humiliating conclusion. On the whole, even subtle opponents like d'Eichthal and Quatrefages rejected such overt beliefs that less perfectible races were not fully human. However, d'Eichthal was ready to conclude that blacks could not spontaneously reach civilization.

Most SEP naturalists fervently wished for study of the influence of the physical environment in cases of migration to determine susceptibility of the organism to change. If races had evolved within a single species under climatic influence, there was greater room for development by education, as Quatrefages continually argued. They also hoped to solve whether interbreeding would improve "inferior" races. The evidence of Morton led many among them to refuse to define a species by the

---

119 See Quatrefages's own note in AN, AJ 15 551.

120 *Revue des cours publics* 2, no. 26 (29 juin 1856): 404–7; no. 28 (13 juillet 1856): 23–7, 70; Forest, "De l'abolitionnisme," 88; for the complex views of Serres, see Blanckaert, "La Création," 101–23.

121 *MSAP* 3 (1868–69): xxxvi–xli.

122 Schmidt, *Victor Schoelcher en son temps*, 74. Schoelcher had at one point considered peaceful colonization a corollary to abolition of slavery; see Cohen, *The French Encounter with Africans*, 273.

Labeling People

incomplete sterility of hybrids. They could not resolve, but were continually fascinated by, the question of whether some human varieties indeed constituted distinct species.

The linguistic mode of classification pioneered by Balbi clearly impressed Edwards and d'Eichthal, but by the late 1840s, Vivien was redefining anthropology to focus on physical traits. The linguistic theory had helped promote the Aryan view of European descent, voiced by Courtet, Vivien, Troyer, and Duprat well before the work of Arthur de Gobineau. Exploration of cultural issues and customs, supposedly the major aspect of SEP interests, reached its full potential in works such as d'Avezac's on the Yebu. Even there, d'Avezac did not allow the Yebu slave an authentic, unmediated voice. Cultural surveys such as those of Pavie, Benet, and Löwenstern betrayed a kind of Orientalist notion of contempt or lack of empathy for the other.

The SEP devoted a surprising amount of attention to the discussion of physical features in view of the small section on the physical in the original mission statement. While only Courtet and Dumoutier subscribed fully to phrenology, Edwards, d'Eichthal, and Milne-Edwards had ruminated on its applicability. Most members of the SEP did not accept the doctrines of Gall and Spurzheim, but they continued to believe that organic deficiencies, measurable in some cases by a "prognathic" profile, entailed cultural deficiencies. To Courtet, facial angle, facial features, and head shape were the indispensable indicators of intellectual capacity. The crucial scientific question was whether certain races could spontaneously attain civilization, to what extent, and under what influences. Non-Europeans with deficient profiles could allegedly never achieve the same level of perfectibility. If, as Edwards maintained, types were permanent, ethnology could work against notions of susceptibility to the milieu. This principle of permanence of racial types, even after Darwin's challenge to the entire notion of fixed species, had great resonance even later in the century.

Despite some ethnologists' opposition to slavery, such views could give comfort to American pro-slavery theorists who would postulate inferiority of Africans and increased infertility of "mixed" people of colour. The arguments about Egyptian monuments were also a nineteenth-century version of the debates about how civilized Africans were, and what their influence was in Egypt and Greece.

There was no direct correlation of political views in the SEP to theories of racial hierarchy. Ultra-conservative pro-Bourbon authors such as d'Eckstein could firmly endorse a hierarchy, but so could Saint-

Simonian progressives such as Courtet. In a milder form than Courtet, d'Eichthal shared a concept of a functional and organic hierarchy. The tradition of anti-clerical scepticism even allowed geographers like Vivien and d'Avezac to cry for scientific freedom so polygenism could challenge the religious constraints of a Prichard.

Within the SEP, the Saint-Simonian influence was ambivalent. As a new religion of social reform, it attacked privilege and fostered opportunities for women and workers. Rodrigues illustrated its egalitarian potential. But Courtet and d'Eichthal more typically represented the principle of Saint-Simonian functional hierarchy, with blacks indelibly subordinate or patronizingly analogous to women. Their organic society was meritocratic, dynamic, and somewhat sympathetic to Islam, but still resolutely Eurocentric.

Naturalists like Milne-Edwards, Quatrefages, and Dumoutier nominally subscribed to the unity of the species, but not to racial equality. Craniological theories of inequality influenced Milne-Edwards well into the 1880s, while Dumoutier remained convinced that head shapes of races influenced mental capacity. Other members of the Dumont d'Urville expedition, the polygenists Hombron and Jacquinot, eagerly joined the SEP before its demise. Quatrefages may have been a monogenist charitable to "savages" and to increased educational potential of non-Europeans. In notions of ultimate European superiority, though, he differed only marginally from his later anthropological colleagues such as Broca. Geographers such as d'Avezac were receptive to accounts of African culture, but still labeled blacks as aberrant. Even Fourierist radicals such as Duprat and Thomassy constructed a Berber identity that suited French imperial goals. On the other hand, religious conservative monogenists such as de Salle could be more defiantly anti-colonialist. Though de Salle opposed Islam, he was astute enough to see how the arguments of polygenists could serve slaveholders and imperial adventurers.

The real impact of the SEP, with its small contingent of members, cannot be reduced to readers of its publications. Milne-Edwards's illustrated racial caricatures appeared in texts approved for use in the collèges and écoles normales primaires through nearly forty years of French history. Naturalists such as Quatrefages wrote for the *Revue des deux mondes*, which had a small circulation of about 2,000 among opinion leaders. Schoelcher's articles lambasting slaveowners' refusal to allow abolition and their manifold abuses appeared in Alexandre Ledru-Rollin's *La Réforme*, another small-circulation newspaper (also about

2,000). Yet this paper would be a critical vector of discontent in 1848. In 1847, of course, petitions were already circulating among thousands of artisans, clergy, and teachers calling for the abolition of slavery.[123] Radical publications like the *Revue indépendante* were the favoured medium for Fourierist members such as Duprat and Thomassy.[124] Press articles about French expansion elsewhere in the world most likely did not reach a mass audience before the 1880s, when a mass-circulation press began to feature them.[125] Yet the theories voiced in the SEP were important subjects of discussion among the cultural elite – professors of the Muséum and members of the Academy of Sciences (witness Serres's report on Dumoutier). Most important, the SEP bestowed a legacy to future learned societies that enabled theories of racial hierarchy to underpin their view of the world.

While the Muséum courses partly institutionalized anthropology, the SEP played a key role in prefiguring the discourse of the Paris Anthropological Society. In 1889 linguistic anthropologist Abel Hovelacque considered equatorial Africans to be "big children," much as Dumoutier had characterized the Pacific islanders. He concluded that since they were "immutable" it was hopeless to try to transmit European civilization to them.[126] The construction of the concept of race may have reflected multiple insecurities of Europeans – the need to protect themselves against turbulent working classes or native peoples, the fear of miscegenation, or fears about varieties of sexuality.[127]

As the cases of Arthur de Gobineau, Robert Knox, Herbert Spencer, and even Broca himself show, the impulse to indulge in rank-ordering of races did not always lead to enthusiasm for colonization.[128] In fact, polygenism could gain support by the concept of lack of adaptability of Europeans to other climates. This alleged difference in species could be less conducive to imperial adventure than a monogenism that permitted

123 Seymour Drescher, "British Way, French Way: Opinion Building and Revolution in the Second French Slave Emancipation," *American Historical Review* 96, 3 (1991): 709–34, reprinted in his *From Slavery to Freedom*, 158–95.

124 For circulation figures, see Ian McKeane, Institute of Irish Studies, University of Liverpool, "Selective Bibliography."

125 Schneider, *An Empire for the Masses*; Hale, "Races on display."

126 Desmet, "Abel Hovelacque," 77.

127 See Young, *Colonial Desire*, 142–82; on the social context of British racism, Lorimer, "Theoretical Racism," esp. 428–30; Lorimer, "Science and the Secularization," esp. 228–9.

128 Cohen, *The French Encounter with Africans*, 260–1 argues that racism did not arise merely as a rationalization for imperialism since racists were divided on empire before the 1880s, but I would add it still functioned as an effective rationalization.

successful migrations of peoples.[129] But such racial classification, endemic in the SEP statement of mission, continued to be a principal concern of anthropologists later in the century. The image of inferior Pacific islanders and Africans purveyed by geographers and ethnologists could certainly facilitate the appropriation of more naval stations and missions of conquest or civilization in west and central Africa. A recent study of Algeria demonstrates how military medical personnel often became politically influential promoters of colonization because of their ethnological research.[130] "Race" allowed allegedly objective physical criteria to be linked to the moral and intellectual capabilities of humans. Hence, Henry Louis Gates, in arguing for the constructed nature of "race," has called it a "dangerous trope."[131]

Theories of racial hierarchy had permeated the elite, helped justify the continuing saga of French domination of Algeria, and could become a condition for a more aggressive age of imperial expansion. While abolition of slavery had ended one era, even the most ardent abolitionists contemplated the necessity of stopping the internal slave trade by European intervention to "civilize" the natives, including possibly colonizing them. With the extension of French interests in the Pacific and southeast Asia, and eventually the annexation of territory in the interior of sub-Saharan Africa, French administrators had at their disposal a convenient rationale of racial superiority.

129 Blanckaert, "La Crise de l'Anthropométrie," esp. 114–22.

130 Harvey, "Races Specified, Evolution Transformed" 115, 134; Lorcin, *Imperial Identities*; Lorcin, "Imperialism, Colonial Identity" argues that French physicians in Algeria, including some Saint-Simonians, reputed to be civilizing and humanitarian agents, contributed to the "categorization and marginalization" of the indigenous population; see 662 for the report of the military surgeon Lacger to the SEP in 1841 on the peoples of Algeria, 667 for physicians praised by Broca, 673–4 for activities of Périer and Jean-Christian Boudin.

131 Blanckaert, "Le système des races," 36; Gates,"Writing 'Race' and the Difference It Makes," in his *"Race," Writing, and Difference*, 1–20, esp. 5.

6

Constructing the "Other" in the Early Social Sciences

The learned societies discussed so far each played a critical role in the formation of disciplinary domains of the early social sciences. The activity of the Société phrénologique de Paris anticipated at some crude, elemental level neuroscientific principles of cerebral localization, by aspiring to relate brain organs to intellect and personality. The reading of head shapes dimly foreshadowed the more sophisticated quantitative techniques of testing for intellectual and psychological dispositions. Of course, modern psychologists find phrenology extravagant, laughable, and unprovable. But in its cultural context, it both created a sensation and assumed the dimensions of a serious scientific activity. Thereby it became a favourite subject of discussion (pro or con) in the earliest scholarly societies of medical psychology. In seeking to diagnose dispositions to individual eccentricity, it resembled later nineteenth-century efforts to read the limitations of character from symptoms of degeneration or from a "criminal" visage. At one remove from the early years of French empirical psychology in the 1870s, it helped solidify the claim that some of the most important individual inclinations were hereditary.

The Société de géographie de Paris stimulated interest not only in cartography and physical geography but also in voyages of reconnaissance that observed inhabitants of distant regions. The excitement about economic or imperial opportunities in these areas, along with anguish about defeat by Germany in 1870, propelled the fascination for societies of commercial geography. In turn, the atmosphere of expanding markets and more colonial possessions helped institutionalize the study of geography in universities. The Société ethnologique de Paris debated the nature of the human species and propounded doctrines of racial hierarchy in a discourse surprisingly continuous with the early debates of the Société d'anthropologie de Paris. The anthropologists who so reluctantly acknowledged their predecessors established a teaching institution in anthropology, a prelude to the post-World War I institutes and university courses that established a recognized discipline of anthropology.

As Edward Said and other theorists of construction of the "Other" have argued, each group created an image that often deprived the human objects of their studies of authentic voices. The learned societies produced doctrines that suited the purpose of those fearful of social deviancy or those who justified domination of non-European peoples. In the Foucauldian sense, their knowledge did help constitute the not always beneficent exercise of power. In a few cases, phrenologists actually did exercise medical administration of an asylum or prison. Imperial administrators were less likely to be imbued with theories of ethnology or anthropology. But they participated in a cultural complex in which there was ceaseless denigration of the savage or of the uncivilizable people. Scientific theories supported the apparent rationality of these labels. If the most reputable students of human nature believed in racial hierarchy, the subordination of other peoples could be a logical (though certainly not inevitable) next step. To acknowledge these realities means raising caveats about the intentions of the social sciences without necessarily agreeing with Foucault that any social science is simply a category mistake or a kind of knowledge constituted concurrently with a will to power.

This account of the pretensions of the discourse of the early social sciences investigates one basic assumption – that some external appearance or internal inherited indicator could signal the state of intellect and character. Almost all proponents recognized, as do recent *Bell Curve* theorists, that intelligence and behaviour result from a mix of innate dispositions and environmental effects (or circumstances for expression of genes). But the dispositions allegedly observable by scientific methods in head shape, facial angle, or similar indices were an open invitation to normalization and domination.

Before the era of Darwin and social pessimism, amid the ostensible idealism of Romantic reformers, learned society members asserted the limits of equalizing opportunities for other "races" and the disturbing consequences of European contact. The phrenologists' map of individual diversity was ambivalent about social mobility. They assessed other peoples as tainted with organic deficiency. The geographers and ethnologists applied the concepts of racial theorists that assumed European superiority.

The following sections will link the conclusions of this study of the era before 1848 to other scholars' perceptions of analogous attitudes in the last third of the nineteenth century. After the failures of the Second Republic, the military defeat of the Franco-Prussian War, and the tragic dénouement of the Paris Commune, the French cultural community was haunted by forebodings of national decline and social insecurity. Just as there was a concern for correlation of all social handicaps during the *Bell Curve* controversy, the resulting uneasiness led to a so-called "linking of all the deviancies." French social scientists searched for the individual and social flaws that were producing a declining birth rate, apparently rising crime, alcoholism, prostitution, and venereal disease.[1] For life scientists attached to neo-Lamarckianism, the theory of inheritance of acquired characteristics, sometimes enhancing the idea of progress, could also bring fears of gradual degeneration of the race. Anthropologists, whether or not they were Darwinist, could foresee the likelihood of extinction of "inferior races," while urging superior Europeans to march to their appointed destiny whatever the cost to others. These exhortations implied "elevating" other races through European guidance or developing the resources of the uncivilizable.

THE LEGACY OF PHRENOLOGY

Like the anthropologists of 1859, the founders of the Société phrénologique as well as its membership were principally physicians. They were, in the words used by Michael Osborne about the Société zoologique d'acclimatation, an "epistemic community" sharing a common intellectual and theoretical commitment.[2] Their influence extended to important converts such as François-Joseph-Victor Broussais and several well-known adherents within the Academy of Medicine. Yet the power brokers in the Academy of Sciences, such as Georges Cuvier and Pierre Flourens, became resolute opponents, and leading experimental physiologists such as François Magendie mocked the claims of phrenology. While young physicians were numerous among the Phrenological Society members, limited data does not reveal a systematic age bias as at Edinburgh, where the supporters of phrenology were more youthful than its opponents. On the whole, phrenologists knocked on

---

1 Nye, *Crime, Madness, and Politics,* xiv, 69, 160–1, 297–9.
2 Osborne, *Nature, the Exotic,* xiv.

the doors of respectability without quite achieving it. Physicians and philosophers interested in psychology would debate their claims.

Phrenologists who precisely correlated physical organs and mental faculties made most conservatives and devout Catholics wary either of alleged materialism or of questioning the integrity of the soul. Yet the assumption that phrenologists were progressive reformers, despite their anti-Bourbon (or even Carbonaro) heritage, needs important qualifications. Gall and Spurzheim already represented, respectively, more pessimistic and optimistic attitudes toward social reform. Gall, however, did not deny the power of education, and Spurzheim found moral education far weaker than proto-eugenic breeding. Some phrenologists seemed to be genuine social radicals with generous liberal or socialist proclivities. J.-B. Mège (within an economic liberal framework), Auguste Luchet, and Adrien Berbrugger, while reading dispositions from cranial protuberances, wished to empower individuals to realize their own potential. Such indeed had been the attraction of phrenology to British artisans and Owenites. Reformers could also hope to mitigate harsh treatments in prisons and asylums with proper classification, as Ferrus proposed. Prison physicians sought to isolate the incorrigible or channel strong inclinations into approved activity.

Yet several impulses in phrenology counteracted social radicalism. A few phrenologists did not hesitate to combine their "science" with the art of physiognomy, which could produce a more indelible portrait of organic limitation. Whatever reforms the conservative prison physician Hubert Lauvergne advocated for the stationary galleys, his harshness anticipated later notions of the incorrigible criminal. The Saint-Simonian impulse evident in several leading phrenologists such as E.-M. Bailly de Blois was often unfriendly to social mobility. Hippolyte Bruyères, Casimir Broussais, and even the ex-Carbonaro J.-L.-A. Fossati offered little hope that the legislators of society would rise from the ranks of the humble. True enough, the banker and Ethnology Society member Olinde Rodrigues derived an egalitarian compassionate attitude from his early Saint-Simonian flirtation. Other former Saint-Simonians would characteristically value the classification of talent by the phrenologist-expert, who would advise all about their appropriate functional niche in an organic society.

Even a virulent anti-clerical and republican such as the elder Broussais could decide that the masses needed most of all to work and learn affection for each other. Like the prison physician Emile Debout, he would maintain both social and racial hierarchy. Liberal or ex-Carbonaro

opponents of the Bourbons, such as Emmanuel de Las Cases, J.-B. Beunaiche de la Corbière, and Fossati were at heart anti-democratic. The
alienist Félix Voisin, chief physician at Bicêtre, once a radical fulminating
against aristocrats and the financial elite, in the end found revolution
frightening and expressed concern about the defence of property. His
own vacillations encapsulate the dilemmas of the phrenologist – environmental influences might profoundly affect criminality, but he would
willingly classify criminals by defective cerebral organization. The more
important the cerebral organs were, the less scope there was for rehabilitation. While Voisin had been sensitive to the handicaps of the impoverished and of the neglected children, he ultimately returned to Guizot's
work ethic.

The classificatory impulses of phrenology applied not only to individuals but also, in a condescending manner, to non-European peoples.
Gall was certainly not overtly racist, but from the founders' generation,
there was greater empathy for American natives than for Africans or
other darker-skinned peoples. Pierre-Alexandre Dumoutier fought against
J.-J. Virey's harsh judgment of the Charruas of Uruguay, but questioned
the maturity of the Marquesas islanders and was clearly contemptuous
of Melanesians. Phrenology also fuelled the extremely rigid view of Victor Courtet de l'Isle, among geographers and ethnologists. For him, racial endowment produced existing castes, so that, like Joseph Vimont,
he could even endorse slavery. The founder of the Société ethnologique
de Paris, William-Frédéric Edwards, who believed in the permanence of
types, dabbled in phrenology before he found it wanting statistically.
Gustave d'Eichthal, the heart and soul of the SEP, would use a phrenological argument in his private correspondence to Enfantin to call forth
the patronizing image of the feminine-black.

With few exceptions, those phrenologists and geographers who discussed gender roles repeated conventional cultural stereotypes. They
judged women, like blacks, to be predominantly sensitive and affective,
incapable of the highest exercise of reflective faculties. Explorers in the
Geographical Society reacted to the reception women gave them, and
reported voyeuristically on the contours of their bodies. There were
contradictory observations of the uniformity of the eternally feminine
with the peculiarly "disgraced" nature of the "savage" woman, hardly
more delicate than her male relatives. Hence, civilization in that latter
sense created notions of the "feminine."

The Société phrénologique de Paris seems to have collapsed in the
spring of 1848. There were sporadic, largely unsuccessful efforts to

revive phrenology during the Second Empire, often with concessions to Catholic spiritualism. The popularizers who employed physiognomy, such as Victor-Frédéric-Alexandre Ysabeau and Isidore Bourdon, remained active in the 1860s. There were also faddists who sold phrenological wigs, assorted magnetizers, and the hilarious "phrenyogénie" of Bernard Moulin (1868). This latter art, described by Renneville, intended to give aptitudes to children according to the thoughts of the partners during the sexual activity when the children were conceived.[3]

DEGENERACY AND THE "BORN CRIMINAL"

To round out discussion of the legacy of phrenology, we shall reflect on previous scholars' studies of theories of heritable dispositions after 1850 – degeneracy theory and the criminal as atavism. Work on the prehistory of psychiatry has assessed the rise of degeneracy theory as ensuring the survival of this emerging profession, for in the 1850s, clerics still attacked alienists for their suspected materialism and politically liberal critics thought asylum therapy had failed. Degeneracy theory also appears to have given evidence of pervasive cultural fears as important as the power/knowledge strategies highlighted by Foucault.[4]

Voisin joined the Société médico-psychologique, a group animated by the reformist Catholic physician Philippe Buchez that became a clearinghouse of ideas for medical psychopathology. While their journal, the *Annales medico-psychologiques*, began appearing in 1843, by the time of the definitive organization of the Société in 1852, phrenology was a spent force and its critics were paramount in the new society. In the 1850s, the conservative Catholic alienist Bénédict-Augustin Morel (1809–73), a member of Buchez's circle and of the Société médico-psychologique, purveyed doctrines of the heritability of nervous pathology and its dangers for the production of "sickly varieties of the human species." Having studied "cretins" and worked with Jean-Pierre Falret and Guillaume Ferrus, Morel, the director of the Saint-Yon asylum near Rouen, produced a major treatise on intellectual, moral, and physical degeneracy in 1857.[5] Visible signs were an important component of this diagnosis. There was no one head type yielding degeneracy, but a poor

3 Renneville, *Le Langage des cranes*, 275–7, 279–84; see also ch. 3.
4 Dowbiggin, *Inheriting Madness*, 5–6; see also Pick, *Faces of Degeneration*, 41; Goldstein, *Console and Classify*, 339–76.
5 Pick, *Faces of Degeneration*, 44–59; Renneville, *La Médecine du crime*, 2:544, 551–6.

conformation of the head, along with short stature or other signs of arrested development, were telltale indicators. For example, a small, narrow, and prominent forehead was a "vicious conformation of the head" indicating bad tendencies.[6] In 1864 he commented further on the detrimental effects of exaggerated upper jawbones, prominent lips, and a flat nose.[7] Morel helped inaugurate the concept of a domestic degenerate akin to a savage or primitive, which stimulated study of a criminal anthropology of the "dangerous classes."[8]

The causes of degeneracy could be inherited, but could also be a variety of environmental "intoxicants," such as alcohol, narcotics, swampy soil, or dietary deficiency. Sections of his treatise would be unremarkable today in studies of iodine deficiency or fetal alcohol syndrome. There were in addition the "mixed" physical and moral factors of overcrowded or unsanitary urban or factory milieus, permeated by alcoholism, malnutrition, and the temptations of poverty. The significant aspect of degeneracy and the profound social fear was that, whatever the cause, it was a slippery slope. Each succeeding generation could depart more from the normal human type. These "profound, permanent" changes "transmissible by heredity" could lead from mental disturbance to imbecility and eventually sterility, and would be almost impossible to reverse.[9]

Morel's neo-Lamarckianism was double-edged. On the one hand, he always claimed to be interested principally in prevention and remedial approaches to the mentally or physically ill. His Christian convictions placed much faith in the efficacy of preaching, temperance, improvements in diet – in short, physical and moral hygiene.[10] On the other hand, Morel saw the victims of degeneracy as beyond help (other than prison or asylum regimen) once they were born with or acquired

6 Morel, *Traité*, 62, 68–70, 489; see also Atlas, plate 10, fig. 2, cited in Heilmann, "Die Bertillonnage," esp. 39–40.

7 Morel, *De la formation du type dans les variétés dégénérées ou nouveaux éléments d'anthropologie morbide pour faire suite à la théorie des dégénerescences dans l'espèce humaine* (1864), cited in Renneville, *La Médecine du crime*, 2:556–60.

8 Morel, *Traité*, 461, 687 on degenerate or degraded "classes"; Blanckaert, "Des sauvages," esp. 63.

9 Morel, *Traité*, 125, 438; Renneville, *La Médecine du crime*, 2: 552–4; Dowbiggin, *Inheriting Madness*, 151–4.

10 Morel, *Traité*, 326, 332, 356–7, 397 on morality; 604–9 on public health measures; Pick, *Faces of Degeneration*, 59–67; Dowbiggin, *Inheriting Madness*, 127–39; Renneville, "De la régénération," 16–17.

the tainted disposition. The non-receptivity to education was in fact the marker of whether the individual was truly degenerate.[11]

Interestingly enough, Morel's fervent Christian faith induced him to proclaim, against Virey and Bory, the unity of the human species. He believed in the educability of "natural" (not degenerate) varieties, including "Hottentots" and "Eskimos," and waxed eloquent about the efforts of missionaries in French Guiana and Greenland.[12] Had he been in the Anthropology Society, he would have sided with the monogenists on the perfectibility of all races, without subscribing to the equality of their intellectual faculties. However, somewhat like Spurzheim earlier, he admitted that such educability would be very slow, and the surest means of elevating a race would be interbreeding under the right moral and religious conditions. Furthermore, some barbarous races were predestined to disappear since they lacked the aptitudes to flourish when confronted by civilization. "Morbid heredity" was therefore a challenging subject of study for anthropologists.[13]

Not only was Morel's work highly influential on a generation of French alienists, but the heritability of psychological inclinations became a cornerstone for the work of the founder of French empirical psychology, Théodule Ribot. While Ribot read many British and German psychologists, his concept of "morbid heredity" of dispositions to hallucinations or mania owed much to the French "alienist" tradition, including Jules Baillarger and Falret. The heredity of acquired characteristics, as with Morel, remained a linchpin of Ribot's biological thought. His controversial thesis on "psychological heredity" (1873) outlined a theory of the heritability of penchants or instincts, including inclinations analogous to Gall's dispositions to steal and murder.[14] Political views might shape the response to hereditary pathology (preaching and moralization for the conservatives, public action against pathological environments for the progressives). The resemblance to phrenology was not only in the search for visible cranial signs but also in the conviction that an innate individual disposition could come to control intelligence and character.

11 Morel, *Traité*, 467.

12 Ibid., 16n., 41, 441–2, 471.

13 Ibid., 440, 497, 519, 523; on the parallelism of physical degeneracy and racial degeneration, see also Blanckaert, "L'ethnographie de la decadence," esp. 61, 64–5.

14 Nicolas et Murray, "Le fondateur de la psychologie," 1–42; Nicolas, "L'Hérédité psychologique," esp. 307–10, 323, 331–2; see also Renneville, *La Médecine du crime*, 2:623.

The concurrent debates of the 1870s and 1880s all over Europe and in North America over the "born criminal" (a term invented by Enrico Ferri) identified by the physician Cesare Lombroso (1835–1909) perpetuated the search for "stigmata" on the face or other body parts. Lombroso's reading of Darwin stressed atavisms or "throwbacks" to previous human or animal-like states. Studying soldiers and prisoners, he contended that a considerable and most violent proportion of the criminal population had hereditary inclinations to their crime. Claude Blanckaert has pointed out that theories of atavism flourished in response to the new findings of "primitive" European human fossils, the pathology of small-brained "microcephalics," and of mixed-race individuals.[15]

The anti-clerical Lombroso derived ideas both from Morel and from Paul Broca's craniometry. In *L'uomo delinquente* (1876), Lombroso had carefully catalogued stigmata including small cranial capacity, a sugar-loaf head shape, and various curves of the skull or cephalic indices, in which criminals might be comparable to "primitive" peoples such as "Hottentots and Bushmen."[16] Other indicators were the receding forehead, a "prognathism found in Negroes and animals," strong canine teeth, a flattened nose and high cheekbones, an occipital depression in the cranium, the shape of arms and ears, prehensile toes, or flat feet. Lombroso also included such cultural phenomena as tattooing and argot, which he classified as atavistic.[17] In his opinion, savages were naturally inclined to steal or kill, so what was reproved in civilization was normal for them.[18] Lombroso's system tended to single out those who today would be labeled "dangerous offenders" and assumed that a skilled analyst could identify them.[19]

In later years, Lombroso's views mellowed to the extent that he acknowledged only one-third of all criminals, albeit the most violent and the recidivists, were "born" as such.[20] The consequence was that society would be compelled to sentence more harshly, to isolate, perhaps even transport, or prevent from reproducing, these atavistic types.

---

15 Blanckaert, "Des sauvages."

16 Lombroso, *Criminal Man*, xii–xiii; Gould, *The Mismeasure of Man*, 151–72; Pick, *Faces of Degeneration*, 113–52.

17 Lombroso, *Criminal Man*, xxv, 7; Pick, *Faces of Degeneration*, 122–6; Renneville, "La réception," 110.

18 Lombroso, *Criminal Man*, xxiv, 126–30; Boetsch et Fonton, "L'Ethnographie criminelle."

19 Lombroso, *Criminal Man*, 231–42.

20 Ibid., xiv–xv, xxvii, 8.

Lombroso defended himself against French criticism by admitting the importance for the creation of many criminals of poor education, urban overcrowding, rootlessness, and poverty.[21] His prescriptions were not always repressive. Indeed, he thought divorce would help prevent crimes of passion and freedom of the press would avert the dangerous activities of anarchists. But the balance of his theories fell more on the side of biological determinism than of environmental influence.

One of his most famous French critics was the editor of the *Archives d'anthropologie criminelle* (founded in 1885), Alexandre Lacassagne (1843–1924), a Lyon Medical Faculty professor of legal medicine. Lacassagne notoriously asserted, "the social milieu is the broth of criminality; the microbe is the criminal, an element of no importance until the broth makes him ferment." In theory, Lacassagne was thus a strong proponent of changing the social environment to fight crime. However, Renneville and Mucchielli have shown that his concept of the social corresponded more to the hygienic influences of climate and diet, and their effects in turn on the brain and body.[22] Despite French opposition to Lombroso at the International Congresses of Criminal Anthropology in 1885 and 1889, the debates were quite deceptive. Lacassagne was not at all averse to physical indicators of hereditary criminal dispositions. At one time, he even supported Lombroso's measurements of arm length and height, as well as the analogy to primitive races. Lacassagne also praised phrenology, which he most likely learned from Gall's Lyon disciple Fleury Imbert.

In 1884 Lacassagne accepted Pierre-Louis Gratiolet's threefold classification of races: (1) those with most active organs in the frontal brain (the most developed intelligent and sociable upper classes and the European races, or criminals of calculation); (2) activity in the parietal brain (an intermediate group and the Mongolian race, or of criminals of passion), and (3) activity in the occipital brain (illiterate lower classes and "Negroes with animal instincts," or criminals of instinct). While Lacassagne rejected the concept of atavism, he extended Lombroso's domestic savage idea to characteristics of the lower social classes in France.[23]

21 Ibid., 150–201.

22 For a summary of this view of the heredity-milieu debate, see Nye, *Crime, Madness, and Politics*, 97–133; Renneville, "Alexandre Lacassagne," esp. 128 for citation from Lacassagne, "Les transformations du droit pénal et les progrès de la médecine légale de 1810 à 1912," *Archives de l'anthropologie criminelle* (1913): 364; see also Mucchielli, "Hérédité et milieu social."

23 Renneville, "Alexandre Lacassagne."

While no longer accepting the multiplicity of brain organs in Gall and Spurzheim, Lacassagne thus carried into the twentieth century an interpretation of criminality that stressed hereditary brain configuration. As late as 1909, he was still discussing prominent cheekbones and heavy jaws. Like Morel, Lacassagne believed in the pathological heredity of criminals and hereditary transmission of vices, though some derived from climate, diet, or the habits of city life.[24] This archetypical representative of the "French school," a conservative Gambettist in politics, did admit that social action was needed to fight epidemics and alcoholism. Yet he was harsher than Lombroso himself in his eventual attitude toward capital punishment and penalties for the pathological.[25]

Morel, the Lombrosians, and their French critics such as Lacassagne all sought heritable external characteristics or heritable internal nervous pathology, each with a somewhat different relative weight for the environment. They carried on the tradition of physiognomists and phrenologists – reading dispositions by head shape with potential applicability to social deviants. Neo-Lamarckians such as Morel could fear a gradual spread of degeneration affecting population growth and social ills such as alcoholism. The truly degenerate, stigmatized, or misshapen were domestic savages. While one should not exaggerate their influence on actual legislative debate, Lacassagne supported the law of 1885 in France on "relegation" (deportation without loss of civil rights) of recidivists.[26] So, even without a Lombrosian criminal "type," there was a considerable distance between the heirs of phrenology and the Durkheimian belief in social causes of crime.[27] Study of physical indicators remained a tempting instrument to label individuals.

Only a few anthropologists began to move away from this temptation by questioning anthropometry and the use of all anatomical indicators to reach definitive conclusions about intelligence and character. One of the most vehement opponents of Lombroso and indeed of all biological determinism was Léonce Manouvrier (1850–1927), the most active anthropogist in the Laboratory of the École d'anthropologie and an advocate of civil and political equality for women. By 1893, he clearly

24 Ibid., 130; see also Blanckaert, "Des sauvages" on the French physician Arthur Bordier, 67.

25 Renneville, 124, 136–7; on the continuing primacy of hereditarian explanations in Lacassagne and the Lyon school, see Mucchielli, "Hérédité et milieu social" Renneville, "La réception," esp. 115–16.

26 Renneville, "Alexandre Lacassagne," 136.

27 Mucchielli, "Hérédité et milieu social," 205.

believed that the conditions of the milieu would direct the utilization of individual organic aptitudes.[28]

THE GEOGRAPHICAL SOCIETY AND EMPIRE

The Geographical Society was far more the preserve of amateurs and hobbyists than was the Phrenological Society. Political luminaries, government officials, and lawyers would join the scholars, linguists, cartographers, and explorers who helped found the Society. Human geography was only one of its interests amid classical erudition, maps, statistics, and physical geography.

From the earliest years, Society members such as Edme Jomard, a veteran of the Egypt expedition, and textbook author C.-A. Walckenaer demonstrated their concern for commercial opportunities in the Sudan. In west Africa, east Africa, and the Pacific, strategic rivalry with Britain was often a principal motive in searching for territories appropriate for French expansion. To this end, both travel literature and systematic geographic knowledge were indispensable prerequisites for power politics. The search for a penal colony also stimulated Pacific island expeditions, whatever the possible threat to the survival of indigenous populations. While France seized Pacific bases in response to the British appropriation of New Zealand, annexation policies in Africa were more cautious before 1848. Even then, the search for a mine or the next upriver trading post in the Senegambia region could mean the need for effective French influence and the desirability of territorial control. Where such control was impracticable, as in Abyssinia, commercial opportunities were prime objectives.

From the eighteenth century, geographers as well as ethnologists had the vision of a common, unilinear path to civilization, with increasing sophistication from hunting and gathering societies through pastoral stages through "civilized" agricultural or commercial societies. In the 1847 discussion, the ethnologists idiosyncratically reversed pastoral and agricultural stages so that the Fulani, or Foulah, could be considered a more advanced people than other Africans. But, on the whole, a march to civilization model, without necessarily the same stages, persisted fitfully throughout the nineteenth century, as in the evolutionist anthropology of

28 On the fascinating figure of Manouvrier, see Hecht, "Anthropological Utopias," 159–200, and revised in "A Vigilant Anthropology"; Blanckaert, "La Crise de l'Anthropométrie," 132–59; and Mucchielli, "Sociologie versus anthropologie raciale," esp. 89–90.

Charles Letourneau (1831–1902). This retardation model could function best where the inhabitants seemed closer to European norms of facial features, and favoured attempts to "civilize" and "assimilate" indigenous peoples. Even in west Africa, and particularly Senegal, where quasi-European appearance seemed to coexist with darker skin colour, Geographical Society members perceived sagacious people who could benefit from European guidance.

On the whole, the ethnologists were more eager to place all "Negroes" in a category of limited intellectual capacities, with due allowance for their affective and empathetic nature. Hence, the SEP commission of 1847 eagerly adopted Gustave d'Eichthal's contentions that only contact with Europeans or with Islamic peoples could explain the more rapid progress of coastal African peoples. Abyssinians benefited from the cultural kinship of a common religious heritage, but, except for a few distinct "savage" groups, escaped the perceived disadvantage of a purely African heritage.

The surgeons who traveled on the expeditions of founding members of the Geographical Society, such as J.-R.-C. Quoy and J.-P. Gaimard, eagerly used facial angles as an index of intellectual capacity and assumed that they could discern Gall's penchants to steal or to ferocity as badges of inferiority. R.-P. Lesson's description of the various peoples of the Pacific islands, like the accounts dating from the eighteenth century, produced major modifications of racial theory since they seemed to show that climate was insufficient to differentiate groups. For his part, Lesson had contempt even for Polynesians just a few years before the French annexations of Tahiti and the Marquesas. J.-S.-C. Dumont d'Urville had great respect for the vigorous, dignified New Zealanders and avoided belief in polygenism. But he gave a pretext for Courtet's postulation of a graduated scale of superiority from black to yellow to white races. The aftermath of Dumont's voyage produced an outpouring of polygenist speculation as well as Dumoutier's contempt for Melanesians. No doubt the militant abolitionism of the 1840s helped stimulate this reaction. While not all geographers of this era wrote off the civilizability of these peoples, they were sure that the "savage" was doomed to perish on European contact. Both explorers and armchair geographers helped justify European tutelage or domination whenever the government felt inclined to act.

As geography struggled to find a suitable paradigm for its discipline, the Geographical Society became more and more interested in French expansion. The Navy and Colonies minister from 1860 to 1867, marquis Prosper de Chasseloup-Laubat, served as president of the Society for nine consecutive years from 1864. During his tenure, missionary work, commercial influence, and possible territorial expansion in southeast Asia were at the forefront of his agenda. There was a pattern of interest in commercial and "civilizing missions" in the presidential addresses of the Society in the 1850s and 1860s. The map curator of the military archives, Charles Maunoir, presided over the Society for thirty years after 1867, a period when it expanded from 300 to 2,000 members, with a higher proportion of military and naval officers.[29] Members of the Society boosted the careers of African explorers Henri Duveyrier and Pierre Savorgnan de Brazza, heard memoirs from Navy officer Francis Garnier in Indochina, pressured the government to finance exploration, and opposed the evacuation of Gabon.[30]

As France looked outward after its defeat in the Franco-Prussian War, the Geographical Society obtained official government patronage of expeditions to Africa and support in the chambers of commerce for imperial ventures.[31] 2,500 members flocked to the Paris Society in 1885 and twenty-seven provincial societies boasted 16,000 members in 1891.[32] With more and more members who were civil servants and with high aristocratic patronage, the Paris Geographical Society became a modest pressure group for encouraging explorers and missionaries to find territory for France to annex and conquer.[33]

Lejeune charts the veritable triumph of the colonial idea in the society from 1875 to 1878, with the enthusiastic backing of its President, Clément de la Roncière-Le Noury.[34] Further territorial appropriation in Africa and Indochina, as well as associated international commercial and imperial expositions, heightened public interest in the exoticism and practical importance of empire.[35] One of the best-known advocates of associationist colonial policies in the early twentieth century, the naval physician and governor of Indochina, Jules Harmand, was also an active member of the Geographical Society.[36] Historians such as Andrew

---

29 Taylor, "The Geographical Society of Paris"; Lejeune, *Les sociétés de géographie*, 134.

30 Fierro, *La Société de Géographie*, 50–4; Lejeune, *Les sociétés de géographie*, 97–8.

31 McKay, "Colonialism."

32 Ibid., 225–6.

33 Lejeune, *Les sociétés de géographie*, 81, 101–3, 107, 110–12; see Conklin, *A Mission to Civilize*, 12.

34 Lejeune, *Les sociétés de géographie*, 73–75, 134.

35 Schneider, *An Empire for the Masses*.

36 Fierro, *La Société de Géographie*, 99; Adas, *Machines as the Measure of Men*, 321–2 for Harmand's influence upon administrators.

and Kanya-Forstner have spoken of the direct incitement to imperial expansion coming from the "periphery" – prestige-hunting military commanders and colonial administrators, rather than Paris policymakers or public opinion. The "Parti Colonial" of 1890 to 1914 had significant business interests, and penetrated crucial cabinet and parliamentary positions. But these same historians also showed that 108 of 200 lobbyists of the committee of the "Parti Colonial," and 45 of its 58 leaders, belonged to the Paris Geographical Society. The prince d'Arenberg, a major figure in the Comité de l'Afrique française, edited an independent periodical, the *Revue de géographie*; coal and steel patron Florent Guillain was active in the Paris Geographical Society; and shipping magnate Jules Charles-Roux was president of the Marseille Geographical Society.[37]

By 1873, ship owners and merchants in Lyon and Bordeaux were eager not only to establish provincial societies but also to hasten the introduction of geography courses in the schools. The Paris Society established a Commercial Geography committee in 1873, which metamorphosed into a separate society in 1876. By 1880, under the pressure of influential business people, the Ministry of Public Instruction founded university chairs in the provincial faculties in Lyon, Bordeaux, and Caen.

Paul Vidal de la Blache, the acknowledged founder of the new academic discipline, began lecturing in Nancy in 1872 before his move to the Ecole normale in Paris in 1877 and to the Sorbonne in 1898. Two kinds of geography emerged – "popular" geography, very much concerned with exoticism and empire, and academic geography, concerned with the physical geography of landforms and new physical criteria for geographic regions. There was some degree of overlap. Vidal's first coeditor of the *Annales de géographie*, first published in 1891, was Marcel Dubois, who occupied the chair of colonial geography funded by the Ministry of Colonies at the Sorbonne.[38] Both Dubois and Vidal investigated social facts, and in subsequent years, some human geographers drew closer to the circle of Emile Durkheim at the *Année sociologique*.[39]

37 For the centre-periphery thesis, see Andrew and Kanya-Forstner, "Centre and Periphery"; for their analysis of the Parti Colonial, Andrew and Kanya-Forstner, "The French Colonial Party"; see also the businesss connections of *parti colonial* committee members in Abrams and Miller, "Who Were the French Colonialists?" esp. 721–5.

38 Dory, "Géographie et colonisation."

39 Mucchielli, *La Découverte du social*, 392; Broc, *Regards sur la géographie française*, and "L'Établissement de la géographie en France," esp. 552; see also Berdoulay, *La Formation de l'École française*; essays in Claval, *Autour de Vidal de la Blache*; Claval, *Histoire de la géographie*.

The new academic geography considered its primary interest to be the ecological relationship between the activity of human groups and the physical environment, or the spatial arrangements that groups organized. Ethnography was complementary to human geography, but was not its proper object. The human geographer Jean Brunhes pointed out the difference: "ethnographic facts in separating themselves from the essential facts of human geography, are more and more distant from geography proper, while being subjected to the legitimate preoccupations of geographic localization and distribution."[40] However, Brunhes agreed to join the resurrected Society of Ethnography in 1913, and wrote several articles for its new journal, *L'Ethnographie*. There he pointed out that geographers would look at the spatial distribution of houses in a city, while ethnographers might investigate the particular form and techniques of constructing the rooftops.[41]

The learned societies had helped promote interest in imperial expansion, which itself stimulated the institutionalization of geography as an academic discipline. Even before 1848, the geographers' classification of peoples helped provide the intellectual justification for imperial ventures. The attacks on the egalitarian ethos began with the upsurge in polygenism promoted by explorers and by the reception within the Geographical Society of their ethnographic dispatches. In and of itself, polygenism did not necessarily imply imperialism, nor did it exhaust all the implications of a drift in imperial policy from "assimilation" to "association." But the geographers helped confirm the prejudices that some peoples would always be retarded or uncivilizable. In this manner, imperial control became conceivable.

THE CONTINUITY OF
ANTHROPOLOGICAL DISCOURSE

In 1859, two very different societies fragmented the discourse of a science of human beings into preoccupation, first, with physical features of the species and, second, with the study of languages, localized customs, and archaeology. Some members of the Société ethnologique de Paris, such as the geographer Edme Jomard, the historian of medieval folklore Alfred

---

40 Claval, "Le Rôle de Demangeon, de Brunhes et de Gallois dans la formation de l'Ecole française: Les Années 1905–1910" in Claval, *Autour de Vidal de la Blache*, 149–58, citation on 153; Robic, "L'Invention de la « géographie humaine » au tournant des années 1900: Les vidaliens et l'écologie" in Claval, *Autour de Vidal de la Blache*, 137–47.

41 Brunhes, "L'ethnographie," esp. 31.

Maury, the Hindi and Arabic linguist Joseph-Héliodore-Sagesse-Vertu Garcin de Tassy, and the historian Charles Lenormant, joined such renowned authors as Ernest Renan in the new Société ethnographique orientale et américaine, under the direction of Léon Rosny a linguist of Japanese.[42] The former SEP members, however, were not the principal guiding spirits of this new society. Our primary argument here in any case concerns the continuity in discourse on perfectibility of races between the Société ethnologique de Paris (SEP) and the Société d'anthropologie de Paris (SAP), founded by the physician Paul Broca, for the place of the SEP in the institutionalization of French anthropology rests principally upon this latter relationship.

Broca, a republican in 1848 and anti-clerical, was never indifferent to political issues, but his disillusionment with the Revolution of 1848 led to a desire to purge overt politics from scientific discussion. The pretext for founding the Société d'anthropologie was the furor over Broca's attempt to assert his polygenism in a paper on hybridity at the Société de biologie in 1858. Broca was well aware of the theories of hybridity of Samuel George Morton, who had also inspired the members of the SEP. Broca wished to establish the fertility of the rabbit-hare hybrid. In turn, the fertility of hybrids removed an obstacle to the belief in more than one human species: humans could interbreed, remain fertile, yet still come from different species. Broca's willingness to discuss the implications for the human species scandalized the officers of the Société de biologie in 1858, since they feared the Second Empire government would perceive an assault on Biblical monogenism, and they therefore suspended the reading of his paper.[43] Broca then worked diligently to gain support from a group of physicians, naturalists of the Muséum, and medical journalists to found the Société d'anthropologie in 1859. It prospered, with 300 members by 1865.[44]

In discussing human hybridity, Broca argued that only crossings between closely related types such as the Celts and Kymris in ancient France would produce a flourishing people.[45] He also believed Ameri-

---

42 Preliminary studies of the society in Stocking,"Qu'est-ce qui est en jeu dans un nom?"; Lacombe, "Essai sur les origines," 330–3; Williams, "The Science of Man," 150–75; and Chailleu, "La Revue orientale et américaine."

43 Schiller, *Broca*, 128–35.

44 Williams, "The Science of Man," 81–2; *MSAP* 1 (1860–63): 1; *Statuts, règlement et liste des membres* (Paris: Henneyer, 1868).

45 Broca, *Hybridity*, 21–4; Harvey, "Races Specified, Evolution Transformed"; Jean-Louis Fischer, "Espèce et hybrides: A propos des léporides," in Atran, ed. *Histoire du concept d'espèce*, 256.

can pro-slavery theorists when they argued that black-white crossings (mulattos) were weaker and eventually might become sterile.[46] To support these views, he adduced evidence from Quoy, Gaimard, and Lesson, though he thought Bory and Desmoulins had divided humans into too many species. The paradox of Broca's hierarchical racial theory was that polygenism seemed to him less insulting to "inferior" races than the monogenist story of degeneration from a primitive superior type. As he concluded, "To be inferior to another man either in intelligence, vigour or beauty is not a humiliating condition."[47] However, Broca clearly wished to constitute a racial hierarchy based on cranial capacity and such features as prognathous facial appearance.

Broca's political radicalism, at least before 1848, and his anti-slavery sentiment did not interfere with his allegedly "scientific" questioning of racial equality. He believed that "science may claim its rights [polygenism] without caring for the sophisms of the slaveholders ... [since] the difference of origin by no means implies the subordination of races."[48] On other social issues, he remained convinced that "social selection" by providing services for the sick and weak had to counteract natural struggle (about which he had reservations in any case), and that mass education was progressive and required for both men and women.[49]

Broca himself was a great anatomist who studied brain localization, notably the link between aphemia (later called aphasia) and the language area. But even as he revived cerebral localization, Broca kept his distance from phrenology. Although he assigned to Gall the "incontestable merit of proclaiming the great principle of cerebral localizations, point of departure for all discoveries of our century on brain physiology," Gall's "applications were almost entirely erroneous," with an insufficient anatomical basis and too many specialized organs. Nor was Camper rigorous enough, since he did not consider the width of the forehead. Still, there was a rough correspondence of facial angle to intellectual capacity, since the forehead related to the obliquity of the facial line.[50] Broca challenged Pierre-Louis Gratiolet's critique of the significance of brain weight in itself but accepted Gratiolet's

46 Broca, *Hybridity*, 33–60; Blanckaert, "L'esclavage des Noirs"; *cf* Forest, "De l'abolitionnisme," 88.

47 Broca, *Hybridity*, 3, 6, 11.

48 Ibid., 68–71.

49 Broca, "Les sélections," *Revue d'anthropologie* 2 (1873): 241–54, reprinted in Broca, *Mémoires d'anthropologie*.

50 *BSAP* 2 (1861): 191–2, 197–8.

classification, used by Lacassagne, of frontal, parietal, and occipital races.[51] Hence, cranial capacity remained a cornerstone of discourse about intellectual prowess within the SAP.

Broca painstakingly attempted to correlate cranial capacity or cranial form with the capacity for civilization, defined as the ability for scientific, philosophical, industrial, literary, and artistic achievement.[52] Gould and Blanckaert have elaborately shown his enthusiasm for craniometry, and SAP physicians brought craniometry to a quantitative precision undreamed of by the SEP. When less advanced peoples displayed larger brains than Europeans, Broca retreated to the principle that size works better in ranking the smaller-brained. He found various explanations for the small brains of eminent men and the larger ones of criminals. When buried Parisians from earlier centuries had larger brains, he tried to explain the difference by their social class or argued that the sutures closed earlier in those races he assumed were inferior. Otherwise, the position of the foramen magnum was recessed in inferior races, meaning there was less room for the important frontal brain functions.[53]

Even after 1868, Broca's concessions to the transformation of species through hybridization still allowed for human "types" (a less charged and more ill-defined term than race or species) to be considered separate without common ancestry.[54] Despite Darwin's questioning of the permanence of species, most members of the SAP continued to postulate a racial hierarchy in the 1860s, with a linear, evolutionary Chain of Being and in some cases parallel, non-convergent polygenist branches.[55]

Developments in other sciences assured some differences in subject-matter between the SEP and SAP. Among the anthropologists in the era of Darwin and Thomas Huxley, there was far more painstaking analysis of the differences between humans and apes. New discoveries of human fossils placed prehistory on the agenda both for craniometry and for

---

51 *BSAP* 2 (1861): 139–203 and summary by Eugène Dally in *MSAP* 2 (1863–65): lvi; for Gratiolet, see *BSAP* 2 (1861) 72, 79, 243; *cf* Gould, *The Mismeasure of Man*, 115–16, 139. The physician Auguste Coudereau was one of the few Society members who proudly invoked the legacy of Gall and Spurzheim as late as 1880, in referring to the continuing quest for cerebral localization – see Hecht, "Anthropological Utopias," 109.

52 *BSAP* 2nd sér. 7 (1867): 629–30.

53 Gould, *The Mismeasure of Man*, 114–35.

54 Blanckaert, preface to Broca, *Mémoires d'anthropologie*, xxiv–xxviii.

55 Cohen, *The French Encounter with Africans*, 248 may underestimate the viability of racism by parallel polygenism even among French Darwinists after 1880.

evolutionary theory. From the institutional viewpoint, the SAP was far more successful. They established their own laboratory in the Ecole pratique des hautes études in 1867 and in 1876, with support from the City of Paris, founded a teaching institution, the Ecole d'anthropologie. The naturalists Armand de Quatrefages and Isidore Geoffroy Saint-Hilaire were among the few direct links between the SEP and the SAP.

But our main argument is that Broca himself wished to magnify the differences between the societies, which were not so great as he contended. He declared ethnology a mere subdivision of anthropology that classified races and determined the influences of climate, education, and external conditions on them. The broader discipline of anthropology placed human beings in nature and studied the first appearance of the human species.[56]

The SAP members in the circle of Gabriel de Mortillet in the 1870s and 1880s later dreamed of a politicized anthropology destined to combat clericalism and obsolete metaphysics. Broca and Quatrefages both liked to make the obviously inflated claim that the new Society, unlike the SEP, was free from non-scientific cultural assumptions. Quatrefages had refused to contradict traditional scientific and Biblical accounts by admitting transformation of species. Broca argued that the anthropologists could debate monogenism or polygenism with scientific objectivity and without anti-slavery passions because "there were no political or religious preoccupations in our discussions." Science was an "august goddess reigning over humanity to direct it, not follow it."[57]

Despite this mask of neutrality, there was an evident continuity with the SEP on the subject of the perfectibility of races. The extensive debate in the SAP from June to August 1860 resembled arguments in the SEP discussion of 1847. Among the participants, besides Broca, were a polygenist military physician (of the Invalides) with experience on the Scientific Commission for the Exploration of Algeria, Joanny-Napoléon Périer, and a staunchly polygenist natural history museum curator from Rouen, Henri-Charles-Georges Pouchet, a student of the physician Charles Robin. On the monogenist side were the ex-physician to the viceroy of Egypt and ally of Quatrefages, Austrian-born Franz Pruner-Bey; the former Martinique physician and future lecturer on acclimatization

56 MSAP 2 (1863–65): vii–viii, xlii.

57 MSAP 2 (1863–65), xliii; MSAP 3 (1868–69), cxiv–v; for one of the few direct involvements of the SAP in a political issue – the equitability of the height minimum for military conscription on populations of different areas of France – see Blanckaert, "La Crise de l'Anthropométrie," 106–11.

Etienne Rufz de Lavison; and the alienist Louis-Jean Delasiauve. Broca, in comparing the advanced Hawaiians and the perpetually savage Australians, argued that races had "innate and different aptitudes," varying as much as anatomy, "which facilitate, oppose, or entirely prevent efforts at civilization." Therefore perfectibility was unequally distributed.

Quatrefages had been a member of the Institute since 1852 and anthropology professor at the Muséum since 1855. With some support from Rufz and Martin de Moussy, in this debate he would not "admit any race refractory to civilization," even the Australians. Any differences between Australians and Polynesians were due to milieu. However, after insisting on universal susceptibility to development, Quatrefages agreed that "races are unequal in respect of perfectibility and that these unequal aptitudes are in addition hereditary." In addition, Pruner-Bey had alleged the potential of the Australians for civilization and had contested the use of the term "savage" for any people in the "state of nature," since all have some laws and sociability.[58] Isidore Geoffroy Saint-Hilaire similarly remained true to monogenism, although he established the "Hottentots" as a new extreme of racial inferiority.[59]

In the anthropology lectures at the Muséum in 1861, Quatrefages would insist that the fertility of interracial marriages proved the unity of the species. But he accepted the Swiss-American polygenist Louis Agassiz's view that there might be more than one centre of creation, or centre of appearance, as he called it. This concession did not turn Quatrefages into a true polygenist. He amended Agassiz's opinion to argue that humans could migrate successfully, rather than being restricted to a particular "province" or zone. The next year he admitted, like d'Eichthal and contrary to Broca, that even the offspring of distant human varieties, such as mulattos, had a great future, since they were as intelligent as whites and could flourish in the tropics.[60]

In the SAP discussions, Périer denied perfectibility to blacks with old clichés about organic deficiencies making them incapable of science, philosophy, and literature.[61] Similarly, he thought it a mistake to try to

---

58 *BSAP* 1 (1859–60): 338, 347–50, 358–9, 375–9, 389; for Pruner-Bey, 493–4; see also Blanckaert, "La naturalisation de l'homme," 21; Williams, "The Science of Man," 92–5.

59 *MSAP* 1 (1860–63): 125–44.

60 AN AJ 15 551, *Discours d'ouverture du cours d'anthropologie*, extrait de *La Gazette médicale*, 5, 8 and *Discours d'ouverture* of 1862; for scepticism on descent from one couple, see Quatrefages, *Rapport sur les progrès de l'anthropologie*, 121.

61 *BSAP* 1 (1860): 421–7; *cf BSAP* 1 (1860): 330 and Williams, "The Science of Man," 95–6.

assimilate South American natives with inferior aptitudes. He singled out that old supporter of Biblical monogenism, Eusèbe de Salle, for unfairly charging that belief in inequality would promote slavery. Quatrefages replied that polygenists in the United States had used their theories to justify slavery.[62]

Georges Pouchet repeated the contention that Egyptians were not black.[63] Quatrefages had contended that the stable Egyptian milieu explained why Egyptians looked the same now as on their monuments.[64] Pruner-Bey added the argument that German explorer Heinrich Barth had discovered African civilizations in medieval Mali and Ghana.[65]

In fact, in a dictionary article of 1866 on "Anthropology," Broca summarized a position that could have been articulated by many members of the SEP: "Never has a people with dark skin, woolly hair, and a prognathous [prominent jaw, receding forehead] face been able spontaneously to elevate itself to civilization; the African Negroes, who are far from the lowest rank in the human series, have never given their societies stability, the essential condition of progress; and one has never seen any government unite as a nation the savage tribes of Australians and Pelagian or Melanesian Negroes."[66]

Between in 1865 and 1868, the SAP continued to discuss civilizability by racial aptitude. Broca's disciple, the positivist, polygenist physician Eugène Dally, ultimately became an adherent of transformism in the world of animal species, but he refused to see any kind of evolution or progress within races. "Uncivilizable and immutable" races were always such, and even Europeans had not progressed in wisdom or courage since the ancient Greeks. Influenced by the pessimism of Arthur de Gobineau, Dally saw no conceivable evolution of "incomplete" inferior races, whose destruction was merely part of the natural process. Such an outlook, thought Dally in 1881, was insurance against the sentimentality

---

62 *BSAP* 1 (1860): 428–32; also in Quatrefages, *Unité de l'espèce humaine*, 71.

63 *BSAP* 1 (1860): 432–5.

64 Quatrefages, *Discours d'ouverture du cours d'anthropologie*, extrait de *La Gazette médicale* 1861 in AN AJ 15 551.

65 *BSAP* 1 (1860): 480, 489–91; Pruner-Bey, "Mémoire sur les nègres," *MSAP* 1 (1862): 293–333 on prognathism and peripheral nerve capacity.

66 See Harvey, "Races Specified, Evolution Transformed," 210, 279 for contributions of the physician Charles Letourneau and of Broca's ally Eugène Dally; for Broca, see "Anthropologie," in Paul Broca, *Mémoires d'anthropologie* 1 (Paris: Reinhalt, 1871): 33, cited in the preface to the re-edition by Blanckaert, viii; see also Cohen, *The French Encounter with Africans*, 226; also partly cited in Gould, *The Mismeasure of Man*, 116.

of those who think that colonized peoples may be treated as brothers.[67] On the whole, Dally was even harsher than the commissioners of the SEP in 1847 since he did not conclude that European guidance could at least assist Africans. His outlook also strangely resembles those present-day believers in an ethnically stable IQ pattern, which is not expected to improve.

The case of the physician and would-be sociologist/cultural anthropologist Charles Letourneau is more complex. In 1867, Letourneau enthusiastically reviewed Jean-Baptiste Delestre's essay on the "new physiognomy" since it contributed to comparative racial craniology. For Letourneau, the "moral was clearly the slave of the physical." As a "scientific materialist," he clearly championed the idea of a biological approach to human capability based on a system of human needs. He would classify peoples and races as if they all went through the stages of individual development. Although this idea in its embryonic form had been popularized by Ernst Haeckel, the concept that "savages" were retarded, as if children in a world of adults, went back at least to Joseph-Marie Degérando at the turn of the century. In a kind of combination of the old temperament idea with head shapes, Letourneau saw large occipital development in races confined to the simplest "nutritive" needs, while those more "affective," such as the African and the European woman, would have larger parietal development. Like Morel, Letourneau suggested that criminals might have specific facial traits.[68]

Elsewhere Letourneau elaborated his concept of a "progressive social evolution" from peoples in the nutritive phase of development, such as Eskimos and Australians, to peoples in a "sensitive" phase, such as Tahitians and Polynesians, and to others in the "affective" or final "intellectual" phase, which no one had completely attained but which was within the grasp of Europeans.[69] Letourneau's evolutionism, as Blanckaert has argued, was qualitatively different from the rigidities of Dally because all peoples, even inferior races, were educable, and their acquired habits were partly in heritable. Even the Australian aborigines would arrive at civilization, were they not being supplanted by Europeans. Letourneau was also a polygenist, so he could assume parallel development of races created in different places.

67 Blanckaert, "Le premesse"; see 61–3 for citations of Dally's remarks in the *BSAP* 6 (1865): 670–1 and 2nd sér., 3 (1868): 321 and other comments as late as 1882.

68 Letourneau on Delestre, *Physiognomonie BSAP* 2nd sér., 7 (1867): 179–80; Blanckaert, "Le premesse," 56, 60–2; see Degérando, *The Observation of Savage Peoples*.

69 Letourneau, *BSAP* 2nd sér., 7 (1867): 378–82 on social phases.

On the surface, this was a far more open-minded view than that of Dally and even more tolerant than the SEP commissioners, for it allowed spontaneous development, not just European guidance. In practice, however, Letourneau did not necessarily believe in intellectual equality among the races, so the kinds of civilization they would attain might not be equivalent. Then, too, whatever his humanitarian concerns about the disappearance of peoples, these "inferior beings" were still condemned to accept European civilization or die without the luxury of their own timetable for development. So the views of Letourneau expressed in the 1880s did not crystallize in opposition to European colonialism.[70] In a work on Africa published in 1889, the linguistic anthropologist Abel Hovelacque cited Letourneau's comments that Africans were only "big children."[71] How little such appraisals had changed since the days of Virey and the epithets of Lesson and Dumoutier on Pacific islanders!

Several SAP members expressed a far more tolerant perspective. Among them was the materialist physician Charles Coudereau, who provided one of the strongest arguments against rigid division among humans. Coudereau believed that even animal societies could display traits of civilization, and that any people with "a willed tendency toward progress" could be called civilized. His colleague, a Fourierist physician and medical geographer of Montrouge and brother-in-law of the positivist Emile Littré, Charles Pellarin, adopted the evolutionary view of degrees of civilization commencing in savagery and pastoral patriarchy and culminating in civilization. But he would not condemn "inferior races as uncivilizable since I believe that with intelligent, devoted, and beneficent assistance they will arrive at a social harmony that we ourselves have not yet reached."

Unlike the Christian monogenists of the SEP, the relatively tolerant members of the SAP were often anti-clericals who did not view Christianity as a net gain for indigenous peoples. Pellarin even thought that Europeans were a bad influence on the coastal societies they met. Within Europe, he was sensitive to the ravages of "poverty, bankruptcies, and moral corruption," for which he recommended social insurance and retirement funds.

In the discussion of 1866, the linguist Pierre-Louis-Jean-Baptiste Gaussin had also questioned the radical opposition of savage and civilized with the contention that it all was a matter of degree, but he was

70 Blanckaert, "Le premesse," 66–7.
71 Desmet, "Abel Hovelacque," esp. 77–8.

content to use the word "savage" for the "first phases of social development" while "civilized" could be employed for those peoples approaching European development. The conservative archaeologist Alexandre
Bertrand concluded the next year that civilization was a vague, unscientific term. But none of these doubts halted the tendency of the Society
to see some peoples or races as inherently retarded or incapable of at-
taining European levels of achievement.[72]

On one issue, discussions in the SAP were more complex than in the
SEP. The SEP already expressed interest in whether crossbreeding or climate change modified transplanted peoples (such as the West Indian
slaves). If we assume that polygenists were the more virulent racists and
monogenists more disposed to assume the civilizability of all peoples, the
conclusion might be that polygenists were the more enthusiastic imperialists. However, the attitude of the anthropologists toward empire from
1860 to 1880 was more subtle than that of the geographers. Polygenists
often believed that each race was suited only to its own climatic zone. One
could even hope to prove diversity of species by the inability to move to
other climates. Therefore, the high disease mortality figures for French
soldiers and colonists in Algeria or Madagascar seemed to confirm their
fears (or hopes) that European acclimatization in the tropics was questionable. Since these susceptibilities were inherent in the race, large-scale
occupation and settlement might be achievable only at the high cost of
continued replenishment of troops and settlers from France. Both Périer,
for example, and the Marseille military physician and medical geographer Jean-Christian-Marc Boudin insisted that races were not cosmopoli-
tan. Boudin argued that Africans would not long retain their health in the
West Indies. In a curious way, monogenists such as Quatrefages might
have been more receptive to colonization. His entire assumption was that
human beings could migrate and adapt successfully in different zones, albeit only after a long period of adjustment. Acquired disease immunity
and improvements in the milieu could thus improve survival rates.[73]

Michael Osborne has studied the Société zoologique d'acclimatation
(SZA), founded in 1854, which included Quatrefages as vice-president
and president of the permanent commission on colonies and foreign

72 Pellarin, *BSAP* 2nd sér., 7 (1867): 426, and Coudereau, in the same issue, 512–18,
524; for Gaussin see *BSAP* 2nd sér., 6 (1866): 365–9, esp. 369; for a contrasting view on
the tolerance of the anthropologists for "savagery," see Bullard, *Exile to Paradise*, 23–5, who
cites the discussions of 1860, 1866, and 1867 in the Société d'anthropologie.

73 Blanckaert, "La Crise de l'anthropométrie," 114–22, esp. 116 on Quatrefages, 119
on Périer.

lands.[74] This group was deeply committed to converting commercial products (mostly from Algeria) into desired raw materials for the French economy by adapting plant and animal species to the foreign (usually Algerian) climate. They based their scientific theories on the limited variability of types (compatible with monogenism in humans) propounded by Isidore Geoffroy Saint-Hilaire and accepted by Quatrefages.[75] Naturalists from the Muséum were thus giving informal support to colonialism in the 1860s just as the geographers were becoming more active.

Where the issue was the feasibility of the settlement of Algeria, this constellation produced a curious reversal of the positions on racial hierarchy. For example, many in the SZA supported the migration of French peasants to Algeria, while Boudin opposed such measures. He thought that without racial crossing, Europeans could not subsist in such tropical milieus.[76] In response to such perceptions, the French army decreased terms of service in Algeria, acclimated its forces in southern France, or enlisted native soldiers.

However, as Osborne himself admits, such debates were very much tied to the issue of settler colonies.[77] The arguments did not inhibit French expansion in Africa, southeast Asia, or the Pacific, where there was only a token settler immigration to New Caledonia. Nor did the theories of racial hierarchy that led to associationism inevitably ease the plight of indigenous peoples. Even Boudin himself argued that Europeans could adapt more easily in the south Pacific or Australia. And by the 1880s SAP members Dally and Gabriel de Mortillet were advocates of an associationist policy: they assumed that the less developed nervous systems of non-Europeans could never lead to their uncomplicated adoption of European civilization.[78]

Illustrious colonial administrators, such as Louis-Léon-César Faidherbe, the former governor-general of the Sudan, and Paul Bert, future governor-general of Indochina, also found a willing reception in the SAP. Furthermore, some naval physicians and surgeons trained in an-

74 Osborne, *Nature, the Exotic*, 74.

75 Ibid., 62–97.

76 Ibid., 91; see also Osborne, "Acclimatizing the World," 135–51, esp. 139–40.

77 Osborne, *Nature, the Exotic*, 176.

78 Blanckaert, "La Crise de l'anthropométrie," 136–9; Benoît Massin, "L'anthropologie raciale comme fondement de la science politique; Vacher de Lapouge et l'échec de l'anthroposociologie en France (1866–1936)" in Blanckaert, ed. *Les politiques de l'anthropologie*, 269–334, esp. 294.

thropometry at the Paris Medical Faculty lab of the École d'anthropologie after 1876. They furnished a contingent of corresponding members of the SAP who measured skulls and promoted theories of racial inferiority throughout the French empire.[79]

Whether racial theories postulated the uncivilizability of indigenous peoples or their retardation as savages, French administrators' colonial attitudes toward such races could sometimes be singularly callous. Commodore J.E. du Bouzet, the naval governor of the French Pacific islands, was able to declare in 1855, shortly after the French annexation of New Caledonia: "it is a universally acknowledged principle that when a maritime power takes possession of any land never yet occupied by a civilized nation and inhabited only by savage tribes, the said act of taking possession abrogates all former contracts passed by the natives with any other person." The capacity to view the Kanaks as savage or uncivilizable encouraged increasingly repressive land purchase and reserve policies in subsequent decades.[80] Military commandant Testard, posted to New Caledonia in the late 1850s, thought the Kanaks should be wiped out. Henri Rivière, the commandant during the 1878 insurrection, also justified a policy of destruction with his epithet of a "race just above animals" with no hope of perfectibility, indifferent to civilization.[81] Civilian governor Paul Feillet, who arrived in 1894, thought the Kanaks were doomed to extinction. Missionaries, government commissioners for the defence of the indigenous, and General A. de Trentinian, author of a report on the troubles of 1879, were more generous, but did not change government policy.[82]

79 Harvey, "Races Specified, Evolution Transformed" 115, 133–8.

80 Bulletin Officiel de la Nouvelle-Calédonie, Archives nationales, Section Outre-Mer, FM-SG-NCL/67, cited by Mummery, "The Struggle for Survival," 97 for du Bouzet, 70–3 on Rochas, 74–8 on Bourgarel, 91–3 on Rivière, 126–31 on governor Feillet; Mummery's thesis profited a great deal from Bullard, "Becoming Savage?"; Bronwen Douglas, "Conflict and Alliance in a Colonial Context," *Journal of Pacific History* 5 (1980) 30–1; essays in Bronwen Douglas, *Across the Great Divide: Journeys in History and Anthropology – Selected Essays* (Amsterdam: Harwood, 1998) and Joel Dauphiné, *Les Spoliations foncières en Nouvelle-Calédonie (1853–1913)* (Paris: L'Harmattan, 1989). See also the litany of racist stereotypes in Bensa, "Colonialisme, racisme et ethnologie," 188–97.

81 Rivière, *Souvenirs de la Nouvelle-Calédonie* (Paris, 1881) cited in Mummery, "The Struggle for Survival," 91.

82 For a parallel discussion of attitudes to "civilization" and "savagery" with respect to New Caledonia, see Bullard, *Exile to Paradise*, esp. 166–7 on land policy. Bullard outlines the rhetorical manipulation of concepts such as civilization and savagery to denigrate the Kanak, but places insufficient emphasis on previously existing concepts of racial theory. She also stresses the relative tolerance of some members of the Société d'anthropologie de Paris rather than the more negative views of equally significant Society members.

The cultural attitudes of racial hierarchy drew scientific prestige from the naval surgeons Adolphe Bourgarel and Victor Rochas, who in the early 1860s measured the crania of New Caledonians as correspondents for the Société d'anthropologie.[83] Rochas classified them as dolicho-prognathic with a facial angle of 77°. This estimate placed them superior to the Australians but inferior to the Polynesians.[84] Rochas thought that their long nursing period for children and the unhealthful climate threatened their fertility. Bourgarel analysed fifty-seven skulls with comparative arm and foot measurements for Melanesians, Polynesians, and Europeans. He also measured the average New Caledonian facial angle at 76°, compared to 78° for the Polynesians, and claimed their canine teeth resembled those of carnivorous animals. He blamed the New Caledonian decline not only on climate and diet but also on a physical deficiency – incompletely developed sexual organs. He held little hope that their "lazy, deceitful, arrogant" savage behaviour was amenable to civilization.[85] Both Bourgarel and Rochas thought that an allegedly primitive communist society could be saved from degeneration only by the civilizing influence of a market economy. In discussing Rochas's findings at the SAP, the very champion of non-cosmopolitanism, Boudin, reported that, since intermittent fevers did not flourish in these Pacific islands, French troops did not suffer high mortality. The implication was that the much-vaunted barriers to French occupation did not affect the Pacific colonies.[86]

A recent examination of nineteenth-century Tahiti shows that the perception of civilizability of peoples affected French land policy in the Pacific. The French dealt with the existing Tahitian monarchy and legislative assembly and had to purchase and negotiate for land. By contrast, in New Caledonia they created reserves for the indigenous people that severely disrupted existing customs and social structure. In 1880, Tahitians also received French citizenship. As the authors argue, "behind the attitude to colonization in Tahiti, we sense the dream of the New Cythera."[87]

The prestigious *Revue d'anthropologie*, founded in 1872 by Paul Broca, in 1875 published almost a stereotypical account of a Navy physician, Laurent-Jean-Baptiste Bérenger-Féraud, about the Oulofs of Senegal.

83 *MSAP* 1 (1860–63): 250–92; *MSAP* 2 (1863–65): 375–416.

84 *BSAP* 1 (1859–60): 390, 430.

85 Bourgarel, *MSAP* 1 (1860–63): 257–9; 2: 396; *BSAP* 1 (1860): 450–2; Rochas, *BSAP* 1 (1860): 430; see Mummery, "The Struggle for Survival," 75; Bullard, "Becoming Savage?," 347.

86 *MSAP* 1 (1860–63): 394, 401.

87 Pillon and Sodter, "The Impact of Colonial Administrative Policies," esp. 167.

While acknowledging their superiority to other Africans, the author peppered his observations with clichés about their childishness and vanity. He concluded that they "constitute an inferior class of workers and producers who would certainly be useful to us in an environment which is eminently harmful to us and consequently they can substitute for us in several occupations."[88]

If anything, members of the SAP in the 1880s and 1890s became more open to colonization as Spencerian influence declined and the race for empire became more intensified. Ernest-Théodore Hamy, founder of the Musée d'ethnographie, in 1882 worried that indigenous races needed to be studied before they disappeared.[89] While the disillusionment with measuring heads and with the hierarchical ranking of innate aptitudes was setting in with such anthropologists as Léonce Manouvrier already in the 1890s, not until the Durkheimian reaction against racism was there a strong attack on the kind of anthropology that justified domination. When the future leading ethnologist Marcel Mauss lectured at the Ecole pratique des hautes etudes on the "history of uncivilized peoples" in 1900–01, he included in his inaugural lecture the maxim, "there are no uncivilized peoples, only peoples with a different civilization."[90] In fact, the essay of Durkheim and Marcel Mauss on primitive forms of classification would argue that classification itself, like so many other fundamental categories, is always socially constructed.[91] Without completely surrendering all hierarchical and colonialist thinking, the founders of the new Institut ethnographique international (founded late in 1910), European folklorist Arnold Van Gennep and Africanist and colonial administrator Maurice Delafosse, shared attitudes that would end the invidious distinctions among civilized and non-civilized peoples.[92]

88 Bérenger-Féraud, "Étude sur les Ouolofs (Sénégambie)," esp. 469, 484, 494.

89 Blanckaert, "Le premesse," 67.

90 See note 23 above and such articles as Manouvrier, "Les aptitudes et les actes"; Mauss, *Oeuvres*, 3:229–30, reprinted from "Leçon d'ouverture à l'enseignement de l'histoire des religions des peuples non-civilisés." *Revue de l'histoire des religions* 45 (1902): 36–55; also cited in Mucchielli, "La dénaturalisation de l'homme," esp. 50.

91 Durkheim and Mauss, "De quelques formes primitives de classification," reprinted in Durkheim, *Primitive Classification*, trans. Edward Sagarin (Chicago: University of Chicago Press, 1963); *cf* Mucchielli, *La Découverte du social*, 327–8.

92 For a discussion of the change from social evolutionism to a functionalist approach in British and French ethnographic discourse, see Hoyt, "The Reanimation of the Primitive."

Yet the persistence of the old clichés amid the survival and defence of empire was apparent at the Colonial Exposition at the Musée de l'homme in 1931. The aging professor of sociology at the Ecole d'anthropologie, Georges Papillault, a domestic conservative opposed to social insurance, was still discussing the aptitude and value of colonized races. He perceived a correspondence between the evolution of organs in each racial group and their intellectual and moral capabilities. In his view, the north Africans and Syrians might be "assimilated" by the French, and intermarriage with them was feasible, whereas others such as the "Negroids" of Africa and the Pacific and the Indochinese were educable at the individual level but impossible to assimilate.[93]

CONCLUSION

This study has stressed the possibility that phrenology could limit the social mobility of individuals and the intellectual capacity of races by applying a standard of measurement based on cranial capacity. Though it gave indicators for multiple intelligences rather than a single variable, in practice (especially when combined with physiognomy and the facial angle), phrenology could designate underdeveloped or overdeveloped regions of the brain. These appraisals cast summary aspersions on intelligence and character. As with the Saint-Simonian tradition, ambivalence in phrenology could lead to a more optimistic portrait of empowerment and self-development in line with a given individual potential. We have not explored in detail the medicalization of the image of deviants in asylums or prisons, which has constituted a major portion of Renneville's work, but the legacy of phrenology to the late nineteenth century was precisely that rationalization of social fears that resurfaced in the studies of degeneracy and the "born criminal." Like many uses of genetic coding today, the reference to head shapes, facial angles, and cephalic indices could be a force for optimism, but it could also designate an unalterable fate for the poorly shaped (prognathous peoples with frontal deficiencies), who could not develop beyond their limited capacities. Such diagnostic tools could be manipulated to justify harsh punishment or to question the ability of entire peoples.

93 Benoît de l'Estoile, "Des races non pas inférieures, mais différentes: de l'exposition coloniale au Musée de l'homme" in Blanckaert, *Les Politiques de l'anthropologie*, 391–473, esp. 424–6.

Historians of geography have identified it as the colonial science par excellence because explorers and cartographers furnished the raw materials for empire. They often contributed to images of peoples as permanently primitive. For the polygenists among geographers and ethnologists, some species were intermediate between humans and apes or deviations from the ideal forms of the white European male. If peoples did not degenerate from this ideal, they still might not be able to emulate it. Neither ethnologists nor anthropologists were infallibly oriented to conquest and imperial domination. In the early years of the Anthropology Society, polygenism could inhibit migration of European settlers. More generally, though, polygenism implied a worse fate for colonized peoples. The strange alliances and paradoxes within the ethnological and anthropological societies revealed that conservative Christians could have deeper feelings for human brotherhood than secularists, as well as an obvious commitment to the missionary impulse. On the other hand, some of the "progressive" authors who wished to protect the weak, sick, and impoverished at home had little concern for the fate of non-European peoples. Even if they were not crude Darwinists stressing the inevitable struggle for existence that would eliminate the weak, they created derogatory texts about the "Other."

In this theatre of European operations, there could be only three possible dénouements. One, ostensibly the most benevolent, was aiding people to accede to European civilization. Before the late nineteenth century, this viewpoint could also imply a readiness in theory (if rarely in practice) to assimilate peoples as French citizens. In the heyday of colonialism, it may have appeared unrealistic, as the development of inferior races would take many generations and European demands were simply too overbearing. A second, intermediate position was allowing people to develop to their full capacity, which implied educability but a perpetual gap with Europeans. Anthropologists like Charles Letourneau endorsed aspects of both these positions. The third outcome, uncivilizability, undermined the egalitarian assumptions of an assimilationist policy, and implied perpetual European domination without scruples about exploitation.[94]

Other studies will no doubt illustrate how colonial administrators applied these discourses and how they were diffused in the popular press.

94 Blanckaert's citation of physician Jean-Louis Fauvelle in the *BSAP* 3rd sér., 8 (1885): 724 in "Le premesse," 67 is particularly instructive in this regard.

A recent thesis on "Africanists" has concluded that colonial administrators near the end of the nineteenth century were often genuinely concerned to learn about subject peoples and eager to practice a kind of scientific ethnography. They may have helped re-orient ethnologists in Paris after 1900 to a more tolerant position.[95] But this development could not immediately change the dominant models of late nineteenth-century Parisian geographers and anthropologists. Another analysis of the utility of twentieth-century ethnology to colonial administrators examines its role not only as a tool for political and economic control but also for legitimation of colonial rule by the very act of practising "superior" Western science. As late as 1930, the justification of the "civilizing mission" appeared in the evolutionist schemes articulated by the governor-general of French West Africa: "If one admits that more evolved peoples and more retarded races exist, and that it is of general interest that the latter rise to the level of the former, colonialism is implicitly justified in principle."[96] Our assumption has been that there is value in assessing the thinkability, the conditions of possibility, of hierarchical attitudes to the "Other."

All of these emerging social sciences recognized a continuum of influences from the innate to the milieu. Nothing could be more implausible than denying either pole of the nature versus nurture debate of such influences today. The authors of the *Bell Curve* freely admitted that only a certain, and highly indefinite, portion of IQ test results could be traced to a heritable variable of general intelligence. But the abyss of invidious distinctions opens in just that critical portion. In the nineteenth century, the critical search was for just the right protuberance in the cranium, just the right physiognomy or facial angle.

While recognizing such dangers, scholars have understated the continuity of the early nineteenth-century thought with post-Darwinian social pessimism, racism, and imperialism. The Romantics reveled in their enthusiasm for diversity against Enlightenment universalism, in their quest for the exotic and the distant origins of European civilization. In fact, the professor of Chinese at the Collège de France, Jean-Pierre Abel Rémusat

95 Sibeud, "Les constructions des savoirs africanistes"; see also the same author's "La fin du voyage, De la pratique coloniale à la pratique ethnographique (1878–1913)" in Blanckaert, ed. *Les Politiques de l'anthropologie*, 173–98 and "La naissance de l'ethnographie africaniste."

96 L'Estoile, "Science de l'homme et 'domination rationnelle,'" esp. 306–7.

(1788–1832), articulated a fine example of European respect for the "Other" and almost a prophetic satire of the more conventional opinion:

Let the industry of all those peoples (Chinese, Hindu, Eskimo, etc.) yield to Occidental industry, let them renounce in our favour their ideas, their literature, their languages, all that makes up their national individuality. Let them learn to think, feel, and speak like us, let them pay for those useful lessons by abandoning their territory and independence, let them be obliging to the desires of our academicians, devoted to the interests of our merchants, gentle, docile, and submissive; at that price we will grant that they have taken a few steps toward sociability, and we will allow them to take their rank, but at a great distance, after the privileged people, the race par excellence, to whom it was given to possess, dominate, know, and instruct.[97]

Rémusat was not the dominant voice either among Orientalists or social scientists. The desire for willful domination and the limitations of the Saint-Simonian organic model were already evident among the reformist phrenologists. The joy of discovery among the geographers was as much a search for commercial and imperial opportunity as idle erudition. The ethnologists were humanitarians in their objections to slavery, but, like the abolitionists, believed that European intervention in the rest of the world was necessary to parry further evils. They envisaged such "accession" to European civilization as beneficial to the assisted peoples. They did not foresee that the theories of racial hierarchy justifying their intervention could undermine the existence of indigenous peoples. Hence, the era of the revolution of 1848 was not just the great watershed between optimism and pessimism about French society or about the European role in the world. The bright hopes launched in the Romantic era of receptivity to the exotic "Other" had their sombre side of social fear and exploitation.

---

97 Jean-Pierre Abel Rémusat, *Mélanges asiatiques* (Paris: Dondey-Dupré pére et fils, 1829), 244, cited in Morel, *Traité*, 473–4n.

APPENDICES

APPENDIX 1

Active Members of the
Société phrénologique de Paris
or supporters of phrenology

	AGE IN 1831
Andral fils, Gabriel, 1797–1876, internal pathology Paris Fac. Med.	34
Appert, Benjamin, 1797–1873, prison inspector	34
Bailly de Blois, Etienne-Marin MD, 1796–	35
Belhomme, Jacques-Etienne MD 1800–80	31
Bérard, Pierre-Honoré, 1797–1858, prof. École de médecine MD	34
Berbrugger, Adrien, 1801–69	30
Beunaiche de la Corbière, Jean-Baptiste, 1801–78	30
Bouillaud, Jean-François, 1796–1881	35
Bourdon, Isidore, 1796–1861	35
Brierre de Boismont, Alexandre-Jacques-François, 1798–1881, MD	33
Broussais, Casimir-Anne-Marie, 1803–47, Mil. hospital of Gros-Caillou	28
Broussais, François-Victor-Joseph, 1772–1838, Fac. de Médecine	59
Cloquet, Jules, 10 mai 1790–1883, Fac. Med.	41
David d'Angers, Pierre-Jean, 1788–1856, sculptor	43
Dumoutier, Alexandre, 1797–1871	34
Falret, Jean-Pierre, Salpêtrière, Vanves, 1794–1870	37
Faucher, Léon, 9 Aug. 1831, 1803–1854	28
Ferrus, Guillaume, 1784–1861, Bicêtre	47
Foissac, Pierre, 1801–86	30
Fossati, Giovanni, 1786–1874	45
Foville, Achille Louis, 1799–1878, alienist at Rouen 12 April	32
Gerdy, Nicolas, 1797–1856	34
Harel, Charles, 1771–1852	60
Las Cases fils, Emmanuel, 1800–54, deputy	31

Lasteyrie du Saillant, 1759–1849	71
Lauvergne, Hubert, 1796–1859	35
Le Rousseau, Julien, 1812–? (not a member)	20
Lucas, Prosper, 1805–85 (not a member at first)	26
Luchet, Auguste, 1806–72 (joined later)	25
Marchal de Calvi, Charles-Jacob, 1815–73 (joined later)	16
Mège, Jean-Baptiste, 1787–186?	44
Royer-Collard, Hippolyte-Louis, 1802–50, MD	29
Sarlandière, Jean-Baptiste, 1787–1838	44
Scoutetten, Henri, 1799–1871 (not in Paris)	32
Spurzheim, Johann Gaspard, 1776–1832 (hon. member who resigned)	55
Ternaux, baron Guillaume-Louis de, 1763–1833, former deputy	58
Trélat, Ulysse, 1795–1879 (not a member)	36
Vimont, Joseph, 1795–1857 (honorary member)	36
Voisin, Félix, 1794–1872	37
Ysabeau, Victor-Frédéric-Alexandre, 1793–1873 (not a member)	38
Average age	36.85

OPPONENTS	AGE IN 1831 OR WHEN OPPOSED TO GALL
Cerise, Laurent, 1807–69	24
Cuvier, Georges, 1769–1832 (39 when opposed Gall)	62
Debreyne, Pierre-Jean-Corneille, 1786–1867	45
Dubois d'Amiens Frédéric, 1799–1873	32
Flourens, Marie-Jean-Pierre, 1794–1867	37
Lélut, Louis-Francisque, 1804–77	27
Leuret, François, 1797–1881	34
Magendie, François, 1783–1855	48
Moreau de la Sarthe, L.-J., 1771–1826 (when wrote against Gall)	33
Average age	38

Source for members: "Liste des membres de la Société phrénologique de Paris," *Journal de la Société phrénologique de Paris* 1 (1832): 21–8

APPENDIX 2

Société de géographie de Paris Founders

1	Laplace	noble, Institute
2	de Rosily-Mesros vp comte	noble, Navy Marine archives Institute
3	Chateaubriand vp	noble and peer Institute
4	Pastoret, Amédée sec.-gen.	noble, Justice official
5	Delessert, Benjamin – scrutineer	noble baron, banker
6	Ternaux – scrutineer	noble baron, ex-deputy
7	Chapellier treasurer	notary (law)
8	Champollion-Figeac – archivist	Institute corr. and Egyptologist librarian, archivist

CENTRAL COMMISSION

9	Langlès	Institute and professor and librarian
10	Barbié du Bocage, JD	noble, Institute and prof.
11	Jaubert, Amédée	law – maître des requêtes – Turkish professor
12	Héricart de Thury – vicomte	Quarries inspector official, noble masters of requests law, deputy
13	Letronne	classicist and Institute
14	Jomard	Institute and Egyptology
15	Walckenaer	Seine official and noble, Institute
16	de Rossel	noble, Navy, Institute
17	de Freycinet	noble, Navy
18	Malte-Brun	geographer (letters)

19	Eyriès	geographic journalist
20	Lapie	ing.-geog.-military
21	Baron Denon	noble, Institute
22	Humboldt Alex.	noble, Institute
23	Guilleminot, comte	war archives military, noble
24	Girard	Institute
25	Beautems-Beaupré	Institute
26	Coquebert de Montbret	noble, Institute, official
27	Jacotin	military – ing.-geog.-Egypt
28	Warden	ex-US consul
29	Roux	For. Affairs official
30	Puissant	military – ing.-géog.
31	Castellan	Institute
32	Champollion jeune	Egyptology – scholar
33	Cuvier, baron	noble – council of State, Institute
34	Cirbied	Oriental langs. professor
35	Tromelin, baron	noble, military
36	Bajot	Navy official and Annales Maritimes ed.
37	Chateaugiron marquis	noble and Seine official
38	Pastoret, comte de	noble, master of requests law, and scholar
39	Verneur	prefecture Seine official, editor Journal des voyages
40	Férussac, baron	noble, army, and scholar
41	Barbié du Bocage	noble and scholar
42	Vauvilliers	Navy official

OTHER FOUNDERS

43	Cadeau d'Acy	noble
44	Aguillon	
45	Ailly, baron d'	noble
46	Allard maire Saint-Mandé	official
47	Andréossy, comte	general-military
48	Bailleul	law
49	Balbi, Adrien	prof., statistics and geog.
50	Barbié du Bocage JG	For. Affairs official, noble
51	Barnet	
52	Barrière	Seine prefecture official
53	Beauveau, prince Edmond de	noble

54	Bellart	proc. gen. – law, deputy
55	Bérard	law, master of requests
56	Bérard de Pithon	noble, letters
57	Berthollet, comte	noble, peer, Institute
58	Bianchi	Oriental langs. interpreter
59	Bocher	military officer
60	Boissy, comte Octave de	noble
61	Bonnard de	noble, mining eng.
62	Bonne, chevalier	noble, ing.-geog. – military
63	Bonnelier	
64	Bordet	teacher, letters
65	Borel de Bretizel-	noble, deputy, Court Cass. Law
66	Bottin	publisher
67	Bourboulon de Saint-Edme	noble, receiver general
68	Boué	physician
69	Boulard père	ex-notary law
70	Boullée	Council of State official
71	Bowdich, Edwards	
72	Brousseaud	military – ing.-géog.
73	Brué	geographer
74	Cadet de Metz	noble, letters
75	Caïx	teacher and librarian
76	Capelle, baron	noble – council of State, official
77	Chabaud-Latour, baron	noble, deputy
78	Chabrol de Volvic, comte	noble, official, prefect, eng.
		military officer
79	Chapsal	letters
80	Chateaugiron, marquis	noble, Seine official
81	Chaudoir, baron	noble
82	Coraboeuf	military – ing.-geog.
83	Cottin	notary – law
84	Courcier	
85	Cousinery	Institute corr., ex-consul
86	Dalberg, duc de	noble, peer, minister
87	Danemarck Chrétien Fred.	noble – foreign
88	Dechabrefy	
89	Delaborde, comte, Alex	Institute, law – noble
90	Delagonde, baron	noble, city official
91	Delalive, baron	noble, Royal official
92	Delcros	military – ing.-geog.

93	Del'or	military – ing.-geog.
94	Denaix	military
95	Desain de Saint-Gobert	noble, city official
96	Desmoulins	Bordeaux customs
97	Devilliers	Ponts et Chaussées eng.
98	Dezoz de la Roquette	noble, Aff. Etr. official
99	Didot, Firmin	publisher
100	Doudeauville, duc de	noble, peer
101	Ducros	avocat – law
102	Dufour	géographe
103	Dumont d'Urville	noble, Navy
104	Duperrey	noble, Navy
105	Esquirol	physician
106	Everat	publisher
107	Eymery	publisher or bookseller
108	Eyriès	letters – geographer
109	Eyriès	négociant – Havre
110	Fenwick	ex-US consul, Bordeaux
111	Feutrier	church
112	Fitz-James, duc	noble, peer
113	Flury	council of state, for. affairs
114	Fourier, baron	noble, Institute
115	Frazans, chevalier	noble, law court councillor
116	Froment	
117	Funchal, comte	noble
118	Gail	Institute, prof. Collège de France
119	Gareau	law
120	Garnier	law
121	Gasteros	
122	Gauttier	Navy
123	Gay-Lussac	Institute
124	Gentil	official
125	Gérard van Dertaoleon	drawing teacher
126	Gide père	geog. publisher
127	Gourcuff, de	noble, banker
128	Guilleminot, comte	noble, army war archives mil.
129	Guyonnet de Sénac	noble, physician – oculist
130	Guys	vice-consul in Syria, banker
131	Hauterive, comte d'	noble, Institute, For. Affairs and Council of State

132	Haxo, baron	noble, mil. eng.
133	Hell, de	noble, Navy
134	Hély d'Oissel, baron	noble, council of state
135	Henry	military – ing.-geog.
136	Henry	
137	Hericart-Ferrand de Thury, vicomte	noble
138	Herbin-Dehale	official forestry
139	Hottinguer	banker
140	Humblot-Conté	deputy
141	Ilinski, count Jmes	Russian noble, academician
142	Isambert	law
143	Jehannot	treasury official
144	Jullien MA	editor
145	Lainé	minister, deputy
146	Lapeyrière, de	noble, Seine receiver
147	Lapie fils	military – ing.-geog.
148	Largé	collège teacher
149	Las Cases, comte	noble
150	Las Cases, Emmanuel	noble, man of politics
151	Lebeau	law, Seine dept.
152	Lecousturier aîné	postal official
153	Lemaître	military eng. officer
154	Leroy	ex-consul
155	Lesecq	math. teacher
156	Lesueur	cadaster engineer
157	Lesur	letters
158	Llorente	letters
159	Maffioli	law – Cour des Comptes
160	Marcellus, vicomte	noble, dipl. sec.
161	Marcescheau	vice-consul in Arta
162	Marcotte	munic. treasury official
163	Marcotte-d'Argenteuil	noble, forest admin.
164	Mauger	philos. prof.
165	Maurice-Geneva	
166	Maurice baron	noble, Institute
167	Mège	physician of Talleyrand
168	Michel	engraver, mapmaker
169	Michu	physician
170	Miel	Seine official
171	Mollien, comte	noble, explorer

172	Mongeot	law
173	Montbrun des Bassayns de	Legion of honor
174	Moreau	négociant
175	Morier	
176	Morin de Sainte-Colombe	noble
177	Mosbourg, comte	noble
178	Mounier, baron	noble, peer, police official,
179	Museux	law, map author
180	Pastoret, marquis de	noble, peer, law
181	Perré	négociant
182	Picquet père	geographer
183	Picquet fils	geographer
184	Pille, comte de	noble, lt. gen. military
185	Plaisance, duc de	noble
186	Portal, baron de	noble, Marine and Colonies minister
187	Portal fils	
188	Puillon Boblaye	military – ing.-geog.
189	Rataud jeune	customs official
190	Rauzan, duc de	noble
191	Rayneval, de	noble, For. Affairs deputy minister
192	Regnier	lower court judge
193	Renaudière, de la	noble, letters
194	Reiset	Seine-Inf. official
195	Richelieu, duc de	noble, prime minister
196	Ripault	Institut d'Egypte – so eng.?
197	Rochefoucauld-Liancourt, duc de	noble, peer
198	Roger	noble, colonial admin. official
199	Rothschild	banker
200	Saldanha de Gama, comte	noble
201	Saulty, de	regent Bank of France, receiver, noble
202	Schonen, baron de	noble, counselor
203	Senonnes, vicomte de	Ministry Royal Household, noble
204	Servois	Cambray clergy
205	Sidney-Smith	Navy admiral
206	Silvestre	Institute

207	Smith S.	printer
208	Staël-Holstein, baron de	noble
209	Sorgo, comte de	noble
210	Soustains, de	noble, Eure receiver
211	Souza, de	noble
212	Sueur-Merlin	admin. of customs
213	Symonet	deputy, mayor
214	Tarbé de Vauxclairs, chevalier de	noble, master of requests, Civil Eng. inspector
215	Tardieu, Ambroise	engraver – geog.
216	Tardieu, Pierre	engraver – geog.
217	Tupinier, baron	noble, Navy ministry ports and constructions
218	Vauvilliers	Navy ministry sec.-gen.
219	Vindé, comte de	noble, peer
220	Vivien de Saint-Martin	noble, geographer

nobles with particle or otherwise identifiable 89/220= 40.9%
officials in high or lower admin. 33/220= 15%
peers 4.5%
deputies 3.6%
2.7% bankers, even fewer négociants
3.6%Naval officers
7.2% teachers, professor, men of letters
9.5% mil., engineers or other officers
2.3% physicians
10.9% Institute members or correspondents
9% Law

Source: *Bulletin de la Société de Géographie de Paris* 1 (1822): 10–24.

APPENDIX 3

Members of the Société ethnologique de Paris

BUREAU	
PRESIDENT	Prince de Joinville-Protector
	William-Frédéric Edwards-died 1842, replaced in turn by Santarém 1843, Henri Milne-Edwards, Charles Lenormant 1847
VICE-PRESIDENT	Manuel Francisco de Barros e Sousa, vicomte de Santarém-Institute-pres. in 1843, later honorary president
VICE-PRESIDENT	Marie-Armand-Pascal d'Avezac-Société de Géographie, SG*
	Joseph-Héliodore-Sagesse-Vertu Garcin de Tassy 1843
	Alcide d'Orbigny 1847
SECRETARY	C. Imbert des Mottelettes, SG
	Gustave d'Eichthal, 1846 SG
ASSISTANT SECRETARY	d'Eichthal 1841
	Victor Courtet de l'Isle 1846,
	Pascal Duprat 1847
TREASURER	M.A. Noël Desvergers-SG

FONDATEURS-16

Edwards	physician, naturalist, Acad. Moral and Political Sciences
Santarém	
d'Avezac	Naval ministry archives
C. Imbert des Mottelettes	
Filon	prof. École normale

* SG = member of the Société de Géographie

Garcin de Tassy	Institute Acad. Inscriptions, V.P. in 1843, Hindi scholar
Henri Milne-Edwards	Acad. Scis.-pres. 1844-prof. MHN
Jules Michelet	Institute, Acad. Moral and Polit. Scis. historian
Jean-Antoine Letronne	Acad. Inscriptions geographer and classicist
David (d'Angers)	Institute-sculptor, Acad. Fine Arts
Marie-Jean-Pierre Flourens	Acad. Scis. physiologist
Lenormant	Bibl. Royale curator and administrator Prof. History, Egyptology, Sorbonne
Sabin Berthelot	SG
Alcide d'Orbigny	SG, botanist, Pres., Geological Society
Achille-Louis-François Foville	chief physician, Maison royale de Charenton, Academy of Medicine
Charles-Emmanuel	

COMITÉ CENTRAL

Milne-Edwards as of 1845	
Lenormant	
Santarem	
d'Avezac	
Imbert des Mottelettes	
Garcin de Tassy	
Michelet	
Filon	
Alcide d'Orbigny	
Foville	
Berthelot	
d'Eichthal	
Noël Desvergers	SG, wrote instruction with Edwards and de Bertou
Eugène Froberville	SG, Madagascar exploration
Philippe Lebas	Institute Acad. Inscriptions historian
Benet	SG, ex-royal physician, Lahore
Matter	Inspector-general of studies
Troyer	Asiatic Society – in bureau 1847
de Bonnechose	château de Saint-Cloud, librarian

MEMBERS RECEIVED AT MEETINGS-53

Henri Ternaux-Compans	SG, director of Nouvelles Annales des Voyages
de Bertou	SG, helped write Instruction
Noël Desvergers	SG, helped write Instruction
Achille Comte	Natural History Society, zoologist, Académie de Paris
Amédée Jaubert	Acad. Inscriptions, Persian professor, Collège de France
James Orchard Halliwell	Royal Society, London
Frederic Forbes	physician of India-died by 1845
Gustave d'Eichthal	SG
Victor Courtet de l'Isle	SG, entrepreneur, racial theorist
Eugène de Froberville	SG
Philippe-François de LaRenaudière	SG
Alphonse Toussenel Verolot	history, collège Charlemagne
Isidore Geoffroy Saint-Hilaire	Academy of Sciences, naturalist
Euryale Cazeaux	Dir., d'Arcachon Co.
J. Desjardins	Soc. Hist. Naturelle Mauritius-died by 1845
Alexandre-François Barbier du Bocage	SG, ancient geography scholar
Alex. Brongniart	Academy of Sciences, botany
Louis Mandl	physician
Louis Dussieux	
Le Breton	physician
Le Roi	physician
Fourcault	physician
Da Gama Machado	Legation of Portugal
de Bonnechose Ditchfield	librarian, château Saint-Cloud
Ami Boué	physician
Hippolyte Fortoul	archivist
A. Thomassy	SG (same as Raymond Thomassy?)
Matter	inspector-general of studies

Werner, painter	Jardin des Plantes
Hocquart	
Ernest Breton	Soc. des Antiquaires de France
Auguste Le Duc	SG
Saint-Elme Le Duc	SG
Desnoyers	physician, SG and librarian, Muséum d'histoire naturelle
Lebas	Institute Acad. Inscriptions
Benet	SG
Montefiore	SG
de Brière	Société des Antiquaires, SG
capt. Troyer	retired mil. Officer, SG
Aurélien de Courson	
Louis-Francisque Lélut	chief physician of "aliénés"-Salpêtrière-Jan. 1841
Louis Vivien de Saint-Martin	SG, received Jan. 1841 – letters, geography
Dulaurier	prof. of Malay, École spéciale de langues orientales
de Schoenfeld	Jan. 1841
Eugène Sicé	
Victor Lanjuinais	deputy, Loire-Inférieure
Sucquet	naval surgeon
Rey	
Adolphe Guéroult	consul of France, Tampico
Constant Sicé	
Isidore Löwenstern	traveler to US, Cuba, and Mexico, SG

NEW ORDINARY MEMBERS-1845 AND AFTER-114

comte de Castelnau	traveler to America, SG
Edouard Biot	
Alex. Exarque	
Gen. de Yermoloff	Russian army general
C.-Claude Pierquin de Gembloux	teacher, physician
Xavier Raymond	
Ober Müller (Obermüller?)	

Pierre-Alexandre-Marie Dumoutier	physician of ship *Astrolabe*, naturalist
Auguis	deputy
Eusèbe de Salles	Langues orientales, Marseille
abbé Jean-Joseph-Léandre Bargès	Hebrew professor, Sorbonne
Armand Demarquay	architect, Saint-Germain railway
Alfred Maury	Société des Antiquaires de France, man of letters
Casimir Guérin	
Adolphe d'Eichthal	banker
Clapeyron	mining engineer
Frédéric Ayrton	Asiatic Society of London
Mallat	Indochina – on mission
Armand de Quatrefages	naturalist and prof. of zoology-Feb. 1844
Duvernois	Collège de France-Feb. 1844
Jules Guérin	physician, La Muette orthopedic establishment
Achille Valenciennes	préparateur, Muséum national d'histoire naturelle
Edouard Rodrigues	broker-1844
Eugène de Mofras	embassy attaché
Eugène de Maizan	ship's ensign
René de Semallé	teacher, SG
Dally	ex-prof.-Athénée de Bruxelles
chevalier Ferrao de Castelbanco	
Anne-Jean-Baptiste Raffenel	naval officer, explorer, SG-Sept. 1844
Haight	
James Haywood	
Gabriel Lafond de Lurcy	long voyage cpt.
Liger de Libessart	ship's ensign
1846-Emile Péreire	banker, Saint-Germain railway director
Isaac Péreire	banker, Saint-Germain railway director
Victor Schoelcher	art critic, journalist
1847-Michel Chevalier	councillor of state, political economy prof., Collège de France

Eugène Burnouf	Institute Acad. Inscriptions, Collège de France Sanskrit literature
Pascal Duprat	journalist
Olinde Rodrigues	banker
Henri Rodrigues	broker
Hippolyte Rodrigues	broker
Hennecart	deputy
Emile Paton	man of letters
Toussaint	sculptor
Adolphe Vieyra	broker
Baron Ferdinand d'Eckstein	man of letters, India enthusiast
Ritt	school inspector of primary schools
Lallemand	physician, Academy of Sciences
Paul Delaroche	painter, Academy of Fine Arts
Bourgeois	property owner
Ernest Gouin	civil engineer
Cheuvreux	wholesale merchant
Raymond-Bonheur	painter
Dejean de la Bâtie	delegate, Colonial Council, Ile de Bourbon (Réunion)
Charles-Jacob Marchal de Calvi	physician-physiology at Hôpital de Val de Grâce
Girard	painter
Cumberworth	sculptor
Ferdinand Moreau	agent de change
Adolphe Moreau	proprietor
Lemaître	lawyer (avocat)
Mathieu-Joseph-Bonaventure Orfila	dean, École de médecine
Horace Vernet	painter, Institute, Acad. Of Fine Arts
Léopold Javal	banker
Dr. Petit	physician, of waters of Vichy
Jules Benique	surgeon
de Reiset	delegate, Colonial Council, Guadeloupe
Emile Thomas	teacher, civil engineer
Feuilherade, late 1847	Île de France, lawyer (avocat)
Dumas	Acad. Sciences and dean, Faculty of Sciences

Jules Mohl	Institute and secretary, Asiatic Society
Blandin	Hôtel-Dieu surgeon, École de médecine
	Trousseau prof., École de médecine
Lebret	medical student
Urbain of Geneva	interpreter, Ministry of War
Denonvilliers	prof. anatomy, École de médecine
Lorette	cpt. mil. eng.-Sci. Commission of Algeria
Jourdan	deputy director, Comité des Annon.

ADDITIONAL MEMBERS ON 1847 LIST

de Lisboa	Brazil legation attaché
Ayerton	Asiatic Society, London
Duvernoy	prof., Collège de France
Furnari	physician
de Mauroy	founder, *Revue des deux mondes*
Dunlop	founder of Temperance Society, London
Leclère	physician
Amédée Courty	physician
Dr. Pierre Rayer	Institute member, Academy of Scis.
Carette	engineering cpt., Comité scientifique d'Algérie
Adolphe Moreau	proprietor
Ferdinand Moreau	broker
Jacques Hombron	navy naturalist, physician
Honoré Jacquinot	naval surgeon
Génissy de Beaulieu	proprietor
Perinnon	cmdt., naval artillery corps
Rochet d'Héricourt	traveler to Abyssinia, SG
Billiard	prefect in Amiens
Gobert	physician
Eugène de Monglave	
Ebray	civil engineer
Arnoux	naval surgeon
Mericault, employee	Navy ministry
Fleury	man of letters
Cornay de Rochefort	physician
Adolphe Delegorgue	traveler
Francino da Arietos	Havana
Duméril fils	prof., École de médecine, Jardin des plantes

Philippeau	aide-naturaliste, Jardin des plantes
Roberty	painter
D. Barret	
Gosselin	chief of anatomical works, École de médecine
Jean-Jacques Ampère	member of Institute, Acad. Française
Léon Vaïsse	prof., École des sourds et muets

FOREIGN MEMBERS SPONTANEOUSLY ELECTED-73

James Cowles Prichard	physician, Bristol
William Lawrence	physician, London
Karl Ritter	prof. and geographer, Berlin
Eduard Ruppel	Frankfurt am Main
Martius	Acad. Sciences, Munich
Adrien Balbi	Vienna-Imp. Councillor-1845 at Milan
J. Washington	ex-secretary, Royal Geog. Society, London
de Angelis	Buenos-Aires
Franzini	Acad. Sciences, Lisbon
Rafn	Société des Antiquaires du Nord, Copenhagen-
comte Graberg	Florence
de Hamsö	
Finn Magnussen	Copenhagen
Thomas Hodgkin	physician, London
Elias Rodrigues	vice-secretary, Acad. Sciences, Lisbon
Ramon de la Sagra	correspondent Institute; Botanical Garden Havana
Dubois de Monpereux	Neufchâtel
Jacques-Antoine	Fr. consul, Tahiti
Moerenhout	
Corr	1st drogman, French amb., Constantinople
Vilardebo	Museum of Montevideo
Roujoux	director of French Steamships at Athens
James Geel	librarian, Univ. of Leyden
Schroder	rector, Univ. of Uppsala
Thomas Wright	London-1845 correspondent of Institute
A. Asher	Berlin
abbé Arri	Acad. Turin-died by 1845
Rosellini	Pisa
W. Allen	London

Baronet Thomas Fowell Buxton	Society for the Civilisation of Africa
W. Hodgson	ex-consul US at Algiers-now in Savannah
Col. Julian R. Jackson	Sec., Royal Geographical Society, London
Wagner	prof., Göttingen
Haye Horace Wilson	prof., Sanskrit-Oxford
Bodmer	
Biard	painter
Dumoutier	[listed incorrectly as foreign]
Guillaume August de Schlegel	Bonn
Chr. Lassen	Bonn
Adam Mickiewicz	Slavic literature, Collège de France
Kazimirski	drogman, Fr. ambassador to Persia
de Biberstein	
Wallon	
Yanosky	
Wirer	Aulic Councillor, Vienna
Tognio	prof. in Pest, Hungary
Schordan	
Bene	consul
Czermak	professor in Vienna
Kriegk	pres., Frankfurt Society of Geography
Lambert	director, École Polytechnique, Cairo
Claussen	Rio de Janeiro
Wallich	Superintendent, Botanical Garden, Calcutta
W. O'Shaugnessy	secretary, Asiatic Society, Calcutta
1845-Holmboe	Oriental Languages, Christiania, Norway
Joachim Lelewel	Brussels
Samuel Morton	physician, Philadelphia
Anders Retzius	member, Academy of Sciences, Stockholm
Arthur Conolly	died by 1845
Adolphe Quetelet	sec.-perpétuel, Brussels Acad. Scis. 1846
Martinez	sec., Acad. Scis. Madrid?
1847 Elphinston	London
Charles Malcolm	Rear Admiral, London
Albert Gallatin	pres., Ethnological Society, New York
Jean-Baptiste-Julien Omalius d'Halloy	member, Academy of Sciences, Brussels
Richard King	secretary, Ethnological Society, London

Edward Robinson	vice-pres., Ethnological Society, New York
Henry Schoolcraft	vice-pres., Ethnological Society, New York
J.K. Buschmann	
Toby Prinseps	London
James Ferguson	member, Irish Academy, Dublin
George Catlin	painter, United States
De Montigny	consul of France at Shanghai
Boussakis	physician, Athens
prince de Canino	

CORRESPONDING MEMBERS-15

Antoine d'Abbadie	Abyssinia
Charles Deane	India
Ségur Dupeyron	Navy Conseil de santé
Annibal de Grasse	captain
Benit	physician of French Legation, US
Pavie	India
R. Carr Woods	India
Dufoz de Maufras	
Dr. W. Stanger	
Leguével de la Combe	Zeyla, east Africa
Charlemagne-Théophile	
Le Febvre	Abyssinia – SG, naval officer – June 1840
Jean-Antoine-Victor	
Martin de Moussy	physician, Montevideo
Col. Cadazzy	Venezuela
Johann Moritz Rugendas	painter and traveler, South America
1845-Alcide Pelletan	physician, South America

HONORARY MEMBERS-28

Duke of Sussex	pres., Royal Society-died by 1845
Johann Friedrich Blumenbach	naturalist, Göttingen died 1840
Count Munster	pres., Asiatic Society of London-died by 1845
Lord Brougham	Peer
Major Jarvis	surgeon-general, India

Prince Maximilien de Wied-Neuwied	traveler to US
Baron Alexandre de Humboldt	geographer, SG, Council of State, Prussia
Baron de Hammer Pugstall	Aulic Councillor, Vienna
Gen. Van den Bosch	ex-governor, Dutch Indies-died by 1845
Van de Weyer	Belgian minister plenipotentiary to London
Count Ouwarow	Academy of Sciences, St. Petersburg
Count Woronzow	gov.-general, New Russia
Gen. Golowin	Commander-in-chief, Grusie, Armenia, Trans-Caucasia
Count Osterman	Geneva
Steven	Russian Council of State, Simpheropol
de Navarrete	pres., Royal Academy of History, Madrid
conseiller de Macedo	sec., Royal Acad. Sciences, Lisbon
conte Comaldoli	pres., Acad. Sciences, Naples-died by 1845
Gen. Colettis	plenipotentiary of Greece in Paris
Pierre-Etienne du Ponceau	Am. Philos. Society, Boston-died by 1845
Dallas	sec., American Philos. Society
Tiknor	ex-minister, US
Guilermo de Souza	Foreign Affairs Minister, Brazil
de Villela Barboza	de Paranagua-Brazil Navy
Paulo Barboza	sec. to Emperor, Brazil
Vicomte de San Leopoldo	Institute of History and Geography-Rio-Janeiro
conte Santangelo	Interior ministry, Naples

Source: *Mémoires de la Société ethnologique de Paris*, vol. 1 (1841) Bulletin, xvi–xxi vol. 2 (1845): v–ix + *Bulletin de la Société ethnologique de Paris* 1846–47, Archives de la Société d'Anthropologie de Paris, 1847 Liste de membres, Société d'ethnologie

Bibliography

MANUSCRIPTS

Archives, Ministère des Affaires Étrangères (AAE)

Afrique 13, Abyssinie, 1. 1838–50, nos 20,22, 37, 39, 113, 116–40

Archives nationales (AN)

AJ 15 551 dossier de Quatrefages
AJ 15 562 Papiers de Dumoutier
AJ 15 574 Dossier de Gaimard
Marine BB4 998 Voyage de Freycinet
Marine BB4 1000 Voyage de Duperrey
Marine BB4 1002 Voyage de Dumont d'Urville
Marine BB4 1009 Instructions to d'Urville
Marine BB 1014 Abyssinie
F17 17201 Sociétés savantes
F17 3000
F17 3038 Dumoutier's private course
F17 3038 Société phrénologique de Paris
F17 3003B Ministerial subsidies
Marine 5JJ 68 Journal de Raillard, voyage de Freycinet

Bibliothèque de l'Arsénal (BA)

Fonds d'Eichthal, MS. 13741/23 and 13741/37
MS. 13750/170, 13750/211, 13750/250, 13750/265

MS. 13751/1, 16, 56, 65, 76
MS. 13759
MS. 14719, 14720
Fonds Enfantin, MS. 7839/12; 7839/14

Bibliothèque historique de la Ville de Paris

Papiers de l'Athénée de Paris MS. CP 3948; MS. 772, MS. 920

Bibliothèque du Musée de l'Homme

MS. 72, Dumoutier, Journal de son voyage à bord de l'Astrolabe, [1837–40]
Archives de la Société d'anthropologie de Paris (owned by the Society),
unclassified Notes pour les procès-verbaux, M7 1660, MI 1744–5
Correspondance.

Bibliothèque nationale, Cartes et Plans, Archives de la
Société de géographie (ASG)

Colis 3 bis, Colis 4 bis, Colis 18, Colis 19, Colis 21, Colis 26, Colis 65
MS. in-4° 12. Vivien de Saint-Martin, "Études d'histoire générale"
MS. in-4° 34, 1830, 1832 – Liste de présences, réunions de la commission
centrale

Fondation Dosne-Thiers, Fonds d'Eichthal

Carton IV/R2; Carton IV/R6

PRINTED WORKS

Periodicals

Archives générales de la médecine (1825)
Bulletin de l'Académie royale de médecine 1841–42
Bulletin de la Société d'anthropologie de Paris 1859–68 (*BSAP*)
Bulletin de la Société de Géographie de Paris 1821–48, 1855 (*BSG*)
Bulletin de la Société ethnologique de Paris 1846–47. 3 vols (*BSEP*)
La Décade philosophique an IX
Esculape 1839
Gazette de France 1808

Journal de l'Empire 1808
Journal de la Société phrénologique de Paris 1832–35. 3 vols (*JSPP*)
Journal de Paris 1807
Journal universel et hebdomadaire de médecine et chirurgie pratiques 1832
The Lancet 1825, 1835–36
Mémoires de la Société d'anthropologie de Paris 1860–69. vols 1–3 (*MSAP*)
Mémoires de la Société ethnologique de Paris. Paris: 1841–45. 2 vols (*MSEP*)
Nouvelles annales des voyages 1845–48 (NAV)
La Phrénologie. 1837–39. 3 vols
Revue des deux mondes 1841, 1843
La Revue indépendante 1844–45

PRIMARY AND SECONDARY WORKS

Abbadie, Antoine d.' *L'Abyssinie et le roi Théodore*. Paris: Charles-Douniol, 1868.
Abbadie, Arnauld d.' *Douze ans dans la Haute Ethiopie Abyssinie*. Paris: L. Hachette, 1868.
– *Douze ans de séjour dans la Haute-Éthiopie*. eds. Jeanne-Marie Allier and Joseph Tubiana. 4 vols. Vatican City: Biblioteca apostolica vaticana, 1980–1999.
Abrams, L. and D.J. Miller. "Who Were the French Colonialists? A Reassessment of the Parti Colonial, 1890–1918." *Historical Journal* 19 (1976): 685–725.
Ackerknecht, Erwin H. "P.M.A. Dumoutier et la collection phrénologique du Musée de l'homme." *Bulletins et mémoires de la Société anthropologique de Paris* 10th sér., 7 (1956): 289–308.
Adas, Michael. *Machines as the Measure of Men: Scientific and Technological Superiority and Ideologies of Western Dominance*. Ithaca: Cornell University Press, 1989.
Ageron, Charles-Robert. *Modern Algeria: A History from 1830 to the Present*. ed. Michael Brett. London: Hurst, 1991.
Albury, W.R. "Corvisart and Broussais: Human Individuality and Medical Dominance." In Caroline Hannaway and Ann La Berge, eds. *Constructing Paris Medicine*. 221–50. Amsterdam: Éditions Rodopi, 1998.
Aldrich, Robert. *Greater France: A History of French Overseas Expansion*. New York: St Martin's Press, 1996.
Alexandre-Debray, Janine. *Victor Schoelcher ou la Mystique d'un athée*. Paris: Librairie Académique Perrin, 1983.
Andrew, Christopher M. and A.S. Kanya-Forstner. "Centre and Periphery: The Making of the Second French Empire, 1815–1930." *Journal of Imperial and Commonwealth History* 16 (1988): 9–34.
– "The French Colonial Party – Its Composition, Aims and Influence, 1885–1914." *Historical Journal* 14 (1971): 99–128.

Appert, Benjamin. *Bagnes, prisons et criminels.* Paris: Guilbert et Roux, 1836. 4 vols.

Atran, Scott, ed. *Histoire du concept d'espèce dans les sciences de la vie.* Paris: Fondation Singer-Polignac, 1987.

Augstein, Hannah F. "Aspects of philology and racial theory in 19th Century Celticism – the case of James Cowles Prichard." *Journal of European Studies* 28 (1998): 355–71.

Azouvi, François. "La phrénologie comme image anticipée de la psychologie." *Revue de synthèse* 3rd sér., nos 83–84 (1976): 251–78.

Bailly de Blois, Etienne-Marin. "De la physiologie appliqué à l'amélioration des institutions sociales." In *Oeuvres de Saint-Simon et Enfantin* [1865–78] 39 (Aalen: Otto Zeller, 1964): 175–197.

– *L'Existence de Dieu et la liberté morale démontrées par des arguments tirés de la doctrine du Dr. Gall.* Paris: Delaunay, 1824.

Balbi, Adrien. *Introduction à l'Atlas ethnographique du globe.* Paris: Rey and Gravier, 1826.

Banton, Michael. *Racial Theories.* Cambridge: Cambridge University Press, 1987.

Baridon, Laurent and Martial Guédron. *Corps et arts; Physionomies et physiologies dans les arts visuels.* Paris: L'Harmattan, 1999.

Barthez, Paul-Joseph. *Nouveaux élémens de la science de l'homme.* Montpellier: J. Martel, 1778.

Bathily, Abdoulaye."La conquête française du Haut-Fleuve Sénégal 1818–1887." *Bulletin de l'Institut Français de l'Afrique du Nord* 34, sér. B, 1 (1972): 67–112.

Baudin, Nicolas. *The Journal of Post Captain Nicolas Baudin.* Ed. Christine Cornell. Adelaide: Libraries Board of South Australia, 1974.

Baumgart, Winfried. *Imperialism: The Idea and the Reality of British and French Colonial Expansion, 1880–1914.* Oxford: Oxford University Press, 1982.

Bazard, Saint-Amand. *Le Producteur* 4 (1826): 417–18.

Belhomme, Jacques. "Compte rendu des travaux de la société phrénologique pendant le cours de l'année 1839." *Esculape* 1 (1 septembre 1839): 78–9.

Bell, Morag, Robin Butlin, and Michael Heffernan, eds. *Geography and Imperialism, 1820–1940.* Manchester: Manchester University Press, 1995.

Bénichou, Claude and Claude Blanckaert, eds. *Julien-Joseph Virey, naturaliste et anthropologue.* Paris: Librairie philosophique J. Vrin, 1988.

Bensa, Alban. "Colonialisme, racisme et ethnologie en Nouvelle-Calédonie." *Ethnologie française* 18, no. 2 (1988): 188–97.

Berdoulay, Vincent. *La Formation de l'École française de géographie 1870–1914.* Paris: Bibliothèque nationale, 1981.

Bérenger-Féraud, Laurent-Jean-Baptiste. "Étude sur les Ouolofs (Sénégambie)." *Revue d'anthropologie* 4 (1875): 466–94.

Berkhofer, Robert. *The White Man's Indian: The History of an Idea from Columbus to the Present.* New York: Knopf, 1978.

Bernal, Martin. *Black Athena: The Afroasiatic Roots of Classical Civilization.* New Brunswick: Rutgers, 1987–91. 2 vols.

Bertoletti, Stefano Fabbri. "The Anthropological Theory of Johann Friedrich Blumenbach." In Stefano Poggi and Maurizio Bossi, eds. *Romanticism in Science: Science in Europe, 1790–1840.* 103–25. Dordrecht: Kluwer Academic Publishers, 1994.

Betts, Raymond. *Assimilation and Association in French Colonial Theory 1890–1914.* New York: Columbia University Press, 1961.

– *Tricouleur: The French Empire Overseas.* London: Gordon and Cremonsi, 1978.

Beunaiche de la Corbière, Jean-Baptiste. *Discours de clôture.* 8 janvier 1844. Paris: Imprimerie E.B. Delanchy.

– *Discours de rentrée prononcé à la Société phrénologique de Paris le 11 janvier 1843.* Paris: P. Renouard, 1843.

– *De l'influence que doit exercer la Phrénologie sur les progrès ultérieurs de la philosophie et de la morale.* Paris: Masson, 1853.

Bichat, Xavier. *Recherces physiologiques sur la vie et la mort* [1800]. Ed. Jacques Ménétrier. Verviers: Gérard, 1973.

Blais, Hélène. "Les voyages français dans le Pacifique. Pratique de l'espace, savoirs géographiques et expansion coloniale" Thèse de doctorat, EHESS 2000. Not consulted.

Blanchard, Emile. *Voyage au Pôle Sud, partie IV. Anthropologie.* Paris: Gide et Baudry, 1854.

Blanckaert, Claude. "1800 – Le moment 'naturaliste' des sciences de l'homme." *Revue d'histoire des Sciences Humaines* no. 3 (2000): 117–60.

– "L'anthropologie en France, Le mot et l'histoire XVIᵉ-XIXᵉ siècle." *Bulletins et mémoires de la Société d'anthropologie de Paris* n.s. 1, nos 3–4 (1989): 13–44.

– "Buffon and the Natural History of Man: Writing History and the Founding Myth of Anthropology." *History of the Human Sciences* 6 (1993): 13–50

– "Contre la méthode: unité de l'homme et classification dans l'anthropologie des Lumières." *Études de lettres* (Lausanne) 12, nos 3–4 (1998): 111–26.

– "La Création de la chaire d'anthropologie du Muséum dans son contexte institutionnel et intellectuel 1832–1855." In Claude Blanckaert, Claudine Cohen, Pietro Corsi, et Jean-Louis Fischer eds. *Le Muséum au premier siècle de son histoire.* 85–123. Paris: Muséum national d'histoire naturelle, Archives, 1997.

– "La Crise de l'Anthropométrie: Des arts anthropotechniques aux dérives militantes (1860–1920)." In *Les Politiques de l'anthropologie, Discours et pratiques en France 1860–1940.* 95–172. Paris: L'Harmattan, 2001.

– "L'esclavage des Noirs et l'ethnographie américaine: Le point de vue de Paul Broca en 1858." In Claude Blanckaert, Jean-Louis Fischer, Roselyne Rey, eds. *Nature, Histoire, Société: essais en hommage à Jacques Roger.* 391–417. Paris: Klincksieck, 1995.

– "L'ethnographie de la décadence, Culture morale et mort des races (XVIIe-XIXe siècles)." *Gradhiva* 11 (1992): 47–65.

– "Méthode des moyennes et notion de "série suffisante" en anthropologie physique 1830–1880." In Jacqueline Feldman, Gérard Lagneau, B. Matalon, eds. *Moyenne, Milieu, Centre. Histoires et usages.* 213–43. Paris: Éditions de l'EHESS, 1991.

– "Monogénisme et polygénisme." In Patrick Tort, ed. *Dictionnaire du Darwinisme et de l'Evolution.* 3021–37. Paris: Presses Universitaires de France, 1996.

– "La naturalisation de l'homme de Linné à Darwin: Archéologie du débat nature/culture." In Albert Ducros, Jacqueline Ducros, et Frédéric Joulian, eds. *La culture est-elle naturelle? Histoire, Epistémologie et Applications récentes du Concept de Culture.* 15–24. Paris: Errance, 1998.

– "On the Origins of French Ethnology: William Edwards and the Doctrine of Race." In George W. Stocking, Jr., ed. *Bones, Bodies, Behavior: Essays on Biological Anthropology.* 18–55. Madison: University of Wisconsin Press, 1988.

– ed. *Les Politiques de l'anthropologie, Discours et pratiques en France 1860–1940.* Paris: L'Harmattan, 2001.

– "Le premesse dell'antropologia 'culturale' in Francia. Il dibattito sul 'Questionnaire de Sociologie et d'Ethnographie' di Charles Letourneau 1882–1883." *La ricerca folklorica* 32 (1995): 51–70.

– "Des sauvages en pays civilisé, L'anthropologie des criminels (1850–1900)." In Laurent Mucchielli, ed. *Histoire de la Criminologie française.* Paris: L'Harmattan, 1994.

– "'Story' et 'History' de l'ethnologie." *Revue de synthèse* 4th sér., nos 3–4 (1988): 451–67.

– "Le système des races." In Isabelle Poutrin, ed. *Le XIXe siècle: Science, politique et tradition.* 21–41. Paris: Berger-Levrault, 1995.

– "'Les vicissitudes de l'angle facial,' et les débuts de la craniométrie 1765–1875." *Revue de synthèse* 4th sér., nos 3–4 (1987): 417–53.

Blumenbach, Johann Friedrich. *The Anthropological Treatises of Johann Friedrich Blumenbach.* ed. Thomas Bendyshe. London: Anthropological Society by Longman, Green, Longman, Roberts, and Green, 1865.

Boetsch, Gilles and Michèle Fonton. "L'Ethnographie criminelle. Les applications de la doctrine lombrosienne aux peuples colonisés au XIXème siècle." In Laurent Mucchielli, *Histoire de la criminologie française.* Paris: L'Harmattan, 1994. 139–56.

Boissel, Jean. *Victor Courtet 1813–1867: premier théoricien de la hiérarchie des races.* Paris: PUF, 1972.

Bonnemains, Jacqueline, Elliott Forsyth, and Bernard Smith, eds. *Baudin in Australian Waters.* Melbourne: Oxford University Press, 1988.

Bory de Saint-Vincent, Jean-Baptiste-Geneviève-Marcellin. *L'Homme (homo) ou Essai zoologique sur le genre humain* [1825]. Paris: Rey et Gravier, 1827.

– "Sur l'anthropologie de l'Afrique française." *NAV* 5ᵉ sér., 6 (1846): 108–24.

Bourdon, Jean-Baptiste Isidore. *La Physiognomonie et la Phrénologie, ou connnaissance de l'homme d'après les traits du visage et les reliefs du crâne.* Paris: Charles Gosselin, 1842.

Brahimi, Denise. "Volney chez les sauvages: un idéologue contre l'idéologie." In Jean Roussel, ed. *L'héritage des lumières: Volney et les idéologues.* 73–81. Angers: Presses Universitaires d'Angers, 1988.

Braunstein, Jean-François. *Broussais et le matérialisme, Médecine et philosophie au XIXᵉ siècles.* Paris: Méridiens-Klincsieck, 1986.

Brissonnet, Lydie. "La Société: The Ethnological Society of Paris, 1839." *The Kroeber Anthropological Society Papers,* no. 59–60 (Spring-Fall 1979): 19–35.

Broberg, Gunnar. "Homo sapiens: Linnaeus's Classification of Man." In Tøre Frangsmyr, ed. *Linnaeus: The Man and His Work.* 157–94. Berkeley: University of California Press, 1983.

Broc, Numa. "L'Etablissement de la géographie en France: diffusion, institutions, projets 1870–1890." *Annales de géographie* 83, no. 459 (1974): 545–68.

– "Les grandes missions scientifiques françaises au XIXᵉ siècle Morée, Algérie, Mexique et leurs travaux géographiques." *Revue d'histoire des sciences* 34 (1981): 318–58.

– *Regards sur la géographie française de la Renaissance à nos jours.* Perpignan: Presses universitaires, 1994. 1:177–205.

Broca, Paul. *Mémoires d'anthropologie.* ed. Claude Blanckaert. Paris: Jean Michel Place, 1989.

– *On the Phenomena of Hybridity in the Genus Homo.* London: Longman, Green, Longman & Roberts, 1864.

Broussais, Casimir. *Hygiène morale, ou application de la physiologie à la morale et à l'éducation.* Paris: J.-B. Baillière, 1837.

– *De la phrénologie humaine et comparée ou Réponse aux objections de MM. Flourens et Leuret.* Discours du 18 décembre 1842. Paris, 1842.

Broussais, François-Joseph-Victor. *Cours de phrénologie.* Paris: J.-B. Baillière, 1836.

Brunhes, Jean. "L'ethnographie et la géographie humaine." *L'Ethnographie* 1 (1913): 29–40.

Bruyères, Hippolyte. *La Phrénologie, Le Geste et la physionomie mis en scène.* Paris: Aubert, 1846.

Buchez, Philippe et Ulysse Trélat. *Précis élémentaire d'hygiène*. Paris: Raymond, 1825.

Buffon, Georges-Louis Leclerc, comte de. *Histoire naturelle générale et particulière*. Paris: Imprimerie royale, 1750–89. 15 vols.

– *Oeuvres de Buffon, avec la synonymie et la classification de Cuvier*. 5 vols. "Premier discours" in *Histoire naturelle générale et particulière* [1749]. ed. J. Pizzetta. Paris: Parent Desbarres, 1868.

Bullard, Alice. "Becoming Savage? The First Step toward Civilization and the Practices of Intransigence in New Caledonia." *History and Anthropology* 10, no. 4 (1998): 319–74.

– *Exile to Paradise: Savagery and Cvilization in Paris and the South Pacific, 1790–1900*. Stanford: Stanford University Press, 2000.

Burke III, Edmund. "Thomas Ismail Urbain 1812–84: Indigénophile and Precursor of Négritude." In G. Wesley Johnson, ed. *Double Impact: France and Africa in the Age of Imperialism*. 319–30. Westport: Greenwood Press, 1985.

Cabanis, Pierre-Jean-Georges. *Oeuvres philosophiques*. ed. Claude Lehec et Jean Cazeneuve. Paris: PUF, 1956. 2 vols.

Caillié, René. *Travels through Central Africa to Timbuctoo: and across the Great Desert, to Morocco: performed in the years 1824–1828*. London: Henry Colburn and Richard Bentley, 1830; London: Frank Cass reprint, 1968. 2 vols.

– *Voyage à Tombouctou* [1830]. Paris: La Découverte, 1996. 2 vols.

Camper, Pierre. *Dissertation sur les variétés naturelles qui caractérisent la physionomie des hommes des divers climats et des différents âges, suivies de Réflexions sur la Beauté*. Paris: H.J. Jansen, 1791.

Carlisle, Robert. *The Proffered Crown: Saint-Simonianism and the Doctrine of Hope*. Baltimore: The Johns Hopkins University Press, 1987.

Cartailhac, Emile. *Notice sur A. de Quatrefages*. Paris: G. Masson, 1892.

Cerise, Laurent-Alexis-Philibert. *Exposé et examen critique du système phrénologique*. Paris: Trinquart, 1836.

Chailleu, Luc. "La Revue orientale et américaine 1858–1879, Ethnographie, orientalisme et américanisme au XIXᵉ siècle." *L'Ethnographie* 86, no. 1 (1990): 89–107.

Chaline, Jean-Pierre. *Sociabilité et érudition dans les sociétés savantes en France XIXᵉ-XXᵉ siècles*. Paris: Éditions du C.T.H.S., 1995.

Chappey, Jean-Luc. "L'Anthropologie et l'histoire naturelle de l'homme en 1801. Les enjeux d'un heritage." *Annales historiques de la revolution française* no. 320 (avril-juin 2000): 47–54.

– "La Société des Observateurs de l'Homme 1799–1804, Genèse, personnel et activités d'une société savante à l'époque consulaire." Thèse Paris-I, 1999. I have seen only the summary.

- "Les sociétés savantes à l'époque consulaire." *Annales historiques de la Révolution française* no. 309 (juillet-sept 1997): 451–72.

Chevalier, Louis. *Laboring Classes and Dangerous Classes in Paris during the First Half of the Nineteenth Century* [1958]. Princeton: Princeton University Press, 1973.

Chevalier, Michel. *Religion Saint-Simonienne, Politique Industrielle et système de la Méditerranée.* Paris: Globe, 1832.

Clarke, Edwin C. and L.S. Jacyna. *Nineteenth-Century Origins of Neuroscientific Concepts.* Berkeley: University of California Press, 1987.

Claval, Paul. *Autour de Vidal de la Blache, La formation de l'École française de géographie.* Paris: CNRS, 1993.

- *Histoire de la géographie française de 1870 à nos jours.* Paris: Nathan, 1998.

Cohen, Mark. "Functional MRI: A Phrenology for the 1990s?" *Journal of Magnetic Resonance Imaging* 6 (1996): 273–4.

Cohen, William B. *The French Encounter with Africans 1530–1880.* Bloomington: Indiana University Press, 1980.

- "French Racism and its African Impact." In G. Wesley Johnson, ed. *Double Impact: France and Africa in the Age of Imperialism.* 305–17. Westport: Greenwood Press, 1985.

- "Imperial Mirage: The Western Sudan in French Thought and Action." *Journal of the Historical Society of Nigeria* 7, no. 3 (1974): 417–45.

Combe, George. *The Constitution of Man considered in relation to external objects* [1828–29]. Edinburgh: Maclachlan and Stewart, 1847. 8th ed. Reprint, Westmead: Gregg Internatonal, 1970.

Combes, Edmond and Maurice Tamisier. *Voyages en Abyssinie, dans le pays des Gallas, de Choa, et d'Ifat* [1838] Paris: L. Passard, 1843, 2nd ed. 4 vols.

Conklin, Alice L. *A Mission to Civilize: The Republican Idea of Empire in France and West Africa, 1895–1930.* Stanford: Stanford University Press, 1997.

Cooter, Roger. *The Culture of Popular Science, Phrenology, and the Organization of Consent in Nineteenth-Century Britain.* Cambridge: Cambridge University Press, 1984.

- "Phrenology and British Alienists, c. 1825–1845." *Medical History* 20 (1976): 1–21, 135–51.

Copans, Jean and Jean Jamin, eds. *Aux origines de l'anthropologie française, les mémoires de la Société des Observateurs de l'Homme en l'an VIII. Les hommes et leurs signes.* Paris: Le Sycomore, 1978.

Courtet de l'Isle, Victor. *Au congrès … Déterminer par l'histoire et par les sciences ce que l'on doit entendre par les mots de genre, espèces, et races appliqués à l'homme.* Paris: Bureau de l'Institut historique, 1835.

- *Mémoire sur les races humaines.* Paris: Baudouin, 1835.

– *Programme de réformes présenté au gouvernement provisoire 10 mars 1848.* Paris: Paulin, 1848.

– *La science politique fondée sur la science de l'homme ou Etude des races humaines sous le rapport philosophique, historique, et social.* Paris: Arthus Bertrand, 1838.

– *Tableau ethnographique du genre humain.* Paris: Arthus Bertrand, 1849.

Curtin, Philip D. *The Image of Africa: British Ideas and Action, 1780–1850.* Madison: University of Wisconsin Press, 1964. 2 vols.

Cuvier, Georges. *Leçons d'anatomie comparée.* Paris: Baudouin, 1800–05. 4 vols.

– *Le Règne animal.* Paris: Fortin, Masson, 1836–49 [1817]. 20 vols.

– *Le Règne animal distribué d'après son organisation.* Paris: Deterville, 1817.

– *Tableau élémentaire de l'histoire naturelle des animaux.* Paris: Baudouin, an VI [1798].

d'Allemagne, Henry-René. *Les Saint-Simoniens, 1827–1837.* Paris: Gründ, 1930.

d'Avezac, Pascal. *Histoire et description de tous les peuples. Afrique. Tableau général.* Paris: F. Didot frères, 1842.

Davis, David Brion. "Constructing Race: A Reflection." *William and Mary Quarterly* 54, no. 1 (1997): 7–18.

– "Looking at Slavery from Broader Perspectives." *American Historical Review* 105, no. 2 (April 2000): 1–34.

– *The Problem of Slavery in Western Culture.* Ithaca: Cornell University Press, 1966.

de Salle, Eusèbe. *Histoire générale des races humaines ou philosophie ethnographique.* Paris: Duprat/Pagnerre, 1849.

Debout, Emile. *Esquisse de la phrénologie et de ses applications exposées aux gens du monde.* Paris: H. Lebrun, 1843.

Debreyne, J.-B. *Pensées d'un croyant catholique.* Paris: Poussielgue-Rusand, 1844.

Degérando, Joseph-Marie. *The Observation of Savage Peoples* [1800]. ed. F.C.T. Moore. Berkeley: University of California Press, 1969.

d'Eichthal, Gustave. *Études sur l'histoire primitive des races océaniennes et américaines.* Paris: Mme. Veuve Dondey-Dupré, 1845.

– *Histoire et origine des Foulahs, ou Fellans.* Paris: Mme. Veuve Dondey-Dupré, 1856.

Delaunay, Paul. "Un Médecin Broussaisien: le Docteur Beunaiche la Corbière." *Bulletin de la Société française d'histoire de la médecine* 20 (1926): 397–428.

– "De la Physiognomonie à la Phrénologie, Histoire et évolution des écoles et des doctrines." *Le progrès médical* no. 29 (21 and 28 July 1928): 1207–11, 1237–41.

Demangeon, Jean-Baptiste. *Physiologie intellectuelle ou développement de la doctrine du Professeur Gall sur le cerveau ...* Paris: Delance, 1808.

Deneys, Anne. "Géographie, Histoire et Langue dans le Tableau du Climat et du sol des États-Unis." *Corpus* no. 11/12 (1989): 73–90.

Desmet, Piet. "Abel Hovelacque et l'école de linguistique naturaliste: De l'inégalité des langues à l'inégalité des races." In Claude Blanckaert, ed. *Les Politiques de l'anthropologie, Discours et pratiques en France 1860–1940.* 55–93. Paris: L'Harmattan, 2001.

Desmoulins, Antoine. *Histoire naturelle des races humaines du nord-est de l'Europe …* Paris: Méquigon-Marvis, 1826.

Dias, Nélia. "Une science nouvelle: la géo-ethnographie de Jomard." In Marie-Noëlle Bourguet, Bernard Lepetit, Daniel Nordman, Maroula Sinarellis, eds. *Invention scientifique de la Méditerranée. Égypte, Morée, Algérie.* 159–183. Paris: Éditions de l'EHESS, 1998.

Dobo, Nicolas et André Rôle. *Bichat, la vie fulgurante d'un genie.* Paris: Perrin, 1989.

d'Orbigny, Alcide. *L'Homme Américain de l'Amérique Méridionale considéré sur les rapports physiologiques et moraux.* Paris: Pitois-Levrault, 1839. 2 vols.

Dory, Daniel. "Géographie et colonisation en France durant la troisième république 1870–1940." In Patrick Petitjean, Catherine Jami, Anne-Marie Moulin, eds. *Science and Empires.* 323–9. Dordrecht: Kluwer Academic Publishers, 1992.

Dowbiggin, Ian. *Inheriting Madness: Professionalization and Psychiatric Knowledge in Nineteenth-Century France.* Berkeley: University of California Press, 1991.

Drescher, Seymour. "The Ending of the Slave Trade and the Evolution of European Scientific Racism." *Social Science History* 14 (1990): 415–50.

– *From Slavery to Freedom: Comparative Studies in the Rise and Fall of Atlantic Slavery.* New York: New York University Press, 1999.

Driver, Felix. *Geography Militant: Cultures of Exploration and Empire.* Oxford: Blackwell, 2001.

Dubois d'Amiens, Frédéric. *Philosophie médicale. Examen des doctrines de Cabanis et de Gall* [1842]. Paris: Germer Baillière, 1845. 2 vols.

Duchet, Michèle. *Anthropologie et histoire au siècle des lumières.* ed. Claude Blanckaert. Paris: Albin Michel, 1995.

Dumont d'Urville, Jules S.-C. *An Account in Two Volumes of Two Voyages to the South Seas by Captain later Rear-Admiral Jules S.-C. Dumont d'Urville of the French Navy to Australia, New Zealand, Oceania 1826–1829 in the corvette Astrolabe.* ed. Helen Rosenman. Honolulu: University of Hawaii Press, 1988. 2 vols.

– *Voyage de la corvette l'Astrolabe, exécuté par ordre du Roi pendant les années 1826, 1827, 1828, 1829: Relation historique.* Paris: J. Tastu: 1830–35. 4 Vols.

– *Voyage au Pôle Sud et dans l'Océanie, sur les corvettes l'Astrolabe et la Zélée exécuté par ordre du Roi pendant les années 1837, 1838, 1839, 1840.* Paris: Gide et J. Baudry, 1842–54. 23 vols., 7 vols. and atlas.

Dumont d'Urville, Eyriès d'Orbigny, A. Jacob, eds. *Histoire générale des Voyages.* Paris: Furne, 1859. 4 vols.

Duperrey, Louis-Isidore. *Voyage autour du monde ... sur la corvette La Coquille.* Paris: Arthus Bertrand, 1826–30. 7 vols.

Duprat, Pascal. *Essai historique sur les races anciennes et modernes de l'Afrique septentrionale.* Paris: Jules Lafitte, 1845.

Durkheim, Emile and Marcel Mauss. "De quelques formes primitives de classification: contribution à l'étude des représentations collectives." *Année sociologique* 6 (1903[actually 1901–2]): 1–72.

Eckstein, Ferdinand d'. *Lettres inédites de baron d'Eckstein. Société et littérature à Paris en 1838–1840.* ed. Louis Le Guillou. Paris: PUF, 1984.

Edwards, William-Frédéric. *Des caractères physiologiques des races humaines considérés dans leurs rapports avec l'histoire.* Paris: Compère jeune, 1829.

– *Fragments d'un mémoire sur les Gaëls.* Paris: Mme. Veuve Dondey-Dupré, 1845.

– *De l'influence réciproque des races sur le caractère national.* Paris: Mme. Veuve Dondey-Dupré, 1845.

– *Lettres sur la race noire et la race blanche.* Paris: Paulin, 1839

Emerit, Marcel. "Diplomates et Explorateurs Saint-Simoniens." *Revue d'histoire moderne et contemporaine* 22 (1975): 397–415.

– "Les explorateurs saint-simoniens en Afrique orientale et sur la route des Indes." *La Revue Africaine* nos 394–5 (1943): 99–100.

– *Les Saint-Simoniens en Algérie.* Paris: Les Belles Lettres, 1941.

Enfantin, Barthélemy-Prosper. *Colonisation de l'Algérie.* Paris: Bertrand, 1843.

Fairchilds, Cissie. "The Production and Marketing of Populuxe Goods in Eighteenth Century Paris." In John Brewer and Roy Porter, eds. *Consumption and the World of Goods.* 228–48. London: Routledge, 1993.

Faivre, Jean-Claude. *L'Expansion française dans le Pacifique de 1800 à 1842.* Paris: Nouvelles Éditions Latines, 1953.

– "Les idéologues de l'an VIII et le voyage de Nicolas Baudin en Australie 1800–1804." *Australian Journal of French Studies* 3 (1966): 3–15.

Faust, Drew Gilpin, ed. *The Ideology of Slavery? Proslavery Thought in the Antebellum South, 1830–1860.* Baton Rouge: Louisiana State University Press, 1981.

Ferrus, Guillaume-Marie-André. *Des prisonniers, de l'emprisonnement, des prisons.* Paris: Germer Baillère, 1850.

Fierro, Alfred. *La Société de Géographie 1821–1946.* Geneva: Droz, 1983.

Flavell, Kay. "Mapping Faces: National Physiognomies as Cultural Prediction." *Eighteenth-Century Life* 18 (1994): 8–22.

Flourens, Marie-Jean-Pierre. *Examen de la phrénologie* [1842]. Paris: L. Hachette, 1851.

Foissac, Pierre. "La tête de Bichat devant la Société anthropologique; et les localisations cérébrales." *Union médicale* 3rd sér., 24 (1877–78): 869–73, 917–22, 941–7, 953–62.

Forest, Luc. "De l'abolitionnisme à l'esclavagisme? Les implications des anthropologues dans le débat sur l'esclavage des Noirs aux Etats-Unis 1840–1870." *Revue française d'histoire d'outre-mer* 85, no. 320 (1998): 85–102.

Fossati, Jean-Antoine-Laurent. *Manuel pratique de phrénologie.* Paris: Baillière, 1845.

– *Questions philosophiques, sociales et politiques traitées d'après les principes de la Physiologie du cerveau.* Paris: Amyot, 1869.

Foucault, Michel. *Discipline and Punish: The Birth of the Prison.* New York: Pantheon, 1977.

– *Les mots et les choses, Une archéologie des sciences humaines.* Paris: Gallimard, 1966.

Fox, Robert. "Learning, Politics, and Polite Culture in Provincial France: The Sociétés Savantes in the Nineteenth Century." In Donald Baker and Patrick Harrigan, eds. *The Making of Frenchmen: Current Directions in the History of Education in France, 1679–1979.* 543–64. Waterloo, Ontario: Historical Reflections Press, 1980.

– "The Savant Confronts his Peers: Scientific Societies in France, 1815–1914." In Robert Fox and George Weisz, eds. *The Organization of Science and Technology in France, 1808–1914.* 241–82. Cambridge: Cambridge University Press, 1980.

Fox, Robert and George Weisz, eds. *The Organization of Science and Technology in France, 1808–1914.* Cambridge: Cambridge University Press, 1980.

Francis, Mark. "Anthropology and Social Darwinism in the British Empire: 1870–1900." *Australian Journal of Politics and History* 40 (1994): 203–15.

Freycinet, Louis de. *Voyage autour du monde, entrepris par ordre du roi.* Paris: de Pillet aîné, 1824–1844. 7 vols in 9.

Gall, Franz Joseph. *Sur les Fonctions du cerveau.* Paris: J.-B. Baillière, 1825–26. 6 vols.

Gall, Franz Joseph and Johann Gaspard Spurzheim. *Anatomie et physiologie du système nerveux en général et du cerveau en particulier.* Paris: Schoell, 1810–19. 4 vols and atlas.

– *Recherches sur le système nerveux en général, et sur celui du cerveau en particulier.* Paris, 1809.

Gallagher, J. "Fowell Buxton and the New African Policy." *Cambridge Historical Journal* 10, no. 1 (1950): 36–58.

Garnot, Prosper. "De l'Homme considéré sous le rapport de ses caractères physiques." Extrait from natural history dictionary. Paris: Cosson, n.d. 13–14.

Gates, Henry Louis Jr., ed. *"Race," Writing, and Difference.* Chicago: University of Chicago Press, 1986.

Girardet, Raoul. *L'Idée coloniale en France de 1871 à 1962.* Paris: La Table Ronde, 1972.

Giustino, David de. *Conquest of Mind: Phrenology and Victorian Social Thought.* London: Croom Helm, 1975.

Godlewska, Anne. *Geography Unbound: The French Geographic Science from Cassinito Humboldt.* Chicago: University of Chicago Press, 1999.

– "L'influence d'un homme sur la géographie française: Conrad Malte-Brun 1775–1826."*Annales de géographie* 100, no. 558 (1991): 190–206.

– "Map, text, and image: The mentality of enlightened conquerors: a new look at the *Description de l'Égypte" Transactions of the British Institute of Geographers* 20 (1995): 5–28.

– "Napoleonic Geography and Geography under Napoleon." *Proceedings of the Nineteenth Consortium on Revolutionary Europe* 1989, 1. Athens, Ga.: University of Georgia Department of History, 1990. 281–302.

– "Napoleon's Geographers (1797–1815): Imperialists and Soldiers of Modernity." In Anne Godlewska and Neil Smith, eds. *Geography and Empire.* 31–53. Oxford: Blackwell, 1994.

– "Traditions, Crisis, and New Paradigms in the Rise of the modern French Discipline of Geography 1760–1850." *Annals of the Association of American Geographers* 79, no. 2 (1989): 192–213.

Godlewska, Anne and Neil Smith, eds. *Geography and Empire.* Oxford: Blackwell, 1994.

Goldstein, Doris S. "'Official Philosophies' in Modern France: The Example of Victor Cousin." *Journal of Social History* 1 (1968): 259–79.

Goldstein, Jan. *Console and Classify: The French Psychiatric Profession in the Nineteenth Century.* Cambridge: Cambridge University Press, 1987.

– "The Uses of Cousinian Pedagogy in Nineteenth-Century France." In Jan Goldstein, ed. *Foucault and the Writing of History.* 99–115. Cambridge, Mass.: Blackwell, 1994.

Gould, Stephen Jay. *The Mismeasure of Man.* New York: Norton, 1996. (2d ed.)

Guillon, Jacques. *Dumont d'Urville 1790–1842.* Paris: Éditions France-Empire, 1986.

Guizot, François. *Mémoires pour servir à l'histoire de mon temps* Paris: Michel Lévy frères, 1858–67. 8 vols in 6.

Gusdorf, Georges. *Dieu, la nature, l'homme au siècle des Lumières.* Paris: Payot, 1972.

Haigh, Elizabeth. *Xavier Bichat and the medical theory of the eighteenth century.* New York: Burt Franklin, 1981.

Haines, Barbara. "The Inter-Relation between Social, Biological, and Medical Thought, 1750–1850, Saint-Simon and Comte." *British Journal for the History of Science* 11 (1978): 19–35.

Hale, Dana. "Races on Display: French Representations of the Colonial Native, 1886–1931." Ph.D. dissertation, Brandeis University, 1998.

Haller, John, Jr. *Outcasts from Evolution: Scientific Attitudes of Racial Inferiority, 1859–1900.* Urbana: University of Illinois Press, 1971.

Hamy, Ernest-Théodore. "Vie et travaux de M. de Quatrefages." In Jean-Louis-Armand de Quatrefages, *Les Émules de Darwin.* cxi–cxl. Paris, 1894.

Hannaford, Ivan. *Race: The History of an Idea in the West.* Washington: Woodrow Wilson Center Press, 1996.

Harvey, Joy Dorothy. *"Almost a Man of Genius": Clémence Royer, Feminism, and Nineteenth-Century Science.* New Brunswick: Rutgers, 1997.

– "Races Specified, Evolution Transformed: The Social Context of Scientific Debates Originating in the Société d'Anthropologie de Paris, 1859–1902." Ph.D. dissertation, Harvard University, 1983.

Hecht, Jennifer. "Anthropological Utopias and Republican Morality: Political Atheism and the Mind-Body Problem in France, 1880–1914." Dissertation, Columbia University, 1995.

– "A Vigilant Anthropology: Léonce Manouvrier and the Disappearing Numbers." *Journal of the History of the Behavioral Sciences* 33, no. 3 (1997): 221–40.

Heffernan, Michael. "The Science of Empire: The French Geographical Movement and the Forms of French Imperialism, 1870–1920." In Anne Godlewska and Neil Smith, eds. *Geography and Empire,* Oxford: Blackwell, 1994.

Heilmann, Eric. "Die Bertillonnage und die Stigmata der Entartung." *Kriminologisches Journal* 1 (1994): 36–46.

Heintel, Helmut. *Leben und Werk von Franz Joseph Gall, Eine Chronik.* Würzburg, 1986.

Herrnstein, Richard J. and Charles Murray. *The Bell Curve: Intelligence and Class Structure in American Life* [1994–95]. New York: Free Press, 1996.

Hervé, Georges and L. de Quatrefages, "Armand de Quatrefages de Bréau, médecin, zoologiste, anthropologue." *Bulletin de la Société française d'histoire de la médecine* 20 (1926): 309–30; 21 (1927): 17–34 and 200–22.

Hippocrates, *The Works of Hippocrates.* ed. W.H.S. Jones. London: Heinemann, 1959–62. 4 vols.

Hombron, Jacques Bernard. *Voyage au Pôle Sud ... Zoologie.* Paris: Gide, 1846. 5 vols.

Horner, Frank. *The French Reconnaissance: Baudin in Australia.* Melbourne: Melbourne University Press, 1987.

Horsman, Reginald. *Josiah Nott of Mobile: Southerner, Physician and Racial Theorist.* Baton Rouge: Louisiana State University Press, 1987.

Hoyt, David L. "The Reanimation of the Primitive: *Fin-de-siècle* ethnographic discourse in Western Europe." *History of Science* 39 (2001): 331–54.

– "The Surfacing of the Primitive: Social Reform, Colonial Administration, and Ethnographic Discourse in Great Britain and France, 1870–1914." Ph.D. dissertation, University of California at Los Angeles, 1999.

Hudson, Nicholas. "From 'Nation' to 'Race': The Origin of Racial Classification in Eighteenth-Century Thought." *Eighteenth-Century Studies* 29, no. 3 (1996): 247–64.

Isambert, François-André. *De la charbonnerie au Saint-Simonisme. Étude sur la jeunesse de Philippe Buchez.* Paris: Les Éditions de Minuit, 1966.

Jacoby, Russell and Naomi Glauberman, eds. *The Bell Curve Debate: History, Documents, Opinions.* New York: Random House, 1995.

Jacquinot, Honoré. *Etudes sur l'histoire naturelle de l'homme.* Paris: Rignoux, 1848.

Jacyna, L.S. "Medical Science and Moral Science: The Cultural Relations of Physiology in Restoration France." *History of Science* 25 (1987): 111–46.

Jennings, Lawrence C. *French Anti-Slavery: The Movement for the Abolition of Slavery in France, 1802–1848.* Cambridge: Cambridge University Press, 2000.

Jordan, Winthrop, Jr. *White Over Black: American Attitudes Toward the Negro, 1550–1812.* Chapel Hill: University of Carolina Press, 1968.

Kistner, Ulrike. "Georges Cuvier: Founder of Modern Biology (Foucault) or Scientific Racist (Cultural Studies)?" *Configurations* 7, no. 2 (1999): 175–90.

Lacaze, Louis de. *Idée de l'homme physique et moral.* Paris: H.-L Guérin et L.-F. Delatour, 1755.

Lacombe, Robert. "Essai sur les origines et les premiers développements de la Société d'Ethnographie." *Ethnographie* n.s. 76, no. 83 (1980): 329–41.

Lantéri-Laura, Georges. *Histoire de la phrénologie.* Paris: PUF, 1970; 2d ed. 1993.

Laurens, Henry, Charles Coulston Gillispie, Jean-Claude Golvin, and Claude Traunecker. *L'Expédition d'Égypte, 1798–1801.* Paris: Armand Colin, 1989.

Lauvergne, Hubert. *Les forçats considérés sous les rapports physiologiques, morales, et intellectuels observés au bagne de Toulon.* Paris, 1841; reprint Grenoble: J. Millon, 1991.

Lavater, Gaspard. *L'Art de connaître les hommes par la physionomie.* eds. Jacques-Louis Moreau de la Sarthe and J.-P. Maygrier. Paris: Depélafol, 1820 [1st ed. 1806–09]. 10 vols in 5.

– *Essays on Physiognomy calculated to extend the Knowledge and Love of Mankind.* ed. C. Moore. London: Symonds, 1797. 4 vols.

Le Rousseau, Julien. *Notions de phrénologie.* Paris: Librarie Phalanstérienne, 1847.

Lefebvre, Théophile. *Voyage en Abyssinie exécuté pendant les années 1839, 1840, 1841, 1842, 1843.* Paris: Arthus Bertrand, 1845–51. 8 vols.

Lefkowitz Mary R. and Guy MacLean Rogers, eds. *Black Athena Revisited.* Chapel Hill: University of North Carolina Press, 1996.

Lejeune, Dominique. *Les sociétés de géographie en France et l'expansion coloniale au XIXe siècle.* Paris: Albin Michel, 1993.

Lélut, Louis-Francisque. *De l'organe phénologique de la destruction chez les animaux.* Paris: J.-B. Baillière, 1838.

– *La Phrénologie: Son histoire, ses systèmes, et sa condamnation* [1853]. Paris: Delahays, 1858.

Lenormant, Charles. *Cours d'histoire ancienne professé à la Faculté des Lettres, Introduction à l'histoire de l'Asie occidentale et l'Égypte.* Paris: J.-J. Angé, 1837.

– *Musée des Antiquités Égyptiennes* Paris: Leleux, 1841.

Lesch, John. *Science and Medicine in France, The Emergence of Experimental Physiology, 1790–1855.* Cambridge: Harvard University Press, 1984.

Lesson, René-Primevère. *Compléments de Buffon, races humaines et mammifères.* Paris: Peurrat, 1838. 2 vols.

– *Oeuvres complètes de Buffon … Complément par Lesson* Paris: Pourrat frères, 1838–1839. 7 vols + 6–7 *Compléments de Buffon par R.P. Lesson.*

– *Voyage autour du Monde … sur la corvette* La Coquille. Paris: Pourrat frères, 1838–39. 2 vols.

L'Estoile, Benoît de. "Science de l'homme et 'domination rationnelle,' savoir ethnologique et politique indigène en Afrique coloniale française." *Revue de synthèse,* 4th sér., nos 3–4 (2000): 291–323.

Leterrier, Sophie-Anne. *L'institution des sciences morales, l'Académie des sciences morales et politiques, 1795–1850.* Paris: L'Harmattan, 1995.

Leuret, François. *Anatomie comparée du système nerveux considéré dans ses rapports avec l'intelligence.* Paris: J.-B. Baillière, 1839. 2 vols.

Liebersohn, Harry. *Aristocratic Encounters: European Travelers and North American Indians.* Cambridge: Cambridge University Press, 1998.

Linné, Carl von. *A General System of Nature …* London: Lackington, Allen, 1802–06. 7 vols.

Livingstone, David N. *The Geographical Tradition.* Oxford: Blackwell, 1992.

– "The moral discourse of climate: historical considerations on race, place, and virtue." *Journal of Historical Geography* 17, no. 4 (1991): 413–34.

Lombroso, Cesare. *Criminal Man.* [1911] ed. Gina Lombroso-Ferrero. Reprinted Montclair: Patterson Smith, 1972.

Lorcin, Patricia. *Imperial Identities: Stereotyping, Prejudice and Race in Colonial Algeria.* London: I.B. Tauris, 1995.

– "Imperialism, Colonial Identity, and Race in Algeria, 1830–1870." *Isis* 90 (1999): 653–79.

Lorimer, Douglas. "Science and the Secularization of Victorian Images of Race." In Bernard Lightman, ed. *Victorian Science in Context.* 212–35. Chicago: University of Chicago Press, 1997.

– "Theoretical Racism in Late Victorian Anthropology, 1870–1900." *Victorian Studies* 31 (1988): 405–30.

Lovejoy, Arthur O. *The Great Chain of Being: The Study of the History of an Idea.* New York: Harper and Row, 1965.

McGiffert, Michael. "Editor's Preface." *William and Mary Quarterly* 54, no. 1 (1997): 3–6.

McKay, Donald Vernon. "Colonialism in the French Geographical Movement 1871–1881." *Geographical Review* 33 (1943): 214–32.

McKeane, Ian. "Selective Bibliography of the French Press, 1825–1848." http://www.bris.ac.uk/dix-neuf/presse.html.

McKechnie, Sue. *British Silhouette Artists and their Work 1750–1860.* London: Philip Wilson for Sotheby Park Bernet, 1978.

McLaren, Angus. "A Prehistory of the Social Sciences: Phrenology in France." *Comparative Studies in Society and History* 23 (1981): 3–22.

McWilliam, Neal. *Dreams of Happiness: Social Art and the French Left.* Princeton: Princeton University Press, 1993.

Magendie, François. *Précis élémentaire de physiologie.* Paris: 1816–17. 2 vols.

Malécot, Georges. *Les Voyageurs français et les relations entre la France et l'Abyssinie de 1835 à 1870.* Paris: Société française d'histoire d'outre-mer, 1972.

Malik, Kenan. *The Meaning of Race: Race, History and Culture in Western Society.* New York: New York University Press, 1996.

Malte-Brun, Conrad. *Précis de géographie universelle.* Paris: F. Buisson, 1810–29. 8 vols.

Manouvrier, Léonce. "Les aptitudes et les actes dans leurs rapports avec la constitution anatomique et avec le milieu extérieur." *Bulletin de la Société d'anthropologie de Paris* 4th sér., t. 1 (1890): 918–51.

Manuel, Frank E. "From Equality to Organicism." *Journal of the History of Ideas* 17 (1956): 54–69.

– *The New World of Henri Saint-Simon.* Cambridge: Harvard University Press, 1956.

– *The Prophets of Paris: Turgot, Condorcet, Saint-Simon, Fourier, and Comte.* Cambridge: Harvard University Press, 1962.

Mauss, Marcel. *Oeuvres.* Paris: Éditions du Minuit, 1969. 3 vols.

Maza, Sarah. "Luxury, Morality, and Social Change in Prerevolutionary France." *Journal of Modern History* 69 (1997): 199–229.

Meek, Ronald. *Social Science and the Ignoble Savage.* Cambridge: Cambridge University Press, 1976.

Mège, J.-B. *Avis aux patriotes.* Paris: Eluard, 1843.

– *Manifeste des principes de la Société phrénologique de Paris.* Paris, 1835. Supplément to vol. 3 of *JSPP*, 21, 27–9.

– *Des principes fondamentaux de la phrénologie appliquées à la philosophie.* Paris: Guiraudet et Jousaust, 1845.

Meijer, Miriam Claude. "Petrus Camper On the Origin and Color of Blacks." *History of Anthropology Newsletter* 24, no. 2 (1997): 3–9.

– *Race and Aesthetics in the Anthropology of Petrus Camper 1722-89.* Amsterdam: Rodopi, 1998.

Meyer, Jean, Jean Tarrade, Annie Rey-Goldzeiguer, and Jacques Thobié. *Histoire de la France coloniale: des origines à 1914.* Paris: Armand Colin, 1990–91. 2 vols.

Milne-Edwards, Henri. *Elémens de zoologie.* 2nd ed. Paris: Fortin, Masson, 1840. 3 vols.

– *Leçons sur la physiologie et l'anatomie comparée de l'homme et des animaux.* Paris: V. Masson, 1857–81. 14 vols.

Milne-Edwards, Henri and Achille Comte. *Cahiers d'histoire naturelle à l'usage des collèges et des écoles normales.* 3rd ed. Paris: Crochard, 1836.

Mitchell, Timothy. *Colonizing Egypt.* Berkeley: University of California Press, 1991

Mollien, Gaspard-Théodore. *Voyage dans l'intérieur de l'Afrique aux sources du Sénégal et de la Gambie fait en 1818.* Paris: Veuve Courcier, 1820. 2 vols.

Moravia, Sergio. *Il pensiero degli Idéologues: Scienza e filosofia in Francia 1780–1815.* Firenze: La Nuova Italia, 1974.

– *La scienza dell'uomo nel settecento.* Bari: Laterza, 1970.

Moreau de la Sarthe, Louis-Jacques. "Encore des réflexions et des observations relatives à l'influence du moral sur le physique." *La Décade philosophique*: (20, 30 nivôse an IX): 69–75, 134–41. "Esquisse d'un cours de hygiène ou de médecine appliquée à l'art d'user la vie et de conserver la santé, extrait par Sédillot," *Recueil périodique de la Société de médecine* 8 (an VIII–1800): 75.

– "Exposition et critique du système du docteur Gall sur la cause et l'expression des principales différences de l'esprit et des passions." *La Décade philosophique* t. 40: (30 nivôse an XII): 129–37; 40 (10, 20 pluviôse an XII): 193–202, 257–65.

– "Extrait du Traité médico-philosophique sur l'aliénation mentale par Ph. Pinel." *La Décade philosophique*, no. 26 (20 prairial an IX–1801): 458–67.

– *Histoire naturelle et philosophique de la femme, suivie d'un traité d'hygiène.* Paris: L. Duprat, Letellier, 1803. 3 vols.

– "Mémoire sur plusieurs maladies à la guérison desquelles les ressources pharmaceutiques n'ont pas concouru." *Recueil périodique de la Société de Médecine* 6 (an VII–1799): 389–96.

– "Pinel, Traité médico-philosophique sur l'aliénation mentale, ou la manie." *La Décade philosophique* 20 (prairial an IX): 458–9.

Morel, Bénédict-Augustin. *Traité des dégénérescences physiques, intellectuelles, et morales de l'espèce humaine.* Paris: J.-B. Baillière; H. Bailiière, 1857.

Mucchielli, Laurent. *La Découverte du social,* Paris: La Découverte, 1998.

– "La dénaturalisation de l'homme: Le tournant durkheimien de l'ethnologie française (1890–1914)." In Albert Ducros, Jacqueline Ducros, et Frédéric Joulian, eds. *La Culture est-elle naturelle?* 41–53. Paris: Errance, 1998.

– "'Hérédité' et 'milieu social': le faux antagonisme franco-italien." In *Histoire de la criminologie française.* 189–214. Paris: L'Harmattan, 1994.

– ed. *Histoire de la criminologie française.* Paris: L'Harmattan, 1994.

– "Sociologie versus anthropologie raciale. L'engagement des sociologues durkheimiens dans le contexte "fin de siècle" (1885–1914)." *Gradhiva* 21 (1997): 77–95.

Mummery, Chris. "The Struggle for Survival: The Origins of Racism in New Caledonia, 1843–1902." Master's thesis, University of Calgary, 2000.

Murphy, Agnes. *The Ideology of French Imperialism, 1871–1881.* Washington: Catholic University of America Press, 1948.

Nicolas, Serge. "L'Hérédité psychologique d'après Théodule Ribot, 1873: La première thèse française du psychologie scientifique." *L'Année psychologique* 99 (1999): 295–348.

Nicolas, Serge and David Murray. "Le fondateur de la psychologie 'scientifique' française: Théodule Ribot 1839–1916." *Psychologie et Histoire* 1 (2000): 1–42. Online at http://lpe.psycho.univparis5.fr/membres/nicolas/Nicolas1.htm.

Nott, Josiah and George R. Gliddon. *Indigenous Races of the Earth, or New Chapters in Ethnological Inquiry.* Philadelphia: J.B. Lippincott, 1857.

– *Types of Mankind, or Ethnological Researches based upon the ancient monuments, paintings, sculptures, and crania of races and upon their philological and Biblical history* [1854]. Philadelphia: J.B. Lippincott, 1855.

Nye, Robert. *Crime, Madness, and Politics in Modern France.* Princeton: Princeton University Press, 1984.

O'Brien, Patricia. *The Promise of Punishment: Prisons in Nineteenth-Century France.* Princeton: Princeton University Press, 1982.

Osborne, Michael A. "Acclimatizing the World: A History of the Paradigmatic Colonial Science." *Osiris* 15 (2001): 135–51.

– *Nature, the Exotic, and the Science of French Colonialism.* Bloomington: Indiana University Press, 1994.

Pagden, Anthony. *European Encounters with the New World.* New Haven: Yale University Press, 1993.

Pardailhé-Galabrun, Annick. *La naissance de l'intime: 3000 foyers parisiens, XVIIe–XVIIIe siècle.* Paris: PUF, 1988.

Perrot, Michelle, ed. *L'Impossible prison, Recherches sur le système pénitentiaire au XIXe siècle.* Paris: Seuil, 1980.

Pick, Daniel. *Faces of Degeneration: A European Disorder c. 1848–1918.* Cambridge: Cambridge University Press, 1989.

Pickstone, John V. "How Might We Map the Cultural Fields of Science? Politics and Organisms in Restoration France." *History of Science* 37 (1999): 347–65.

Pierquin de Gembloux, C.-C. *Lettre au général Bory de Vincent, sur l'unité de l'espèce humaine.* Bourges: Manceron, 1840.

– *Traité de la Folie des animaux.* Paris: Béchet, 1839. 2 vols.

Piguet, Marie-France. "Observation et histoire: *Race* chez Amédée Thierry et William F. Edwards." *L'Homme* 153 (2000): 93–106.

Pilbeam, Pamela. *Republicanism in Nineteenth-Century France 1814–71.* London: Macmillan, 1995.

Pillon, Patrick and François Sodter. "The Impact of Colonial Administrative Policies on Indigenous Social Customs in Tahiti and New Caledonia." *Journal of Pacific History* 26 (1991): 151–68.

Pinkney, David. *Decisive Years in France, 1840–1847.* Princeton: Princeton University Press, 1986.

Poliakov, Léon. *The Aryan Myth: A History of Racist and Nationalist Ideas in Europe.* trans. Edmund Howard. New York: Basic Books, 1974.

Poupin, Théodore. *Caractères phrénologiques et physiognomiques des contemporains les plus célèbres selon les systèmes.* Paris: Germer Baillière, 1837.

Prakash, Gyan. "Orientalism Now. A Review of Reviews." *History and Theory* 34, no. 3 (1995): 199–212.

Pratt, Mary Louise. *Imperial Eyes: Travel Writing and Transculturation.* London: Routledge, 1992.

Quatrefages de Bréau, Jean-Louis-Armand de. Conférences d'anthropologie, *Revue des cours publics* 2, no. 2629 (juin 1856): 404–7; no. 2813 (juillet 1856): 23–7, 70.

– *Rapport sur les progrès de l'anthropologie.* Paris: Imprimerie impériale, 1867.

– *Souvenirs d'un naturaliste.* Paris: Victor Masson, 1854.

– *Unité de l'espèce humaine.* Paris: L. Hachette, 1861.

Raffenel, Anne-Jean-Baptiste. *Nouveau voyage dans le pays des nègres.* Paris: N. Chaix, 1856. 2 vols.

– *Second voyage d'exploration dans l'intérieur de l'Afrique.* Extrait de la *Revue coloniale,* 1849.

– *Voyage dans l'Afrique occidentale comprenant l'exploration du Sénégal ... exécuté, en 1843 et 1844* Paris: Arthus Bertrand, 1846. 2 vols.

Raichle, Marcus. "Modern Phrenology: Maps of Human Cortical Function." *Annals of the New York Academy of Sciences* 88, no. 2 1999): 107–18.

Ratcliffe, Barrie M. "Classes laborieuses et classes dangereuses à Paris pendant lapremière moitié du XIXe siècle? The Chevalier Thesis Reexamined." *French Historical Studies* 17 (1991): 542–74.

Ratcliffe, Barrie and W.H. Chaloner. "Gustave d'Eichthal: An Intellectual Portrait." In *A French Sociologist Looks at Britain: Gustave d'Eichthal and British Society in 1828.* 109–61. Manchester: Manchester University Press, 1977.

Renneville, Marc. "Alexandre Lacassagne: Un médecin-anthropologue face à la criminalité 1843–1924." *Gradhiva* 17 (1995): 127–40.

– "Entre nature et culture: le regard médical sur le crime dans la première moitié du XIXe siècle." In Laurent Mucchielli, ed. *Histoire de la criminologie française.* 29–53. Paris: L'Harmattan, 1994.

– *Le Langage des crânes, Une histoire de la phrénologie.* Paris: Sanofi-Synthélabo, 2000.

– *La Médecine du crime, Essai sur l'émergence d'un regard médical sur la criminalité en France 1785–1885.* Villeneuve d'Ascq: Septentrion, 1997. 2 vols.

– "Un musée anthropologique oublié: Le cabinet phrénologique de Dumoutier." *Bulletins et mémoires de la Société d'anthropologique de Paris* n.s. 10, nos 3–4 (1998): 477–84.

– La réception de Lombroso en France (1880–1900)." In Laurent Mucchielli, ed. *Histoire de la criminologie française.* 107–35. Paris: L'Harmattan, 1994.

– "De la régénération à la dégénérescence: la science de l'homme face à 1848." *Revue d'histoire du XIXe siècle* no. 15 (février 1997): 7–19.

– "Un Terrain phrénologique dans le Grand Océan autour du voyage de Dumoutier sur *L'Astrolabe* en 1837–1840." In Claude Blanckaert, ed. *Le Terrain des sciences humaines XVIIIe-XXe siècle.* 89–138. Paris: L'Harmattan, 1996.

Reuillard, Michel. *Les Saint-Simoniens et la Tentation Coloniale.* Paris: Université de Provence, Éditions L'Harmattan, 1995.

Richards, Graham. *Mental Machinery: The Origins and Consequences of Psychological Ideas. Part I. 1600–1850.* Baltimore: The Johns Hopkins University Press, 1992.

Rignol, Loïc. "Anthropologie et progrès dans la philosophie de l'histoire d'Alphonse Esquiros. Le système des *Fastes populaires.*" *Revue d'histoire du XIXe siècle* no. 20–21 (2000): 157–79.

Roche, Daniel. *The Culture of Clothing: Dress and Fashion in the Ancien Régime.* Cambridge: Cambridge University Press, 1994.

Rochet d'Héricourt, Charles-Etienne-Xavier. *Second voyage sur les deux rives de la mer Rouge dans le pays des Adels et le royaume de Choa.* Paris: Arthus Bertrand, 1846.

– *Voyage de la côte orientale de la mer Rouge dans le pays d'Adel et le royaume de Choa.* Paris: Arthus Bertrand, 1841.

Rodrigues, Olinde. *Organisation du travail.* Paris: Napoléon Chaix, 1848.

– *Projet de constitution populaire pour la République française.* Paris: Napoléon Chaix, 1848.

Rôle, André. *Un destin hors série: Bory de Saint-Vincent1778–1846.* Paris: La Pensée universelle, 1973.

Rupp-Eisenreich, Britta. "Des choses occultes en histoire des sciences humaines: Le destin de la 'science nouvelle' de Christoph Meiners." *L'Ethnographie* 79 (1983): 131–83.

– "The 'Société des Observateurs de l'Homme' and German Ethno-Anthropology at the End of the 18th Century." *History of Anthropology Newsletter* 10 (1983): 5–11.

Rushton, J. Philippe. *Race, Evolution, and Behavior: A Life History Perspective.* New Brunswick, N.J.: Transaction Publishers, 1995.

Russett, Cynthia. *Sexual Science: The Victorian Construction of Womanhood.* Cambridge: Harvard University Press, 1989.

Said, Edward. *Orientalism* [1978]. New York: Vintage, 1979.

Saint-Simon, Claude-Henri de. *Oeuvres choisies de C.-H. Saint-Simon.* ed. Charles Lemonnier. Bruxelles: Van Meeren, 1859. 3 vols.

– *Oeuvres de Saint-Simon et d'Enfantin ... publiés par les membres du conseil institués par Enfantin* [1865–78]. Réimpression Aalen: Otto Zeller, 1964. 43 vols in 22.

Sarlandière, Jean-Baptiste. *Traité du système nerveux dans l'état actuel de la science* Paris: J.-B. Baillère, 1840.

Schiebinger, Londa. *Nature's Body: Gender in the Making of Modern Science.* Boston: Beacon Press, 1993.

Schiller, Francis. *Paul Broca: Founder of French Anthropology, Explorer of the Brain.* Berkeley: University of California Press, 1979.

Schmidt, Nelly. *Victor Schoelcher et l'abolition de l'esclavage.* Paris: Fayard, 1994.

– *Victor Schoelcher en son temps: Images et témoignages.* Paris: Maisonneuve et Larose, 1998.

Schneider, William H. *An Empire for the Masses: The French Popular Image of Africa, 1870–1900.* Westport, Conn.: Greenwood Press, 1982.

Schoelcher, Victor. *Des colonies françaises; abolition immédiate de l'esclavage.* Paris: Pagnerre, 1842.

– *L'Égypte en 1845.* Paris: Pagnerre, 1846.

– *Histoire de l'esclavage pendant les deux dernières années.* Paris: Pagnerre, 1846–47. 2 vols.

Scoutetten, Henri. *Leçons de phrénologie.* Metz: Lamort, 1834.

Serres, Etienne. "Rapport sur les résultats scientifiques du voyage de circumnavigation de l'Astrolabe et de la Zélée." In *Comptes rendus hebdomadaires des Séances de l'Académie des Sciences,* 1841, 2nd semestre: 643–59 and 713–14.

Shapin, Steven. "Homo Phrenologicus: Anthropological Perspectives on an Historical Problem." In Barry Barnes and Steven Shapin, eds. *Natural Order: Historical Studies of Scientific Culture.* 41–71. London: Sage, 1979.

– "Phrenological Knowledge and the Social Structure of Early Nineteenth-Century Edinburgh." *Annals of Science* 32 (1975): 219–43.

Shookman, Ellis, ed. *The Faces of Physiognomy: an Interdisciplinary Approach to Johann Caspar Lavater.* Columbia, S.C.: Camden House, 1993.

Shortland, Michael. "Courting the Cerebellum: Early Organological and Phrenological Views of Sexuality." *British Journal for the History of Science* 20 (1987): 186.

Sibeud, Emmanuelle. "Les constructions des savoirs africanistes en France
    1878–1930." Thèse à l'EHESS, 1999. Summary in *Bulletin de la Société Française
    pour l'histoire des Sciences de l'Homme* 21 (2001): 48–50.
– "La naissance de l'ethnographie africaniste en France avant 1914." *Cahiers
    d'études africaines* 34, no. 4 (1994): 639–58.
Signoret, Véronique de. "Moreau de la Sarthe: Idéologue et médecin."
    Unpublished communication, colloque sur les Idéologues et leur postérité,
    Cerisy-la-Salle, 1998.
Sloan, Phillip. "The Idea of Racial Degeneracy in Buffon's *Histoire naturelle*." In
    Harold Pagliaro, ed. *Studies in Eighteenth-Century Culture* 3 (1973): 293–321.
Spurzheim, Johann Gaspar. *Essai sur les principes élémentaires de l'éducation.* Paris:
    Treuttel et Würtz, 1822.
– *Manuel de phrénologie.* Paris: Imprimerie Porthmann, 1832.
– *Observations sur la phrénologie ou la connaissance de l'homme moral et intellectuel.*
    Paris: Treuttel and Wüntz, 1818.
– *Philosophical Catechism of the Natural Laws of Man* [1828]. Boston: Marsh,
    Capen, and Lyon, 1835.
– *Phrenology in Connexion with the Study of Physiognomy.* London: Treuttel, Wurtz,
    and Richter, 1826.
Stanton, William. *The Leopard's Spots: Scientific Attitudes toward Race in America
    1815–1859.* Chicago: University of Chicago Press, 1960.
Staum, Martin S. *Minerva's Message: Stabilizing the French Revolution.* Montreal:
    McGill-Queen's University Press, 1996.
Stepan, Nancy. *The Idea of Race in Science: Great Britain, 1800–1960.* London:
    Macmillan, 1982.
– "Race and Gender: The Role of Analogy in Science." *Isis* 77 (1986): 261–77.
Stocking, Jr. George W. "French Anthropology in 1800." In *Race, Culture, and
    Evolution.* New York: Free Press, 1968. 13–41.
– "Qu'est-ce qui est en jeu dans un nom?: La Société Ethnographique et
    l'historiographie de l''anthropologie' en France." In Britta Rupp-Eisenreich,
    ed. *Histoires de l'anthropologie: XVIᵉ-XIXᵉ siècles.* 421–32. Paris: Klincsieck, 1984.
– *Victorian Anthropology.* New York: Free Press, 1987.
– "What's in a name? The origins of the Royal Anthropological Institute, 1837–
    1871." *Man* 6 (1971): 369–90.
Stoler, Ann. *Race and the Education of Desire: Foucault's History of Sexuality and the
    Colonial Order of Things.* Durham: Duke University Press, 1995.
Sue fils, Jean-Joseph. *Essai sur la physiognomonie des corps vivants considérés depuis
    l'homme jusqu'à la plante.* Paris: Du Pont, an V-1797.
Surun, Isabelle. "De l'explorateur au géographe – La Société de Géographie et
    l'Afrique 1821–54." In Danielle Lecoq and Antoine Chambard, eds. *Terre à
    découvrir, Terres à parcourir.* 259–81. Paris: L'Harmattan, 1998.

Sweet, James H. "The Iberian Roots of Racist Thought." *William and Mary Quarterly* 54, no. 1 (1997): 143–66.

Taylor, Maxine. "The Geographical Society of Paris, 1850–1870." *Proceedings of the Sixth and Seventh Annual Meetings of the French Colonial Historical Society* 6–7 (1982): 36–45.

– "Nascent Expansionism in the Geographical Society of Paris, 1821–1848." *Proceedings of the Annual Meeting of the Western Society for French History* 6 (1979): 229–38.

Temkin, Owsei. *Galenism: The Rise and Decline of a Medical Philosophy.* Ithaca: Cornell University Press, 1973.

– "Gall and the Phrenological Movement." *Bulletin of the History of Medicine* 21 (1947): 275–321.

Thomas, Nicholas. "The Force of Ethnology: Origins and Significance of the Melanesia/Polynesia Division." *Current Anthropology* 30, no. 1 (1989): 27–41.

Thomassy, Raymond. *De la colonisation militaire de l'Algérie.* Paris: Bertrand, 1840.

– *Le Maroc et ses caravanes, ou Relations de la France avec cet empire* [1842]. Paris: Firmin Didot, 1845.

Thomson, Ann. "Bory de Saint-Vincent et l'anthropologie de la Méditerranée." In Marie-Noëlle Bourguet, Bernard Lepetit, Daniel Nordman, et Maroula Sinarellis, eds. *L'Invention scientifique de la Méditerranée.* 273–87. Paris: Éditions de l'EHESS, 1998.

Tytler, Graeme. *Faces and Fortunes: Physiognomy in the European Novel.* Princeton: Princeton University Press, 1982.

van Wyhe, John. "The authority of human nature: the *Schädellehre* of Franz Joseph Gall." *British Journal for the History of Science* 35 (2002): 17–42.

Vergniol, Camille. *Dumont d'Urville.* Paris: La Renaissance du Livre, 1930.

Vermeulen, Hans F. "Origins and institutionalization of ethnography and ethnology in Europe and the USA, 1771–1845." In Hans Vermeulen and Arturo Alvarez Roldán, eds. *Fieldwork and Footnotes: Studies in the History of European Anthropology.* 39–59. London: Routledge, 1995.

Vernon, Richard. "The Political Self: Auguste Comte and Phrenology." *History of European Ideas* 7 (1986): 271–86.

Vimont, Joseph. *Traité de phrénologie humaine et comparée.* Paris: J-B. Baillière, 1832–35. 2 vols.

Vincendon-Dumoulin, C.-A. *Iles marquises ou Nouka-Hiva.* Paris: Arthus-Bertrand, 1843

Virey, Julien-Joseph. *De la femme sous ses rapports physiologique, moral et littéraire.* 2nd ed. Paris: Crochard, 1825.

– *Histoire naturelle du genre humain.* Paris: Dufart, an IX-1800. 2 vols.

– *Histoire naturelle du genre humain* Paris: Couchard, 1824. 3 vols.

Vivien de Saint-Martin, Louis. *Histoire générale de la Révolution française, de l'Empire, de la restauration, de la monarchie de 1830, jusques et après 1841.* Paris: Pourrat frères, 1841. 2 vols.

– *Recherches sur l'histoire de l'anthropologie.* Paris: Arthus Bertrand, 1845.

– *Recherches sur les populations primitives et les plus anciennes traditions du Caucase.* Paris: Arthus-Bertrand, 1847. 2 vols.

Voisin, Félix. *Analyse de l'entendement humain.* Paris: J.-B. Baillière et H. Baillière, 1858.

– *Des causes morales et physiques des maladies mentales.* Paris: J.-B. Baillière, 1826.

– *De l'Homme animal.* Paris: Bechet jeune et Labé, 1839.

Volney, Constantin-François. *Questions de statistique à l'usage des voyageurs* [1795]. Paris: Veuve Courcier: 1813.

– *Voyage en Égypte et en Syrie* [1787]. ed. Jean Gaulmier. Paris: Mouton, 1959.

Walckenaer, Charles-Athanase. *Essai sur l'histoire de l'espèce humaine.* Paris: Du Pont, 1798-an VI.

– *Recherches géographiques sur l'intérieur de l'Afrique septentrionale.* Paris: Firmin Didot, 1821.

Wechsler, Judith. *A Human Comedy: Physiognomy and Caricature in Nineteenth Century Paris.* Chicago: University of Chicago Press, 1982.

Wegner, Peter-Christoph. "Das Ringen um Anerkennung, Drei Briefe Galls an Cuvier," *Medizinhistorisches Journal* 25 (1990): 40–89.

– "Franz Joseph Gall in der zeitgenössischen franzözisher Karikatur." *Medizinhistorisches Journal* 23 (1988): 106–22.

– "Phrenologische Schnupftabakdosen, Ein Beitrag zur« Wirkung Franz Joseph Galls bei seiner Ankunft in Paris." *Medizinhistorisches Journal* 18 (1983): 69–99.

Williams, Elizabeth A. *The Physical and the Moral: Anthropology, Physiology, and Philosophical Medicine in France, 1750–1850.* Cambridge: Cambridge University Press, 1994.

– "The Science of Man: Anthropological Thought and Institutions in Nineteenth Century France." Ph.D. dissertation, University of Indiana, 1983.

Ysabeau, Victor-Frédéric-Alexandre. *Lavater et Gall. Physiognomonie et phrénologie rendues intelligibles pour tout de monde* [1862]. Paris: Garnier frères, 1870.

Young, Robert James Craig. *Colonial Desire: Hybridity in Theory, Culture, and Race.* London: Routledge, 1995.

Young, Robert M. *Mind, Brain and Adaptation: Cerebral Localization and the Biological Context from Gall to Ferrier.* Oxford: Oxford University Press, 1970.

Index